# SOCIAL SERVICE
# IN
# CRIMINAL JUSTICE

**HOWARD ABADINSKY**

*Western Carolina University*

PRENTICE-HALL, INC.
ENGLEWOOD CLIFFS, NEW JERSEY 07632

*Library of Congress Cataloging in Publication Data*

ABADINSKY, HOWARD,
   Social service in criminal justice.

   (Prentice-Hall series in criminal justice)
   Bibliography: p.
   Includes index.
   1. Social work with delinquents and criminals.
2. Crime and criminals.  3. Criminal justice, Adminis-
tration of.  I. Title.
HV7428.A22     364     78-11092
ISBN  0-13-818344-9

*To Donna, Alisa, and Sandi.*

*Editorial production/supervision and interior design by* Wendy Terryberry.
*Cover design by* Richard Lo Monaco. *Manufacturing buyer* Harry P. Baisley.


Prentice-Hall Series in Criminal Justice
James D. Stinchcomb, Editor

Printed in the United States of America

10  9  8  7  6  5  4  3  2  1


Prentice-Hall International, Inc., *London*
Prentice-Hall of Australia Pty. Limited, *Sydney*
Prentice-Hall of Canada, Ltd., *Toronto*
Prentice-Hall of India Private Limited, *New Delhi*
Prentice-Hall of Japan, Inc., *Tokyo*
Prentice-Hall of Southeast Asia Pte. Ltd., *Singapore*
Whitehall Books Limited, *Wellington, New Zealand*

# Contents

# Introduction

Much can be read about criminology, criminal justice, and social service methods. This book provides a blending of information from all of these fields and can be used by people who are working, or are merely interested, in a criminal justice setting. These settings can be as diverse as criminal justice itself—they can vary from prearrest counseling to postincarceration aftercare or parole; they include both public and private agencies. This book draws upon the relevant literature in criminology, psychology, criminal justice, and social service, as well as the practical experiences of criminal justice practitioners, and social service workers in a criminal justice setting. Since this book is designed with a specific focus on criminal justice, only those aspects of theory and practice that are relevant for criminal justice social service have been included.

There are three basic approaches to explaining and responding to crime. (Unless otherwise stated, this book will define "crime" in a narrow legalistic sense—that is, it will define "crime" as a violation of the criminal law.)

1. legal
2. sociological
3. psychological

Within each approach are a variety of "schools," and within each school are various subdivisions whose partisans engage in defending their own, while attacking other, theories about crime and criminals. This book will not deliberately take part in the contest over theory—any theory that is included in this book merely represents a body of information that can be of use to the social service practitioner in a criminal justice setting. While crime and criminal justice are by definition tied to legal, normative structures, our focus will be primarily on sociological and psychological explanations and responses to criminal behavior. The legal structures will provide both the background and framework for our study, while our focus will be delimited to elements that Kittrie believes are controllable.[1]

1. crime as an expression of conditions surrounding man; and
2. crime as a product of man's constitution.

Kahn notes that if theory is to have relevance in criminal justice, it must provide operational definitions which can be useful to the social service prac-

---

[1]Nicholas N. Kittrie, *The Right to Be Different* (Baltimore: Johns Hopkins University Press, 1971), p. 24.

titioner. He recommends that one not choose "between or among delinquency theories on the social-structural, cultural, interpersonal, or intrapsychic levels," but rather one should recognize that each of these levels can provide useful insights for the social service practitioner.[2]

Parsons has observed that psychological thought "has naturally concentrated on the study of the personality of the individual as the focus of its frame of reference," while sociology has "naturally been primarily concerned with the patterning of the behavior of a plurality of individuals as constituting what, increasingly, we tend to call a social system."[3] These differences in perspective, Parsons states, have caused a great deal of misunderstanding. In an effort to ameliorate the differences between social and psychoanalytic theory, Parsons authored several papers which appear in *Social Structure and Personality*.[4] Fromm, in a series of papers appearing in *The Crisis of Psychoanalysis* makes a similar effort: "The thesis that psychology only deals with the individual while sociology deals with 'society' is false."[5] Fromm notes that "just as psychology always deals with a socialized individual, so sociology always deals with a group of individuals whose psychic structure and mechanisms must be taken into account."[6]

In their effort to encourage an "Integrated Theory in Criminology," Wolfgang and Ferracuti state:

> Perhaps fearful of diluting his own approach, each scientist becomes more tenaciously attached to his original framework. The psychiatrist has difficulty in convincing the sociologist that the clinical approach is a useful way of obtaining data or verifying hypotheses. The statistically oriented sociologist or mathematically trained psychologist has difficulty impressing the clinician that sufficiently large groups, representative samples, control groups, and association tests are necessary for the proper testing of hypotheses.[7]

They note that a shortsighted approach has left two vital questions unanswered: (1) Why do not all persons exposed to certain assumed criminogenic factors become criminal: and (2) Why do many pathological personalities remain noncriminal?[8]

Wolfgang and Ferracuti note that the social service practitioner, who must apply the knowledge, has found that sociological formulations are difficult to translate into treatment strategies. On the other hand, they observe, social service workers have failed to develop sophisticated theory or systematic methodology and have been out of touch with sociology:

[2]Alfred J. Kahn, "Social Work and the Control of Delinquency: Theory and Strategy," *Social Work* 10 (April 1965): 8.

[3]Talcott Parsons, *Social Structure and Personality* (New York: Free Press, 1970), pp. 17–18.

[4]Ibid.

[5]Erich Fromm, *The Crisis of Psychoanalysis* (New York: Holt, Rinehart & Winston, 1970).

[6]Ibid., p. 114.

[7]Marvin E. Wolfgang and Franco Ferracuti, *The Subculture of Violence* (London: Tavistock Publications, 1967), p. 2.

[8]Ibid., p. 73.

It was social workers who could have taken up the tradition, the scientific approach, and the theories and empirical studies of sociology and, as carriers of this knowledge, could have applied it in the diagnostic, classification, and treatment quarters of penology. . . . Social workers could have become the functional liaison between disciplines that need one another.[9]

More than one critic has noted that social work has as its central focus the intrapsychic processes of individual clients, "so that the approach is still psychological rather than psychosocial."[10] Handler, however, maintains that social work is placing greater emphasis on institutional or societal factors—social systems that impinge on law violators. Social workers, she states, are looking beyond those factors that operate within the individual actor to those that operate within social systems and which act as generators of crime and delinquency.[11] Kahn states that social workers must be aware of the fact that "delinquency reflects social-structural factors that need to be dealt with at the level of social policy and social provision. To respond only on the level of individual treatment is unsound."[12] Schwartz and Burkhardt, similarly, propose that social workers look more at the problems the client confronts in his environment and "less at the problems that are allegedly within him."[13]

The (New York) Governor's Committee noted the difficulty in bridging the gap between theories that explain how crime develops in society as a general matter and theories that explain the criminality of a given individual:

> Consider, for example, Cloward and Ohlin's theory of Differential Opportunity, which deals with delinquent subcultures rather than with individuals. The theory holds that persons who perceive societal obstacles to legitimate fulfillment of goals generally believed to be accessible to all may adopt illegitimate means of attaining those goals. An important element of the theory is that the individual believes that the obstacles represent injustices created by society and, hence, that he is justified in rejecting society's norms of conduct in pursuing the generally accepted goals. The illegitimate means adopted depend upon the available and accessible opportunities in the particular neighborhood.
>
> The Cloward and Ohlin theory is one way of explaining the phenomenon of crime of a particular type (i.e., lower class youth crime) but it represents a global approach to even that type. One might accept the theory as explaining crime in a certain neighborhood and still have no understanding of why a particular individual in that neighborhood engaged in criminal conduct. To gain such understanding it would be necessary to have knowledge of the individual and to understand the roles played by all of the other factors that might be involved. It might well be that the Cloward and Ohlin theory would explain the individual's criminality, but this cannot be determined without an evaluation of the individ-

---

[9]Ibid., p. 72.

[10]Eckford Voit, "Social Work and Corrections," *Criminology* 13 (August 1975): 259.

[11]Ellen Handler, "Social Work and Corrections," *Criminology* 13 (August 1975): 243.

[12]Kahn, "Social Work and Control of Delinquency," p. 12.

[13]Michael Schwartz and William R. Burkhardt, "Self-Concept in Casework with Adaptive Delinquents," *Social Work* 9 (July 1964): 90.

ual. Thus, such theories may be useful in combatting the general problem of crime and are useful as indicators of factors that may be relevant in treatment of individuals.[14]

The Committee notes that "The criminality of an individual can only rarely be explained by any single factor or by any limited theory."[15] It is only a broader theoretical and methodological approach that will enable the social services to be more responsive to the nuances and variations that are encountered in criminal justice settings. Instead of a model dominated by any one approach or school, the social service worker must be able to "hang loose," remaining eclectic, matching theory to offender, and deriving method from theory. Because of the lack of integration between sociological and psychological approaches, it is the worker who must usually operationalize the theory in ways that are meaningful to his/her setting and clientele. Klenk and Ryan note that treatment or intervention strategies do not flow freely out of the theories and findings of the behavioral sciences: "Whatever action guides they hold have to be teased out and translated into action terms."[16]

[14]Governor's Special Committee on Criminal Offenders, *Preliminary Report*, Albany, N.Y., 1968, p. 289.

[15]Ibid., p. 290.

[16]Robert W. Klenk and Robert M. Ryan, *The Practice of Social Work* (Belmont, Calif.: Wadsworth Publishing, 1970), p. 72.

# 1

# Sociogenic Theories[1] of Crime

## Anomie[2]

Parsons defines anomie as "the disturbance of the state of internalized expectations of persons occasioned by the processes of change in the normative components of the institutionalized culture, and hence in the definition of what can legitimately be expected of individuals and classes of them."[3] Durkheim used the term to describe the "normlessness" which results when the *conscience-collective*, social cohesion, is weakened by some painful crisis or by beneficent but abrupt transitions. At the other extreme from social cohesion is a society in which each individual pursues his own solitary interest.

With the growth of specialization, in the form of a highly developed division of labor, there is a decline in the pervasiveness of the

[1]Theories "clarify and organize events in the world so that they can be placed into perspective; theories explain the causes of past events so that we can predict when, where, and how future events will occur." Johnathan H. Turner, *The Structure of Sociological Theory* (Homewood, Ill.: Dorsey Press, 1974), p. 2; For a discussion of what constitutes sociological theory, see Norman K. Denzin, *The Research Act: A Theoretical Introduction to Sociological Methods* (Chicago: Aldine, 1970), Chapter 2.

[2]From the Greek meaning "lack of law."

[3]Talcott Parsons, *The Social System* (New York: Free Press, 1951), p. 253.

*conscience-collective* and a growth of individualism. Industrialization reduces contacts between workers, between workers and employers—contacts become minimal and socially meaningless. The division of economic functions temporarily outstrips the development of appropriate moral regulation, while work becomes meaningless and degrading. The growth of individualism, while weakening the *conscience-collective* (with the binding force shifting to external powers, i.e., the state) also allows man's insatiable needs to go unbridled: "At the very moment when traditional rules have lost their authority, the richer prize offered these appetites stimulates them and makes them more exigent and impatient of control. The state of de-regulation or anomy is thus further heightened by passions being less disciplined, precisely when they need more disciplining."[4]

Between rapid industrialization and eventual readjustments in the social order is a time lag: when the social scales are upset, time is required for the *conscience-collective* to reclassify men and things and regain social equilibrium. Parsons states that this reorganization "does not occur as an instantaneous adjustment to the major innovations, but is a slow, uneven, and often painful process. In its course, at any one time, there are important elements of indeterminacy in the structure of expectations—not simply in the sense that there are areas of freedom in which autonomous decision is expected, but also in the sense that, where people feel there ought to be guidance, it is either lacking altogether, or the individual is subject to conflicting expectations that are impossible to fulfill all at once."[5]

According to Giddens there is a progressive decline of inequality of opportunity which accompanies the growth of the division of labor. The growth of opportunity, however, cannot match rising aspirations because society is temporarily incapable of exercising a moderating role with respect to these aspirations.[6] In Durkheim's view human nature has unlimited needs, and without a regulating force man's needs are unsatiable. "When this regulation of the individual is upset so that his horizon is broadened beyond what he can endure or contrariwise contracted unduly," anomie results, and the state of anomie is associated with deviant behavior—for Durkheim, in particular, suicide.[7]

In 1938, Robert K. Merton set forth a social and cultural explanation of deviant behavior based on anomie.[8] Like Durkheim, Merton

[4]Emile Durkheim, *Suicide* (New York: Free Press, 1951), p. 253.

[5]Talcott Parsons, *Social Structure and Personality* (New York: Free Press, 1970), p. 171.

[6]Anthony Giddens, *Capitalism and Modern Social Theory* (Cambridge, England: Cambridge University Press, 1971), p. 81.

[7]George Simpson in his introduction to Durkheim's *Suicide*, p. 15.

[8]Robert K. Merton, "Social Structure and Anomie," *American Sociological Review* 3 (1938): 672–82.

emphasized the role of social structures—deviance is a normal response to pressures exerted on certain persons by the social structure. Whereas Durkheim emphasized the deviance of suicide, Merton saw anomie as inducing other forms of deviance, including crime, substance abuse, and mental illness. However, the most important dynamic added by Merton to the theory was the "Americanization" of anomie.

Merton pointed out that no other society comes so close to arguing that success is an absolute value. "There may develop a disproportionate, at times, a virtually exclusive stress upon the value of specific goals, involving relatively slight concern with the institutionally appropriate modes of attaining these goals." Thus, the limiting case in this direction is reached when the range of alternative procedures is restricted only by technical rather than institutional considerations. "Any and all devices which promise attainment of the all important goal would be permitted in this hypothesized polar case." American culture, Merton notes, "has been said to tend in this direction." An "emphasis on the goals of monetary success and material prosperity leads to dominant concern with technological and social instruments designed to produce the desired result, inasmuch as institutional controls become of secondary importance. In such a situation, innovation flourishes as the *range of means* employed is broadened."[9] In American society, "the pressure of prestige-bearing success tends to eliminate the effective social constraint over means employed to this end. 'The-end-justifies-the-means' doctrine becomes a guiding tenet for action when the cultural structure unduly exalts the end and the social organization unduly limits possible recourse to approved means."[10]

Anomie results when numbers of people are confronted by the contradiction between goals and means and "become estranged from a society that promises them in principle what they are deprived in reality."[11] Despite numerous success stories "we know that in this same society that proclaims the right, and even the duty, of lofty aspirations for all, men do not have equal access to the opportunity structure."[12] Merton notes that most people manage to scale down their aspirations, but many find it difficult to do so. "Aberrant conduct, therefore, may be viewed as a symptom of dissociation between culturally defined aspirations and socially structured means."[13] According to Parsons America emphasizes the economic aspects of social structure including

[9]Ibid., p. 673.

[10]Ibid., p. 681.

[11]Robert K. Merton, "Anomie, Anomia, and Social Interaction," *Anomie and Deviant Behavior*, ed. Marshall B. Clinard (New York: Free Press, 1964), p. 218.

[12]Ibid.

[13]Merton, "Social Structure and Anomie," p. 674.

high levels of current family income and the "capitalization" of households through the spread of home ownership, the development of consummer goods, etc. Merton points to the role of the mass media which constantly exposes persons to the "economic aspects of social structure" and the rewards of "fame and fortune."[14]

Anomie is particularly severe within disadvantaged segments of our population. In his discussion of Durkheim's theory, Merton states that a disjunction develops between "aspirations which, even where relatively limited, cannot be approximated, owing in part to socially patterned limitations of access to opportunity."[15] The successful, as Durkheim noted, also suffer from anomia, but, according to the theory it "arises from another kind of seemingly futile pursuit, when progressively heightened aspirations are fostered by each temporary success and by the enlarged expectations visited on them by associates."[16] Thus, anomie has both relativistic and contagious aspects which "can readily create status-anxiety that disturbs the peace of the ostensibly successful."[17] Durkheim refers to this as "overweening ambition" which he notes *always* exceeds the results obtained.[18] The relativistic aspect of anomie is examined by Cohen: "the level of goal attainment that will seem just and reasonable to concrete actors, and therefore the sufficiency of available means, will be relative to the attainments of others who serve as reference objects." Cohen notes that others whom we define as legitimate objects of comparison may adhere to legitimate or illegitimate means—thus, our own choice of means may be affected.[19]

According to Merton contagion results when there is a "mounting frequency of deviant but 'successful' behavior," and this "tends to lessen and, as an extreme potentiality, to eliminate the legitimacy of the institutional norms for others in the system."[20] When there is a breakdown of institutionally accepted means of reaching goals "it affects not only the individuals who first engage in deviant behavior, but also the other individuals in the social system."[21] Merton states that "some individuals are subjected more than others to the strains arising from discrepencies between cultural goals and effective access to their realization."[22] Merton concludes that a growth of "patterns of 'illicit suc-

---

[14]Parsons, *Social Structure and Personality*, p. 156.
[15]Merton, "Anomie, Anomia, and Social Interaction," p. 225.
[16]Ibid., p. 225.
[17]Ibid., p. 221.
[18]Durkheim, p. 253.
[19]Albert K. Cohen, "The Sociology of the Deviant Act: Anomie Theory and Beyond," *American Sociological Review* 30 (February 1965): 6.
[20]Merton, "Anomie, Anomia, and Social Interaction," p. 234.
[21]Ibid., p. 232.
[22]Ibid., p. 234.

cess' may progressively enlarge the degree of anomie in society so that others, who did not at first respond by personal deviant behavior to the initially low degree of anomie, may become liable to deviance as anomie is accentuated, thus in turn creating an anomic situation for still others."[23]

Merton proposes five modes of individual adaptation to culturally prescribed goals of success: conformity, ritualism, rebellion, innovation, and retreatism. Rebellion is conceived of as a transitional response which involves efforts to change the structure rather than make accomodations: "rebellion occurs when emancipation from the reigning standards, due to frustration or to marginalist perspectives, leads to the attempt to introduce a 'new social order.' "[24] To consider this adaptation within the scope of the criminal justice practitioner some statutory violation is necessary. However, the line between lawful protest and officially sanctioned activity is often blurred. In many instances criminal justice practitioner involvement is dependent upon the response of agencies of social control to "rebellious" activity. Therefore, we shall consider only the last two modes of adaptation to be of direct concern to the criminal justice practitioner.

*Innovation* is the adoption of illegitimate means to gain success, an adoption most common in the lower stratum of society. In such a stratum innovation may be a "normal" response to a situation where societal goals have been incorporated and accepted, but where the access to legitimate means for becoming successful are limited. Crime is viewed as basically a utilitarian adaptation.

*Retreatism* is an abandonment of cultural goals and socially accepted practices directed towards reaching these goals. Although the goals have been internalized, their unattainable quality causes them to be rejected in favor of an escape into nonproductive adaptations, e.g., drug addiction and alcoholism.

In the first instance, the criminal justice practitioner is often confronted with clients whose role models are innovative: pimps, racketeers, and drug traffickers. These highly visible criminals often flaunt their financial success in the form of expensive clothes and automobiles, in addition to other status measures of criminal success— women, power, "respect." They provide a form of encouragement for others to innovate, as Merton states, enlarging the degree of anomie in society. Those who are not up to innovation, due perhaps to a lack of intelligence, skill, connections, etc., may move to a retreatist pattern, especially heroin addiction. Several observers have reported that

[23]Ibid., p. 232.
[24]Merton, "Social Structure and Anomie," p. 678.

heroin addiction provides an alternative and attractive life-style. Raymond, for example, describes the narcotic addict as a person for whom narcotics offer a "sense of identity, one with few high or unattainable expectations." He sees addiction as a "career" with its own intrinsic, if not dubious, rewards: "The use of drugs gives him a way of life and 'kicks' that come from running risks required to sustain the habit and being emulated by peers who admire his cunning and courage."[25] Preble and Casey describe the quest for heroin as a search for "a meaningful life." They note that in many high delinquency areas the heroin addict is a hero model: "The appelation of *a real hustling dope fiend* (a successful burglar, robber, con man, etc.) is a mark of respect and status."[26]

Parsons provides an important dimension to the retreatist adaptation, which he labels as *withdrawal*, and which is symptomatic of alienation and passivity. He states that the tendency to withdraw is the most prominent type of deviance in American society; a process which has its origins in the residues of the preoedipal mother-child relationship involving the first time object-attachment. Parsons refers to the "American dilemma" in which the child is encouraged to form an extremely intense attachment to the mother, while at a later age he or she is required to break radically with this early dependence as part of a process of emancipation and independent living. The alienation that results, therefore, involves withdrawal from a set of expectations which put stress on independent achievement.[27] Parsons observes that in American society, which is changing rapidly and "in which there is so much mobility of status, it is only natural that the older generation cannot provide direct guidance and role models that would present the young person with a neatly structured definition of the situation." Instead, the young person "is pushed out of the nest and expected to fly."[28]

Some aspects of anomie present some obvious operational concepts for the criminal justice practitioner. The first relates to persons who have not managed to scale down their aspirations. These individuals have "overadapted" societal goals beyond realistic bounds, and they have adopted innovative or retreatist methods of dealing with the resulting anomic state. In this case the criminal justice practitioner might assist the client to assess goals realistically and help the client to

[25]Frank B. Raymond, "A Sociological View of Narcotics Addiction," *Crime and Delinquency* 21 (January 1975): 14–15.
[26]Edward Preble and John J. Casey, Jr., "Taking Care of Business: The Heroin User's Life on the Street," *The International Journal of the Addictions* 4 (March 1969): 3.
[27]Parsons, *Social Structure and Personality*, pp. 285–86.
[28]Ibid., p. 178.

develop or organize resources that will enable him or her to achieve these goals. A second operational concept relates to Merton's answer to anomie: providing more adequate means for achieving success—opportunities based on merit. The criminal justice practitioner must assess clients' capacities and motivations and, by making use of information on community resources, help to provide a more adequate method for success within the framework of legal structures. In order to advance this treatment goal, the criminal justice practitioner may have to play advocate in order to secure for clients the services and opportunities to which they are entitled. Acting as an advocate the criminal justice practitioner must deal vigorously with such items as prejudice and discrimination against certain racial and ethnic groups, as well as against offenders in general. Artificial (and perhaps illegal) roadblocks to clients seeking socially acceptable and realistic means of achieving goals must be attacked by criminal justice practitioners if they are to be effective social service workers.

## Alienation

Alienation is closely akin to the concept of anomie: some sociologists "have come to use the term 'alienation' to refer, in part, to the subjective aspects of what Merton called anomie."[29] Marx used the term to indicate a separation between the worker and the product of his labor in capitalist society. He saw the material objects produced by the worker becoming treated on par with the worker himself. "The alienation of the worker in the capitalist economy is founded upon this disparity between the productive power of labour, which becomes increasingly great with the expansion of capitalism, and the lack of control which the worker is able to exert over the objects which he produces."[30] Bottomore notes that Marx uses the concept of alienation in order to describe a condition of society in which, although the process of labor should involve the development of man's potentialities and the creation of a world of human enjoyment, it actually produced, through private property, acquisitiveness, exchange and competition, a devaluation and dehumanization of the worker.[31]

While the term has undergone change since its use by Marx, current usage usually contains elements of the original meaning, i.e., isola-

[29]Clinard, Marshall B., ed., *Anomie and Deviant Behavior* (New York: Free Press, 1964), p. 14.
[30]Giddens, p. 11.
[31]Tom Bottomore, ed., *Karl Marx* (Englewood Cliffs, N.J.: Prentice-Hall, 1973), p. 8.

tion, anonymity, impersonalization—in sum, a "disconnectedness" with serious, negative consequences. Clinard states that "the alienated individual is considered marginal, normless and isolated."[32] Keniston states that the term "has become a fashionable catchword for the varied problems and malaises of our age,"[33] while Dressler notes that the term is associated with deviance.[34]

In the following discussion of alienation, I have frequently quoted Melvin Seeman's article, "The Meaning of Alienation."

Seeman distinguishes five types of alienation:[35]

1. Powerlessness
2. Meaninglessness
3. Normlessness
4. Isolation
5. Self-estrangement

*Powerlessness* can be conceived of as "the expectancy or probability held by the individual that his own behavior cannot determine the occurrence of the outcomes, or reinforcements, he seeks." Seeman provides a point that can be useful to the criminal justice practitioner in evaluating a client with respect to this element of alienation: the criminal justice practitioner must determine "the degree of realism involved in the individual's response to his situation." Social service workers recognize this as "reality testing." Seeman notes that it is one thing to feel powerless with regard to such global concerns as war, and quite another to feel powerless in making friends.

*Meaninglessness* is referred to when "the individual is unclear as to what he ought to believe—when the individual's minimal standards for clarity in decision-making are not met." This results in a "low expectancy that satisfactory predictions about the future outcomes of behavior can be made."

*Normlessness* is closely identified with anomie by both Durkheim and Merton. Seeman defines it as a situation "in which there is a high expectancy that socially unapproved behaviors are required to achieve given goals."

*Isolation* is defined in terms of reward values: "The alienated in

---

[32]Clinard, p. 14.

[33]Kenneth Keniston, *Youth and Dissent* (New York: Harcourt Brace Jovanovich, 1971), p. 174.

[34]David Dressler, *Sociology: The Study of Human Interaction* (New York: Knopf, 1976), p. 181.

[35]Melvin Seeman, "The Meaning of Alienation," *American Sociological Review* 24 (December 1959): 783–91.

the isolation sense are those who, like the intellectual, assign low re-ward value to goals or beliefs that are typically highly valued in the given society." Within this type of alienation are two types of adapta-tion referred to by Merton: (1) innovation—using culturally disap-proved means to achieve goals: and (2) rebellion—moving outside the social structure to seek a new, greatly modified, social structure.

*Self-estrangement* means "to be something less than one might ideally be if the circumstances in society were otherwise." Thus, the rewards of a given behavior often lie outside of the activity itself, e.g., the worker who dislikes his job and who works merely for his salary.

Seeman's five types of alienation provide a basis for operationaliz-ing services to the alienated criminal justice client using reeducation. Through the medium of the interview (or group process) the client is taught to recognize that his/her own behavior can influence outcomes and goals, reducing *Powerlessness*. The focus is an ethnomethodologi-cal[36] one, it is attuned to practical actions of everyday life, as opposed to global concerns, e.g., war and peace.

The criminal justice practitioner and the client will isolate spe-cific actions, real if possible, hypothetical if necessary, and follow the results of these actions through to a logical conclusion. The criminal justice practitioner will show the client how to clarify alternatives so that the client can make rational choices, increasing predictive powers and reducing *Meaninglessness*. Dealing with *Normlessness* and *Isola-tion*, both of which have been linked to deviance, is quite difficult. Rewards for unlawful activity abound in our society where cultural folk-heroes are often the likes of a Jesse James or an Al Capone. Persons thus alienated are sometimes referred to as *environmental sociopaths*, and such a person will usually respond only to sanctions and the de-gree of pain that activities incur. Motivation to change with such clients, therefore, must be predicated on the reality of severe sanctions.

Parsons presents a category of alienation which is of direct inter-est to the criminal justice practitioner: the *actively alienated* actor "is predisposed toward individual crime. By virtue of his active orienta-tion he is inclined to defy sanctions, to challenge others to 'do some-thing about.' "[37] Another distinct, although similar, category is the *ac-tively overtly alienated*: This actor maintains an ambivalence about his/her role between conformity and acting out. This actor is inclined to join the criminal or delinquent gang in which partnership in crime "reinforces . . . alienative need-dispositions." By substituting the de-viant subculture for the norms of the social system, this actor can now

[36]See, for example, Harold Garfinkel, *Studies in Ethnomethodolgy* (En-glewood Cliffs, N.J.: Prentice-Hall, 1967), especially pp. 11, 35–36, and 77.
[37]Parsons, *The Social System*, p. 284.

act out both conformative and alienative components—conforming to the deviant subculture while actively rejecting the social system norms. Parsons notes that this "greatly weakens the attitudinal sanctions of the normal instiutionalized structure in that each gang member has an alter to whom he can turn for approval of his action to offset the disapproval of the rest of society."[38]

Sarata presents an *alienation-reduction paradigm*[39] for dealing with delinquency, a paradigm in which the focus is on the situation rather than the individual actor. Defining alienation as "a condition in which there is a disintegration of relations between the person and one or more aspects of his environment," Sarata maintains that alienation precedes delinquent acts. He argues that a paradigm is needed that does not imply blame, but simply recognizes that there is a condition in which meaningful interaction between the delinquent and his environment is "not right." Noting, however, that people, and not situations, commit crimes, Sarata recommends that all treatment approaches make the following communication operational: "You have been convicted of a crime and therefore you will receive punishment. It also seems that some aspects of your life situation are less than satisfactory. Services are available to any citizen in such predicaments and you may wish to avail yourself of the following . . ." Participation in any rehabilitation program that is not voluntary, the author argues, merely increases alienation.

## Differential Association

Most, if not all, rules of probation and parole contain a warning or prohibition against certain associations—for example, with persons who have been convicted of felony crimes. A not uncommon exhortation made by some parents to their children is to stay away from certain company—i.e., keep away from the "bad kids." If there is a theoretical framework that lends support to these rules and exhortations, it would be differential association, which conceives of criminality as a behavior that is learned in interaction with other persons.

This theory, developed by Edwin Sutherland, asserts that the principal part of learning criminal behavior occurs within intimate personal groups based on the degree of intensity, frequency, and duration of the association. The actor learns, in addition to the techniques of committing crime, the drives, attitudes, and rationalizations which add

---

[38]Ibid., p. 286.
[39]Brian P. Sarata, "Alienation-Reduction As A Pardigm for Delinquency Reduction," *Journal of Criminal Justice* 4 (1976): 123–31.

up to a favorable precondition to criminal behavior—the balance between criminal and noncriminal associations. The goal of much criminal and noncriminal behavior is the same, i.e., securing money or status. Differential association accounts for the difference in selecting criminal or noncriminal methods to achieve the goal.

Sutherland presents the nine basics of differential assocation:

1. Criminal behavior is learned.
2. Criminal behavior is learned in interaction with other persons in a process of communication.
3. The principal part of the learning of criminal behavior occurs within intimate groups.
4. When criminal behavior is learned, the learning includes (a) techniques of committing the crime, which are sometimes very complicated, sometimes very simple; (b) the specific direction of motives, drives, rationalizations, and attitudes.
5. The specific direction of motives and drives is learned from definitions of legal codes as favorable and unfavorable. Sutherland notes that in America, attitudes towards rules are usually mixed, and "consequently we have culture conflict in relation to the legal codes."
6. In what Sutherland refers to as *the principle* of differential association, a person becomes delinquent because of an excess of definitions favorable to violation of law over definitions unfavorable to violation of law.
7. Differential association may vary in frequency, duration, priority, and intensity.
8. The process of learning criminal behavior by association with criminal and anticriminal patterns involves all of the mechanisms that are involved in any other learning.
9. Though criminal behavior is an expression of general needs and values, it is not explained by those general needs and values since noncriminal behavior is an expression of the same needs and values.[40]

Taylor, Walton, and Young note that within the theory the actor seems rather limited in his choices: "the resulting behavior appears to be totally determined."[41] They note Sutherland's stress on neighbor-

---

[40]Karl Schuessler, ed., *Edwin H. Sutherland: On Analyzing Crime* (Chicago: University of Chicago Press, 1973), pp. 8–10.

[41]Ian Taylor, Paul Walton, and Jock Young, *The New Criminology* (New York: Harper & Row, 1973), p. 132.

hood environment, "eco-niches," which would appear to severely limit alternatives in the competition between social values.[42]

Sutherland places some qualifications on the theory: "A person may learn, through association with a criminal pattern, a definition of the situation in which it is appropriate to commit a particular crime. He commits this crime, however, only when the situation defined as appropriate arises or can be located."[43] Accordingly, criminal behavior may also result when the alternatives are either not viable or available: even an honest man may steal if the alternative is starvation.[44] Another qualifying variable is "susceptibility": if a person has a low degree of susceptibility it will take a great deal of criminal association to cause him to engage in criminal activities.[45]

Schuessler notes that the theory is tautological: crime causes crime, and thus it fails to explain how crime originates, merely how it is transmitted. The theory is obviously limited to those crimes in which the perpetrators have had extensive criminal contacts prior to the commission of the acts.[46]

Glaser moves Sutherland's theory into what he calls a theory of *differential identification:* "a person pursues criminal behavior to the extent that he identifies himself with real or imaginary persons from whose perspective his criminal behavior seems acceptable." Glaser states:[47]

> Most persons in our society are believed to identify themselves with both criminal and non-criminal persons in the course of their lives. Criminal identification may occur, for example, during direct experience in delinquent membership groups, through positive reference to criminal roles portrayed in mass media,[48] or as a negative reaction to forces opposed to crime. The family probably is the principal non-criminal reference group, even for criminals. It is supplemented by many other groups of anti-criminal generalized others.

Clark, building on Glaser, presents a *reference group* theory of delinquency.[49] His theory provides suggestions for the criminal justice

---

[42]Ibid., p. 128.

[43]Schuessler, p. 34.

[44]Paraphrased from Schuessler, pp. 34–36.

[45]Paraphrased from Schuessler, pp. 42–43.

[46]Ibid., p. xviii.

[47]Daniel Glaser, "Criminality Theories and Behavioral Images," *American Journal of Sociology* 61 (March 1956): 433–44.

[48]Sutherland believed "that the impersonal agencies of communication, such as picture shows and newspapers, play a relatively unimportant part in the genesis of criminal behavior." Schuessler, p. 8.

[49]Robert E. Clark, *Reference Group Theory and Delinquency* (New York: Behavioral Publications, 1972), p. 7.

practitoner who is trying to reform the offender by changing his reference group identification. Clark's theory derives from Glaser's allegorical reference to the theater:[50]

> The image of behavior as role-playing, borrowed from the theatre, presents people as directing their conceptions of how others see them. The choice of another, from whose perspective we view our behavior, is the process of identification. It may be with the immediate others or with distant and perhaps abstractly generalized others of our reference groups. (The "amateur" criminal may identify himself with the highly professional "master"-criminal whom he has never met.) Rationalization is seen as a necessary concomitant of voluntary behavior, particularly when role conflicts exist. Acceptance by the group with which one identifies one's self and conceptions of persecution by other groups are among the most common and least intellectual bases for rationalization by criminals. Role imagery provides the most comprehensive and interconnected theoretical framework for explaining the phenomena of criminality.

Clark advises the criminal justice practitioner to build or encourage desirable identities in the offenders:[51]

1. Make it rewarding for the offender to take on the identity of one who is reformed by (a) making visible the rewards which the reformed receive and (b) granting him the identity of one who is reformed early enough that anticipatory socialization will have its desired effect.
2. Provide status identity which requires lawful behavior, e.g., a position of trust, and then support his efforts to carry out the required roles by showing faith and trust in him.
3. Validate the fact that certain nonmembership groups are realistic aspirations for him. If he is lacking in the skills and training which are required, such training should be provided.
4. Strengthen his aspirations to "make it" as a noncriminal. For example, by showing a parolee others who, like himself, have been able to "make it" after release from prison.
5. Explore with the offender the various identities he is interested in, the priorities of each identity, and the incompatibility of the deviant identities with his primary identity goal of reform.

---

[50]Glaser, "Criminality Theories and Behavioral Images," p. 437.
[51]Clark, pp. 96–97. Reprinted by permission of Human Sciences Press and Robert E. Clark.

According to Sutherland, criminal behavior is learned in interaction with other persons, as is noncriminal behavior. It is this "learning" aspect of the theory which apparently moved Schuessler to assert that if Sutherland were working today he would have availed himself of the reinforcement theories of the behaviorists.[52] This is what Burgess and Akers do in their paper, "A Differential Association-Reinforcement Theory of Criminal Behavior."[53]

Burgess and Akers reformulate Sutherland's basics of differential association into seven statements that center on that part of behavior theory usually referred to as operant conditioning:[54] the law of operant conditioning declares that a reinforcer will increase the rate of occurence of any operant which produces it—a "Skinnerian approach" which merely notes that any action that is rewarded tends to be repeated, and vice-versa. In their reformulation of Sutherland's basic *principle* (number 6) *of differential association*, they state:[55]

> a person will become delinquent if the official norms or laws do not perform a discriminative function and thereby control "normative" or conforming behavior. We know from the law of differential reinforcement that the operant which produces the most reinforcement will become dominant. Thus, if lawful behavior did not reault in reinforcement, the strength of the behavior would be weakened, and a state of deprivation would result. This, in turn, would increase the probability that other behaviors would be emitted which are reinforced and hence would be strengthened and, of course, these behaviors, though common to one or more groups, may be labeled deviant by the larger society. Also such behavior patterns themselves may acquire conditioned reinforcing value and subsequently be reinforced by the members of a group by making various forms of social reinforcement, such as social approval, esteem, and status, contingent upon that behavior.[56]

Burgess and Akers conclude: "Criminal behavior would, then, occur under the conditions in which an individual has been most highly reinforced for such behavior, and the aversive consequences

[52]Schuessler, pp. xvi–xvii.

[53]Robert L. Burgess and Ronald L. Akers, "Differential Association-Reinforcement Theory of Criminal Behavior," *Social Problems* 14 (Fall 1966). Reprinted in *Behavioral Sociology*, ed. Robert L. Burgess and Don Bushell, Jr. (New York: Columbia University Press, 1969).

[54]Behavior theory will be discussed in the section on psychogenic theories.

[55]Burgess and Akers, *Behavioral Sociology*, p. 315.

[56]This last sentence should be considered when subcultural theory is discussed later in this section.

contingent upon the behavior have been of such a nature that they do not perform a 'punishment function.' "[57] That this statement would seem to support a "deterrence" position with respect to criminal justice is obvious. However, Taylor et al., are quite critical of the Burgess and Akers position.[58]

## Differential Opportunity

Cloward and Ohlin present a theory that integrates anomie with differential association.[59] Taylor et al., note that this theory views delinquency as more of a collective endeavor than an individual adaptation.[60] Cloward and Ohlin are concerned with "how delinquent subcultures arise, develop various law-violating ways of life, and persist or change." They distinguish between three types of delinquent subcultures that result from a differential opportunity structure:

1. *criminal subculture*: gang activities devoted to utilitarian criminal pursuits;
2. *conflict subculture*: gang activities devoted to violence and destructive acting out as a way of gaining status; and
3. *retreatist subculture*: activities in which drug usage is the primary focus.

The youths in categories 2 and 3 are actually "double failures"— in both the legitimate and alternative illegitimate criminal worlds. They are the youngsters who proliferate the criminal justice sequence and who make up the overwhelming majority of clients for the criminal justice practitioner.

Cloward and Ohlin state that the dilemma of many lower-class people is that they are unable to locate alternative avenues to success-goals. "Delinquent subcultures, we believe, represent specialized modes of adaptation to this problem of adjustment." The criminal and conflict subcultures provide illegal avenues, while the retreatist "anticipates defeat and now seeks to escape from the burden of the future."[61] However, Cloward and Ohlin add an additional dimension to the dilemma of adaptation: "access to illegitimate roles, no less than

[57]Burgess and Akers, *Behavioral Sociology*, p. 316.
[58]See Taylor et al., pp. 130–33.
[59]Richard A. Cloward and Lloyd E. Ohlin, *Delinquency and Opportunity* (New York: Free Press, 1960).
[60]Taylor et al., p. 134.
[61]Cloward and Ohlin, p. 107.

access to legitimate roles, is limited by both social and psychological factors."[62] They conclude that "there are marked differences from one part of the social structure to another in the type of illegitimate adaptions that are available to persons in search of solutions to problems of adjustment arising from restricted availability of legitimate means."[63] Blacks, for example, have been disadvantaged not only in the legitimate, but also in the illegitimate sector of social mobility: Gage notes that "no door is more firmly locked to blacks than the one that leads to the halls of power in organized crime."[64]

Ianni has observed that organized crime "is a functional part of the American social system, an available means of economic and social mobility."[65] Coser states that crime permits the achievement of social status by persons who, because of their socioeconomic and/or racial status, are deprived of other channels for achieving status.[66] Back in 1943, Whyte noted that the children of immigrants would not have been able to achieve social mobility without gaining control of racket (and political) organizations.[67]

Certain types of criminal activity are quite functional for the offender—*functional* in the literal, as opposed to the psychological, sense of that word—insofar as they can provide handsome economic benefits. The criminal justice practitioner must ascertain the degree to which an offender's criminal activity is functional. In particular, the criminal justice practitioner must be sensitive to the possibility that the offender is involved in organized crime activity or professional criminality. Often it is an impossible, and usually thankless, task to provide alternative means for such clients to reach success-goals.

Short et al., discuss certain aspects of the opportunity structure paradigm which were operationalized in a study of delinquent gangs in Chicago.[68] They compared black and white lower-class gang boys with lower-class nongang boys from the same neighborhoods, and with middle-class boys of the same race. They found that "perception of

[62]Ibid.

[63]Ibid., p. 152.

[64]Nicholas Gage, *The Mafia Is Not An Equal Opportunity Employer* (New York: McGraw-Hill, 1971), p. 113.

[65]Francis A. J. Ianni, *Black Mafia* (New York: Simon & Schuster, 1974), p. 280.

[66]Lewis A. Coser, *Constitution in the Study of Social Conflict* (New York: Free Press, 1967), p. 79.

[67]William Foote Whyte, "Social Organization in the Slums," *American Sociological Review* 8 (1943): 38.

[68]James F. Short, Jr., Ramon Rivera, and Roy A. Tennyson, "Perceived Opportunities, Gang Membership, and Delinquency," *American Sociological Review* 30 (February 1965): 56–57.

*legitimate* opportunities is more strongly associated with delinquency rates than is perception of illegitimate opportunitites." This, they note, is consistant with the theory that when perceived legitimate opportunities have been appraised and found wanting, illegitimate opportunities are then considered and in many cases acted upon. The authors note, however, that within racial categories, perception of illegitimate opportunities does not correspond to delinquency rates: they discovered that "illegitimate opportunities appeared to be open to more Negro than white boys." With respect to legitimate occupational opportunities, they "are perceived as available less often by gang than by nongang boys, and most often by middle-class boys." Differences were also found with respect to race: "White boys are more likely than Negro boys to perceive such opportunities as available in each strata examined."

For the criminal justice practitioner the theory can provide some direction. As with anomie, the worker must analyze the extent to which the offender is reflecting reality with respect to his perceptions of opportunity. It has been the writer's experience that offenders will often overestimate their ability and available opportunities. An offender who does this will soon become quite frustrated, and the resulting hostility can easily convert into further deviant activity. The criminal justice practitioner must help clients to scale down aspirations to realistic levels and then help them to attain success goals. Clients who underestimate their ability or available opportunities must be guided into areas where realistic success goals can be met. The criminal justice practitioner must also be active in the advocate's role by breaking down artificial and/or illegal barriers to opportunity.

## Subcultural Theory

Short explains that "subcultures are patterns of values, norms, and behavior which have become traditional among certain groups. These groups may be of many types, including occupational and ethnic groups, social classes, occupants of 'closed institutions' and various age grades." They are "important frames of reference through which individuals and groups see the world and interpret it."[69] Cohen argues that in certain lower-class subcultures there is a negation of middle-class values, and this negation is a severe handicap. Cohen says that

[69]James F. Short, Jr., *Gang Delinquency and Delinquent Subcultures* (New York: Harper and Row, 1968), p. 11.

there are certain cultural characteristics that are necessary to achieve success and that the middle-class child is more likely to have these characteristics as a result of his upbringing:[70]

> ambition
> a sense of individual responsibility
> skills for achievement
> ability to postpone gratification
> industry and thrift
> rational planning (e.g., budgeting)
> cultivation of manners
> control of physical aggression
> respect for property
> a sense of "wholesome" recreation

Cohen states that class-linked differences "relegate to the bottom of the status pyramid those children belonging to the most disadvantaged classes, not by virtue of their class position as such but by virtue of their lack of requisite personal qualifications resulting from their class-linked handicaps." These children simply lack the attributes listed above.

Cloward and Ohlin note that in a social system that generates severe problems of adjustment for a number of persons, a collective challenge to the legitimacy of established rules and norms will emerge.[71] Those persons sharing a sense of anomie, for example, may reject established norms of the greater culture and devise or adopt delinquent means of achieving success.[72] They note that the discrepency between aspirations and opportunities is not experienced evenly throughout society, and thus "persons in status locations where the discrepency is most acute may develop a common perception and sense of indignation about their disadvantages as contrasted with the advantages of others."[73] This sense of injustice results in acts of deviance and brings the actor into conflict with the official system. The deviant seeks encouragement and reassurance to defend his actions and searches out and joins with others similarly situated. Collectively they provide support for one another in common attitudes of alienation.[74] They form delinquent subcultures whose members have actually

---

[70]Albert K. Cohen, *Delinquent Boys* (New York: Free Press, 1965), p. 86.
[71]Cloward and Ohlin, p. 108.
[72]Ibid., p. 109.
[73]Ibid., p. 108.
[74]Ibid., p. 126.

internalized goals, but because of limitations on legitimate means of access to these goals, instead of revising their aspirations, they become frustrated and reject the middle-class norms of the larger society.[75]

Cohen states that for the child who rejects middle-class morality "there are no moral inhibitions on the free expression of aggression against sources of his frustration."[76] According to Cohen "the delinquent subculture takes its norms from the larger culture but turns them upside down. The delinquent's conduct is right, by the standards of his subculture, precisely *because* it is wrong by the norms of the larger culture."[77] This position is rejected by Short and other authors.[78] Short concludes that the subcultural delinquent gang merely discourages expression of conventional values, and "values which are given active support within the context of gang interaction, for example, toughness and sexual prowess are not conducive to conventional types of achievement."[79]

Cohen emphasizes the totally nonutilitarian nature of most subcultural gang delinquency: it is malicious, negativistic—"stealing 'for the hell of it' and apart from considerations of gain and profit is a valued activity which attaches glory, prowess and profound satisfaction."[80] He notes that rules are not something to be evaded, they are to be *flouted:* there is an element of active spite, malice, contempt, ridicule, challenge and defiance.[81] The sheer strength of this flouting is, at least in part, the result of a *reaction-formation*; the norms of the larger culture are merely repressed, they linger on, unacknowledged "an everpresent threat to the adjustment which has been achieved."[82] For the criminal justice practitioner to deal with the delinquent subculture is problematic, since Cohen notes: "Gang members are usually resistant to the efforts of home, school, and other agencies to regulate, not only their delinquent activities, but any activities carried on within the group, and efforts to compete with the gang for the time and other resources of its members."[83]

[75]Ibid., p. 86.
[76]Cohen, p. 132.
[77]Ibid., p. 28.
[78]See, for example, Robert A. Gordon et al., "Values and Gang Delinquency: A Study of Street Corner Groups," *American Journal of Sociology* 69 (September 1963): 109–28; James F. Short, Jr., et al., "Adult-Adolescent Relations and Gang Delinquency," *Pacific Sociological Review* 7 (Fall 1964): 59–65; Martin Gold, *Status Forces in Delinquent Boys* (Ann Arbor, Mich.: Institute for Social Research, 1963); Taylor et al., pp. 135–36.
[79]Short, p. 16.
[80]Cohen, p. 26.
[81]Ibid., p. 28.
[82]Ibid., p. 132.
[83]Ibid., p. 31.

Cloward and Ohlin state that the first deviant acts are uncertain and filled with fear of disapproval. However, the resulting conflict with official agencies make these early and tentative steps quicken and harden into delinquent careers. Thus, contact with official agencies, i.e., criminal justice agencies, early in the "career" is significant and should be of strategic value to the criminal justice practitioner in his/her efforts to prevent further delinquency and involvement with the criminal justice sequence. Cloward and Ohlin believe that it is the lone delinquent who "is much more likely to experience feelings of ambivalence toward conventional norms of conduct and moral evaluations." Thus, the lone delinquent, and not the gang delinquent, is "more likely to experience guilt reactions and to use various psychological mechanisms for controlling them" such as *reaction-formation*.[84] The subcultural gang delinquent, on the other hand, does not experience guilt feelings and has a stubborn resistance to correction, items that "have earned such offenders the label of 'psychopathic personalities.'" Cloward and Ohlin note that attempts to treat them through conventional therapy usually fail "largely because it is necessary for the 'patient' to have guilt feelings before customary treatment procedures leading to psychological reorganization can be brought into play."[85] They distinguish between subcultural delinquency and delinquent acts "which do not depend upon the prescriptions of a delinquent subculture but are, rather, secondary or incidental to the performance of essentially lawful social roles." They note that neurotic or psychotic youngsters, likewise, may commit delinquent acts without being part of a delinquent subculture since their acting out is not supported and shared by peers.[86]

The delinquent subculture is primarily male and working class, and female delinquency is likely to be related to a girl's adjustment and relationship to boys. Delinquent or acting out behavior will thus often involve sexual misconduct. Cavan reviewed various studies on female delinquency and states that they indicate that the delinquent girls resemble the delinquent boys with respect to age, lower-class background, and disorganized family life.[87] Cavan concludes that girls often strive for middle-class goals in the form of marriage and frequently drop out of school for that purpose. The female delinquent often seeks satisfying relationships with boys in order to escape and offset an unpleasant home environment. She notes that confirmed delinquent girls tend to engage in minor theft and prostitution, or they may assist criminal boyfriends or husbands.

[84]Cloward and Ohlin, p. 137.
[85]Ibid., p. 132.
[86]Ibid., p. 9.
[87]Ruth Shonle Cavan, *Juvenile Delinquency*, 2nd ed. (Philadelphia, Pa.: Lippincott, 1969), Chapter 9.

Miller states that law-violating acts committed by members of adolescent street corner groups in lower class communities have as their dominant component of motivation an attempt by the actor "to adhere to forms of behavior, and to achieve standards of behavior as they are defined within that community."[88] He states that in the case of gang delinquency "the cultural system which exerts the most direct influence on behavior is that of the lower class community itself." Therefore, contrary to Cohen and also Cloward and Ohlin, the delinquent subculture did not rise in conflict with the larger, middle class culture, nor is it "oriented to the deliberate violation of middle-class norms." The focal concerns of the lower-class culture are:[89]

1. Trouble—law violating behavior
2. Toughness—physical prowess, daring
3. Smartness—ability to "con," shrewdness
4. Excitement—thrills, risk, danger
5. Fate—being lucky
6. Autonomy—independent of external constraint

*Trouble* often involves fighting or sexual adventures while drinking; troublesome behavior for women frequently means sexual involvement with disadvantageous consequences. Miller contends that any desire to avoid troublesome behavior is based less on a commitment to legal or larger social order norms than on a desire to avoid the possible legal and other undesirable consequences of the action. There is a potential for internalized conflict for the actor in these circumstances in the opposition of trouble-producing behavior, which is a source of status, and nontrouble producing behavior which is required in order to avoid legal and other complications. Miller notes that this "opposition" has not infrequently resulted in brothers coming out of this milieu, with one becoming a criminal and the other becoming a policeman.[90]

One of the more significant aspects of *trouble* for the criminal justice practitioner is what Miller refers to as "the covertly valued desire to be 'cared for' and subject to external restraint."[91] Thus, *trouble* offers multiple rewards, covert and overt, conscious and unconscious, and the criminal justice practitioner should be aware of the

---

[88]Walter B. Miller, "Lower Class Culture As A Generating Milieu of Gang Delinquency," *Journal of Social Issues* 14 (1958): 5–19.
[89]Ibid., p. 7.
[90]Ibid., p. 8.
[91]Ibid.

possibility that the troublesome behavior of a lower-class client may be symptomatic of a desire for restraint and a need to be cared for.

The emphasis on *toughness* is traced by Miller to the significant proportion of lower-class males reared in predominantly female-dominated households and the resulting concern over homosexuality which "runs like a persistent thread through lower-class culture."[92] Gambling, which is also prevalent in lower-class culture, has its roots in the belief that "their lives are subject to a set of forces over which they have relatively little control,"[93] a symptom of that subjective aspect of alienation referred to as powerlessness.

Miller refers to some of the sentiments commonly expressed in lower-class culture: "No one's gonna push me around," and "I'm gonna tell him to take the job and shove it . . . ." The paradox of *autonomy*, states Miller, is that actual patterns of behavior "reveal a marked discrepency between expressed sentiment and what is covertly valued." He notes that many lower-class persons actually desire highly restrictive social environments with strong external controls over their behavior: military, mental hospital, special school, prison.[94] "While under the jurisdiction of such systems the lower-class person generally expresses to his peers continual resentment of the coercive, unjust, and arbitrary exercise of authority. Having been released, or having escaped from these milieux, however, he will often act in such a way as to insure recommitment, or choose recommitment voluntarily after a temporary period of 'freedom.'" Miller concludes that for the lower-class person "being controlled is equated with being cared for."[95] This suggests an important insight for the criminal justice practitioner relative to setting and enforcing limits:[96]

> attempts are frequently made to "test" the severity or strictness of superordinate authority to see if it remains firm. If intended or executed rebellion produces swift and firm punitive sanctions, the individual is reassured, at the same time he is complaining bitterly at the injustice of being caught and punished.

Miller disagrees with Cloward and Ohlin over the question of labeling subcultural gang members as "psychopathic," but his strongest criticism is over Cohen's assertion that the subcultural delinquent has turned middle-class standards upside down. Instead, Miller

[92]Ibid., p. 9.
[93]Ibid., p. 11.
[94]Ibid., p. 12.
[95]Ibid., p. 13.
[96]Ibid.

asserts that lower-class attitudes, practices, and norms "are designed to support and maintain the basic features of the lower-class way of life," and the violation of middle-class norms is not the dominant component of motivation.[97]

Subcultural theory sensitizes the criminal justice practitioner to some of the potential realities of the life and lifestyle of a great many criminal justice clients. Whether antisocial activity is generated by opposition to the wider society or as a result of a different set of behavioral norms is interesting, but not crucial for the criminal justice practitioner's service task. In his/her relationship with a client, the criminal justice practitioner must deal with reality: without a minimum of conformity to the middle-class norms of the prevailing society, the likelihood of increased criminal justice involvement is probably inevitable.

## Containment Theory

As proposed by Reckless[98] the Containment Theory seeks to bridge the gap between sociological and psychological theory. Reckless feels that sociological theories have failed to account for the self-factor in order to explain differential responses to certain stimuli. He notes that persons enter a world already in existence with a set of norms and expectations; however, alongside these norms exist deviant and illegal models of behavior; the degree to which persons conform to the former and reject the latter is dependent on inner and outer containment.

The diversity and mobility of modern democratic society make alienation from society an ever-present reality, and thus there is a need for strong direction—outer containment. Inner containment represents the ability of a person to follow prevailing norms and provide self-direction. In our modern democratic society, social relations have become more impersonal and self-direction becomes the most important controlling agent: "The more diversity, the more impersonalization, the more away from home base, the self must act as the directional control."[99] Reckless suggests those components of self which are conducive to self-direction:[100]

> a favorable self image, self concept, self perception. The person who conceives of himself as a responsible person is apt to act

[97]Ibid., p. 19.
[98]Walter C. Reckless, *The Crime Problem* (New York: Appleton-Century-Crofts, 1967), Chapter 22.
[99]Ibid., p. 475.
[100]Ibid.

responsibly. The person who conceives of himself as operating within limits is apt to hold himself within limits. The person who perceives of himself as reliable, honest, helpful, cooperative, or unassuming, is more likely to be that way.

Another important component of self, one giving high directional capability, is "goal orientation, especially the orientation of the person toward socially approved goals." This goal orientation enables the self to steer itself in the "right" direction and to avoid deviance. Goals must be realistic and obtainable: "Otherwise an unrealistic aspiration level can lead to collapse of the person." Other important aspects of inner containment are frustration tolerance and an identification with prevailing norms, values, and laws.[101]

Of importance to the criminal justice practitioner are Reckless's observations about treatment:[102]

> Effective treatment of a juvenile or adult offender involves getting him to attach himself to effective reference groups where his participation can be internalized, that is where he can find a sense of belonging and a sense of worth or status. Whether the youthful or adult offender is being handled and treated on probation, in an institution, or during aftercare (parole), these principles of building up an inner and outer containment will apply. Treatment of offenders consists of building up an inner and, hopefully, an outer containment, that is, of making him able to resist the pressures, temptations, and normal restlessness and dissatisfaction that caused him to become an offender.

## Neutralization and Drift

Cohen believes that the delinquent subcultural rejection of middle-class standards is more apparent than real. He contends that the standards actually linger on, requiring, for example, reaction-formation in the form of acts that are grossly antisocial. Miller, on the other hand, asserts that the lower-class culture is distinct, significantly different from the larger middle-class culture. *Trouble* results because of culture conflict: the standards of the middle class emerge as legal codes, thus entangling the lower-class person, who is merely acting according to his cultural standards, in a web of officialdom.

Matza and Sykes maintain, however, that the delinquent actually

---

[101]Ibid., p. 467.
[102]Ibid., p. 481.

retains his belief in the legitimacy of official, middle-class norms: "The juvenile delinquent frequently recognizes *both* the legitimacy of the dominant social order and its moral rightness."[103] The authors argue that "if there existed in fact a delinquent subculture such that the delinquent viewed his illegal behavior as morally correct, we could reasonably suppose that he would exhibit no feelings of guilt or shame at detection or confinement. Instead, the major reaction would tend in the direction of indignation or a sense of martydom."[104] However, they note that many delinquents do indeed experience a sense of guilt, "and its outward expression is not to be dismissed as a purely manipulative gesture to appease those in authority."[105]

Sykes and Matza postulate that (a) the delinquent does not necessarily regard those who abide by the legal rules as wrong or immoral; and (b) it is doubtful if many juvenile delinquents are totally immune from the demands for conformity made by the dominant social order.[106] Therefore, "the juvenile delinquent would appear to be at least partially committed to the dominant social order in that he frequently exhibits guilt or shame when he violates its proscriptions, accords approval to certain conforming figures, and distinguishes between appropriate and inappropriate targets for his deviance."[107] The authors conclude that "the delinquent respresents not a radical opposition to law-abiding society but something more like an apologetic failure, often more sinned against than sinning in his own eyes."[108]

By using various techniques of neutralization the delinquent is able to avoid guilt feelings for his actions. He is able to do this by contending that rules are merely qualified guidelines limited to time-place-persons-conditions. This line of reasoning is in accord with that of our legal code wherein criminal intent must be present for an actor to suffer criminal sanctions. The delinquent justifies his actions in a form that, while it is not valid to the larger society, is valid for him. Sykes and Matza present five types of neutralization:[109]

1. Denial of responsibility—rationalizing that it was not his fault, e.g., a victim of circumstances.

---

[103]Gresham M. Sykes and David Matza, "Techniques of Neutralization: A Theory of Delinquency," *American Sociological Review* 22 (December 1957): 664–70.

[104]Ibid., p. 664.

[105]Ibid., pp. 664–65.

[106]Ibid., p. 665.

[107]Ibid., p. 666.

[108]Ibid., p. 667.

[109]Ibid., p. 667–69.

2. Denial of injury—nobody got hurt; just a prank, or the insurance will cover it.
3. Denial of the victim—he deserved it, e.g., he's a "homo."
4. Condemnation of the condemners—dwells on the weaknesses and motives of those in authority or judgment: police, school principal, judge, etc.
5. Appeal to higher loyalties—had to do it for friends, family, neighborhood, etc.

Empirical data for Matza's thesis rests, to a large extent, on interviews with delinquents at a boys training school.[110] Although Matza entertains the possibility that the responses are not valid he rejects this: "Was I being mislead? I believe not."[111] However, this author, who has worked in a boys training school, finds the interview data questionable. It is difficult to imagine the youngsters' responses not being self-serving, providing just the impression that Matza was looking for, that they were victims of circumstances, actually committed to conventional behavior. Training school youngsters usually recognize that if they do not express such attitudes, their release may be delayed.

Cloward and Ohlin are critical of Sykes and Matza, as well as Cohen:[112]

> They fail to perceive that the individual may regard a given norm as a legitimate guide to behavior under a particular set of circumstances even though at the same time he considers that pattern of action morally inferior to some alternative pattern. He may believe that law-abiding conduct is morally right but inappropriate or impossible in a particular situation. As a consequence of their failure to develop this distinction, Cohen and Sykes and Matza seem to be concerned almost exclusively with the moral judgments of delinquents and the way in which offenders handle problems of guilt.

The question of a "sense of guilt" is important for the criminal justice practitioner. Often, reports prepared in a criminal justice setting, e.g., a presentence report, will contain a reference to signs of "remorse." Knowledge of the "techniques of neutralization" can help the criminal justice practitioner to understand how remorse can present itself. Remorse indicates a desire or potential commitment to alter

[110]David Matza, *Delinquency and Drift* (New York: John Wiley, 1964), pp. 48–50.
[111]Ibid., p. 50.
[112]Cloward and Ohlin, p. 137.

antisocial behavior; thus, recognizing remorse, even if distorted through neutralization, is important for the criminal justice practitioner.

In his book *Delinquency and Drift,* Matza conveys his impression that the delinquent is not fully committed, but instead "he drifts between criminal and conventional action." Matza denies that the picture of a juvenile delinquent as a person committed to an oppositional culture is accurate; instead he notes that the delinquent "reveals a basic ambivalence toward his behavior . . ."[113] Matza believes that juveniles are less alienated than others in society, and that most of the time the delinquent behaves in a noncriminal manner:[114]

> The image of the delinquent I wish to convey is one of drift; an actor neither compelled nor committed to deeds nor freely choosing them; neither different in any simple or fundamental sense from the law abiding, nor the sane; conforming to certain traditions in American life while partially unreceptive to other more conventional traditions; and finally an actor whose motivational system may be explored along lines explicitly commanded by classical criminology—his particular relation to legal institutions.

While Matza does not contradict the idea of a delinquent subculture, he finds that the subculture is not a binding force as other observers would have us believe: "Loyalty is a basic issue in the subculture of delinquency partially because its adherents are so regularly disloyal. They regularly abandon the company at the age of remission for more conventional pursuits."[115] However, while he or she is part of this subculture, the "delinquent is prepared to convert irresponsibility to freedom from moral restraint because his subculture is pervaded by another more profound condition of neutralization."[116] Matza notes that while a sense of injustice is normal in any setting, "its perception is heightened in the subculture of delinquency," which "aggravates and accentuates the sense of injustice among its adherents." Matza provides important operational guidance for the criminal justice practitioner. He stresses the need in the rehabilitation process for delinquents to be able to discover the outlook of their peers, as opposed to the more conventional notion of "insight into self." Thus, there exists a need to work with youngsters in a group setting where they can, under guidance, explore and uncover the actual (conventional) attitudes of

[113]Matza, p. 59.
[114]Ibid., p. 28.
[115]Ibid., p. 158.
[116]Ibid., p. 102.

their peers. Matza refers to this process as overcoming the "system of shared misunderstandings."

Matza provides some insight for the criminal justice practitioner who may observe relatively sudden patterns of conformity among clients moving through adolescence and into a higher level of maturity:[117]

> Masculinity anxiety is somewhat reduced when someone becomes a man rather than being a mere aspirant. Boys are less driven to prove manhood unconventionally through deeds or misdeeds when with the passing of time they may effortlessly exhibit the conventional signposts of manhood—physical appearance, the completion of school, job, marriage, and perhaps even children.

The concept of an "age of remission" often tends to blur research on the effectiveness of certain treatment methods or programs: was it the treatment that caused any positive changes, or was it merely chronological maturity?

## Labeling/Societal Reaction Theory[118]

"Symbolic interactionists suggest that categories which individuals use to render the world meaningful, and even the experience of self, are structured by socially acquired definitions. They argue that individuals, in reaction to group rewards and sanctions, gradually internalize group expectations. These internalized social definitions allow people to evaluate their own behavior from the standpoint of the group and in doing so provide a lens through which to view oneself as a social object."[119] Schur suggests that "the same social structures and value systems that give rise to socially approved conditions and behaviors give rise also to socially disapproved ones," and he notes that the "appraisals of behavior or conditions as socially problematic reflect the social positions, social structures, and rational interests of the apprais-

---

[117]Ibid., p. 55.

[118]Many sociologists prefer the term "perspective" to theory. See, for example, Don C. Gibbons and Joseph F. Jones, *The Study of Deviance* (Englewood Cliffs, N.J.: Prentice-Hall, 1975), pp. 130–33.

[119]Jill S. Quadagno and Robert J. Antonio, "Labeling Theory As An Oversocialized Conception of Man: The Case of Mental Illness," *Sociology and Social Research* 60 (October, 1975): 33.

ers."[120] Labeling perspective focuses not on the behavior of the actor, but on the societal reaction to his behavior: "The labeling perspective considers the question of how social actors become defined and tainted as deviant rather than traditional etiological question of why social actors commit deviant acts."[121] Erikson states that "Deviance is not a property *inherent* in any particular kind of behavior; it is a property *conferred upon* that behavior by the people who come into direct or indirect contact with it."[122] Becker states that "social groups create deviance by making rules, whose infraction constitutes deviance, and by applying those rules to particular people and labeling them outsiders."[123]

The labeling approach focuses on the social audience's (societal) reaction to an individual's behavior rather than on the individual, the content, and cause of his behavior. The societal reaction labels the actor according to his behavior, stigmatizing him, which results in a damaged self-image, deviant identity, and a host of societal expectations which can result in a "self-fulfilling prophesy." Deviance is thus often shaped by the societal reaction to the deviant. As Schur notes: the theory "is more interested in the 'social history' and ramifying effects of deviant behavior than in the basic 'characteristics' of deviating acts or actors."[124]

In 1951, Lemert wrote:[125]

Socially visible deviations stir a wide variety of expressive reactions and attitudes depending upon the nature of the deviations and the expectancies of the conforming majority: admiration, awe, envy, sympathy, fear, repulsion, disgust, hate and anger; these are the elemental stuff from which societal reaction is compounded. A minor violation of legal rules, for example, can provoke stringent penalties. This spurious surplus of societal reaction is an exaggeration and distortion of the facts of deviation, so that a large measure of the deviation becomes "putative," that part of the societal definition of the deviant which has no foundation in his

[120]Edwin M. Schur, "Reactions to Deviance: A Critical Assessment," *American Journal of Sociology* 75 (November 1969): 309.
[121]William J. Filstead, ed., *An Introduction to Deviance* (Chicago: Markham Publishing, 1972), p. 1.
[122]Kai T. Erikson, *Wayward Puritans* (New York:, John Wiley, 1966), p. 6.
[123]Howard S. Becker, Outsiders: Studies in the Sociology of Deviance (New York: Free Press, 1963), p. 9.
[124]Schur, "Reactions to Deviance," p. 310.
[125]Edwin M. Lemert, *Social Pathology* (New York: McGraw-Hill, 1951), pp. 54–56.

objective behavior. Frequently these fallacious imputations are incorporated into myth and stereotype and mediate much of the formal treatment of the deviant.

Two decades later Lemert stated:[126]

The societal reaction is a very general term summarizing both the expressive reactions of others (moral indignation) toward deviation and action directed to its control. In broad purview the societal reaction often presents a paradox in that societies appear to sustain as well as penalize actions and classes of people categorized as immoral, criminal, incompetent, or irresponsible.

One aspect of the societal reaction is the process of attaching visible signs of moral inferiority to persons. These signs may take the form of invidious labels or publicly disseminated information found in trials or newspaper reports. Garfinkel refers to these as *degradation ceremonies*—i.e., "Any communicative work between persons, whereby the public identity of an actor is transformed into something looked on as lower in the local scheme of social types."[127]

Of primary importance to the criminal justice practitioner is the potential impact of the labeling process on the criminal justice practitioner client. Schur writes:[128]

A societal perspective, then is more concerned with what is made of an act socially than with the factors that may have led particular individuals into the behavior in the first place. While these precipitating factors obviously have some importance, the labeling analysts believe they have been overemphasized. Many of the reaction processes that shape deviance situations remain crucial, they argue, *whatever* the precipitating factors in specific cases may be. In particular, the labeling approach stresses that the self-concepts and long-term behavior of rule-violators are vitally influenced by the interaction between them and agents of social control.... There is, then, a complex process of response and counter-response beginning with an initial act of rule-violation and developing into elaborated delinquent self-conceptions and a full-fledged delinquent career.

[126]Edwin M. Lemert, *Human Deviance, Social Problems and Social Control*, 2nd ed., (Englewood Cliffs, N.J.: Prentice-Hall, 1971), p. 64.

[127]Harold Garfinkel, "Condition of Successful Degradation Ceremonies," *American Journal of Sociology* 61 (March 1956): 420.

[128]Edwin M. Schur, *Radical Non-Intervention* (Englewood Cliffs, N.J.: Prentice-Hall, 1973), pp. 119–20.

Schur concludes that "once an individual has been branded as a wrongdoer, it becomes extremely difficult for him to shed that new identity."[129] Once an actor is labeled, as a criminal for example, he is liable to be treated differently from even those who commit similar acts, crimes, but who have not been successfully labeled.

Siporin notes that the diagnostic procedures used by social work and the classification procedures used by agents of social control can easily have a labeling effect.[130] Criminal justice practitioners must try to avoid the labeling of clients, often an impossibility, or learn to soften the results of such a process, no easy task. One area in which the labeling process is of immediate concern to the criminal justice practitioner is in helping clients to secure employment. Experience has shown that most employers are reluctant, perhaps unwilling, to hire those labeled "offender," or "delinquent."[131]

Another result of the societal reaction is referred to by Lemert as *secondary deviance*. The labeled deviant reorganizes his behavior in accordance with the societal reaction and "begins to employ his deviant behavior, or a role based upon it, as a means of defense, attack, or adjustment to the overt and covert problems created by the consequent societal reaction to him."[132] Lemert states:[133]

> Having discovered the prosaic nature of much of his life under a new status, the deviant, like other people, usually tries to make out as best he can. What happens will be conditioned by several factors: (1) the clarity with which a role can be defined; (2) the possession or acquisition of attributes, knowledge, and skills to enact, improvise, and invent roles; and (3) the motivation to play his role or roles.

Heroin addicts provide a most vivid example of secondary deviance. They are excluded from conventional, and even certain sophisticated criminal, occupations, and thus must resort to petty thievery to support a condition (addiction) that is made costly due to the societal reaction to heroin—outlawing it. Thus, a primary deviance, heroin addiction, results in a secondary deviance in the form of criminal activities.

---

[129]Ibid., p. 124.

[130]Max Siporin, "Deviant Behavior Theory in Social Work: Diagnosis and Treatment," *Social Work* 10 (July 1965): 62.

[131]For research in this area see Richard D. Schwartz and Jerome Skolnick, "Two Studies of Legal Stigma," *Social Problems* 10 (Fall 1962): 133–42.

[132]Lemert, *Social Pathology*, p. 76.

[133]Lemert, "Human Deviance," *Social Problems and Social Control*, pp. 82–83.

Quadagno and Antonio state that deviants often reject the label, and, using mental patients as an example, note that: "The labeling process is neither automatic nor self-fulfilling, even for those who have undergone official labeling and institutionalization."[134] Other writers also question the "theory."[135] Bernstein, Kelly and Doyle tested the labeling thesis in an actual criminal justice setting—the New York City Criminal Court. They conclude that the interactionist emphasis on "the role of the deviants' social attributes in explaining variation in societal reaction seems very much overstated."[136] However, for the criminal justice practitioner, an adequate recognition of the problem of stigma is basic to providing social service.

## Radical Theory (The "New Criminology")

While radical theory does not offer an operational basis for the delivery of social services in criminal justice, it does provide insight for the criminal justice practitioner. Radical theory, often referred to as the "New Criminology,"[137] emphasizes political meanings and motives as the bases for criminal behavior and crime control. The "new criminologists" see crime as merely that behavior seen to be problematic within the framework of existing social arrangements.[138] They often extend "crime" to include acts that are not at present considered *legally* criminal, such as racism, imperialism, and labor exploitation (of migrants, for example). The Marxian basis for radical theory is presented by Quinney:[139]

> What, then, is the nature of this ruling class as reflected in criminal matters? It is composed of (1) members of the upper economic class (those who own or control the means of production) and (2)

---

[134]Quadagno and Antonio, p. 42.

[135]See, for example, Jane M. Murphy, "Psychiatric Labeling in Cross-Cultural Perspective," *Science* 12 (March 1976): 1019–28; Milton Mankoff, "Societal Reaction and Career Deviance: A Critical Analysis," *The Sociological Quarterly* 12 (Spring 1971): 204–18: Charles Wellford, "Labeling Theory and Criminology: An Assessment," *Social Problems* 22 (February 1975): 332–45: Prudence Rains, "Imputations of Deviance: A Restrospective Essay on the Labeling Perspective," *Social Problems* 23 (October 1975): 1–12; Taylor et al., pp. 139–71.

[136]Ilene Nagel Bernstein, William R. Kelley, and Patricia A. Doyle, "Societal Reaction to Deviants: The Case of Criminal Defendants," *American Sociological Review* 42 (October 1977): 54.

[137]See Robert F. Meir, "The New Criminology: Continuity in Criminological Theory," *Journal of Criminal Law and Criminology* 67 (December 1976): 461–69.

[138]Taylor et al., p. 282.

[139]Richard Quinney, *Critique of the Legal Order*, (Boston: Little, Brown, 1974), pp. 56–57.

those who benefit in some way from the present capitalist economic system. It is engaged in legal concern for the purpose of preserving the capitalist order, including the welfare state associated with that order. Even when laws regulating morality are made and enforced, the intention is to preserve the moral and ideological basis of capitalism.

Thus, the radical perspective notes:[140] "Many of the most socially and personally damaging acts that are forbidden in United States law are handled as 'civil' rather than 'criminal' issues": job discrimination, industrial safety violations, antipollution violations. Silver, in an article that reviews current approaches to the crime problem, states:[141]

> The new criminology argues that law, especially criminal law, and its administration by officers of the state, especially the administration of criminal justice, is an attempt of those in power and their agents to maintain control over the powerless. Criminality is a cultural device masking the inequities of the social structure. Law enforcement becomes action at the middle levels of power to carry out the policies of the most powerful.

The radical approach eschews theory that treats criminal behavior as a manifestation of individual pathology. Instead, crime is viewed as a phenomenon generated/created by a (capitalist) system of severely differentiated wealth and power. The legal apparatus, including a monopoly over sanctions and the use of force, is used to perpetuate the control by the ruling class. The criminal justice "system" is thus a mechanism through which the self-interests of the ruling class are expressed. Their rule is given legitimacy through ideology, for, as Marx noted, the ideas of the ruling class are always the ruling ideas.

Halleck and Bromberg, both forensic psychiatrists, note that the practitioner "could become an agent of social control in a society in which there was little room for protest, change, or progress. Before behavioral therapies are applied to the criminal it would appear that physicians and social scientists have a moral obligation to carefully examine the consequences of their being used in a coercive manner."[142] Halleck places this concern in a personal perspective:[143]

[140]Center for Research on Criminal Justice, *The Iron Fist and the Velvet Glove: An Analysis of the United States Police* (Berkeley, Calif.: Center for Research on Criminal Justice, 1975), p. 10.

[141]Isidore Silver, "The Crime Problem and Conventional Wisdom," *Law Enforcement News*, May 3, 1977, p. 14.

[142]Seymour L. Halleck and Walter Bromberg, *Psychiatric Aspects of Criminology* (Springfield, Ill.: Charles C. Thomas, 1968), p. 21.

[143]Seymour L. Halleck, *Politics of Therapy* (New York: Science House, 1971), p. 30.

By participating in the punishment process, even as a healer, I loaned a certain credibility to the existing correctional system. . . . In my work in prisons I did little to change an oppressive status quo. In retrospect I am inclined to believe that, although I helped a number of individuals, my presence as a non-militant cooperative psychiatrist tended to strengthen the status quo.

Halleck concludes that the therapist "comes to be viewed as a placator, as an agent of colonization who will provide temporary tranquility while the process of oppression is strenghthened."[144]

Leonard makes a similar observation: "Examination of the philosophy and theory of social work reveals a degree of commitment to bourgeois values and capitalist models of social welfare of which most social workers have themselves been unaware." This is because "more attention is given to methods than to purpose."[145]

Prisons have experienced the "new criminology" in the form of the "radicalization" of inmates who view themselves as political prisoners—not criminals. Russell Oswald, former New York Corrections Commissioner, caustically referred to these inmates as "the new breed of self-proclaimed and self-styled political prisoner."[146] The best known of the "politicized" prisoners was George Jackson whose death in a California prison continues to be a subject of controversy. Articulate and self-educated, Jackson wrote to his attorney in 1970:[147] "criminals and crime arise from material, economic, sociopolitical causes" in a capitalist and racist "Amerika," and "our principal enemy must be isolated and identified as capitalism."

The radical criminologists caution, however, against what they see as the tendency of some to romanticize criminals:[148]

Recent studies in criminology tend to either gloss over the issue of street crime or to portray it in romantic terms. Crime is often characterized as a form of primitive political rebellion or a rational attempt to survive under oppressive conditions. For some activities in specific historical periods, such as the spontaneous

[144]Ibid., p. 52.

[145]Peter Leonard, "Towards a Paradigm for a Radical Practice," In Roy Bailey and Mike Brake, eds., *Radical Social Work* (New York: Pantheon Books, 1975), p. 47 and p. 50.

[146]Russell G. Oswald, remarks made at the Joint First-Second Circuit Sentencing Institute. In *Justice in Sentencing*, Leonard Orland and Harold R. Tyler, eds. (Mineola, N.Y.: Foundation Press, 1974), p. 141.

[147]*Soledad Brother: The Prison Letters of George Jackson* (New York: Bantam Books, 1972), pp. 28, 176.

[148]Editorial in "The Politics of Street Crime," *Crime and Social Justice* 5 (Spring-Summer 1976): 2.

urban rebellions of the 1960s, this is certainly correct. But, for most street crime, this Fanonist imagery serves to distort and glorify acts of reactionary individualism.... The glorification of crime is prevalent among intellectuals and students who are especially susceptible to ideals which are left in form but liberal in substance (radical chic).

Radicals provide some useful observations for the criminal justice practitioner, especially in his role as an advocate: "the social worker should defend his client by acting as lawyer, organizer, and information-provider in helping him to fight the system which created his problem."[149] Leonard states that in residential institutions it may be necessary for the social worker to work to ameliorate the effects of and ultimately change an authoritarian regime. He cautions, however, that the "radical social worker may be relatively protected from the consequences of any particular action compared with other members of the action system, and must take this into account."[150]

Thus, radical theory reminds the social service worker of the need to maintain his own personal integrity by speaking out and otherwise resisting aspects of practice which are unjust, while at the same time remembering his primary interest in the welfare of his client. As we have seen in the discussion of anomie and differential opportunity, a social system creates the soil from which deviance can grow. It is thus the task of the worker to intervene on behalf of clients at times and in ways that are appropriate to the individual situation.

[149]Stanley Cohen, "It's All Right For You To Talk: Political and Sociological Manifestos for Social Work Action," In *Radical Social Work*, p. 89.
[150]Leonard, p. 60.

# 2

# Psychogenic Theories of Crime

## Psychoanalytic Theory[1]

In this section we will distinguish between psychoanalysis as a form of treatment and as a body of knowledge presenting a theoretical basis for understanding crime. Lief points out some of the difficulties involved in using psychoanalytic treatment for offenders:[2]

> As a method of treatment psychoanalysis is applicable to only a small percentage of the general population. It is an excellent form of treatment if the patient is introspective, psychologically minded, reasonably intelligent and has good ego strength. Leaving aside all monetary considerations, there are relatively few people who can profit by psychoanalysis.

Literature on the successful use of psychoanalysis with criminal offenders is best characterized by its paucity. Psychoanalytic theory, how-

---

[1]This chapter presupposes some knowledge of general psychoanalytic theory. For those lacking this background see, for example, Charles Brenner, *An Elementary Textbook of Psychoanalysis* (paper) (Garden City, N.Y.: Anchor Books, 1974).

[2]Harold I. Lief, "Psychoanalysis and Psychiatric Training," *Psychoanalysis in Present-Day Psychiatry*, ed. Iago Galdson (New York: Brunner/Mazel, 1969), p. 24.

.

ever, does provide a conceptual basis for understanding and treating offenders.

Psychoanalytic theory does not make a distinction between behavior that is criminal and noncriminal: "criminality is not a psychological concept; criminality is action contrary to the penal code."[3] Alexander and Staub state that psychological knowledge of crime is "based primarily on the data obtained from our psychoanalytic knowledge of the neuroses."[4] Singh states:[5]

Distinction is often made between crime and psychoneurosis. But from the point of view of their dynamics, they are very similar. Since psychoneurosis and criminality are defects in one's social adjustment, they hardly differ from one another in their respective psychological dynamics. Both the neurotic and the criminal fell victims to their incapacity of finding a socially accpetable solution of the conflicts which the relationships to the various members of the family engendered. The neurotic expresses symbolically by means of his symptoms, which are socially innocuous, the same thing which the criminal does by means of real actions.

The difference between criminal and neurotic behavior relates to alloplastic-autoplastic adaptations. Crime and delinquency are categorized as alloplastic adaptations to aggressive drives caused by stress, which in the neurotic person are directed inward (autoplastic). Alloplastic behavior encompasses the actor's attempt to change his external environment. While there is a continuous interaction between the internal and external environments, Eissler states that delinquencies "are genuinely and primarily alloplastic."[6] Helleck notes that alloplastic behaviors serve two purposes: either gratifying drives or warding off attacks. Whereas alloplastic adaptations can lead to creative activities, art and building for example, in the delinquent the outlets are antisocial.[7] The choice of outlet can be seen as environmentally or socially determined, and can thus be correlated with some of the sociological explanations of crime, e.g., subcultural theory.

Psychoanalytic theory views delinquent behavior as a manifestation determined by early life experiences.[8]

[3]Otto Fenichel, The Psychonalytic Theory of Neuroses (New York: Norton, 1945), p. 505.

[4]Franz Alexander and Hugo Staub, The Criminal, the Judge, and the Public (Glencoe, Ill.: Free Press, 1956), p. 47.

[5]Udai Pratap Singh, Personality of Criminals (Agra, India: Mehra, 1973), p. 8.

[6]Eissler in his introduction to Searchlights on Delinquency, ed. K. R. Eissler (New York: International Universities Press, 1956), p. 9.

[7]Seymour L. Halleck, Psychiatry and the Dilemmas of Crime (New York: Harper & Row, 1967), p. 64. Reprinted by permission of the publisher.

[8]Fenichel, p. 374.

Lack of lasting object relationships in early childhood or an oral fixation and traumatic experiences may make the complete and definite establishment of an effective superego impossible; for example, the parent figures may have changed in such rapid succession that there was objectively no time or opportunity to develop lasting relationships; however, persons of this kind also experience frustrations and develop reactions to them. Their superego is not lacking but imcomplete or pathological, and the reactions of the ego to the pathological superego reflect the ambivalences and contradictions which these persons felt toward their first objects. Psychoanalysis of juvenile delinquents gives various examples of such distorted relations toward the superego.

Alexander and Staub state that a human being enters the world socially unadjusted—as "a criminal:"[9]

During the first years of his life, the human individual preserves his criminality to the fullest degree. His actual social adjustment begins only at the time after the Oedipus complex is overcome. This happens during the so-called latency period which was described by Freud. This period begins between the ages of four and six, and ends at puberty. It is at this period that the development of the criminal begins to differentiate itself from that of the normal. The future normal individual succeeds (mostly in the latency period) in partly repressing his genuine criminal instinctual drives, and thus cuts them out of motor expression, and partly in transforming them into socially acceptable striving; the future criminal more or less fails in carrying out this adjustment.

The authors note the precarious balance between the "normal" and the "criminal:"[10]

a criminal act may be committed out of unconscious noncriminal motives and a socially acceptable act might be dictated by unconscious, unsocial motives. . . . that even as the socially useful act is the resultant of many psychic motives, some of which are partially criminal, so every criminal act is determined by many motives, the majority of which remained buried in the unconscious of the criminal.

Alexander and Staub point to the anal character traits of many criminals, which, it should be noted, resemble some of the characteris-

---

[9]Alexander and Staub, p. 30.
[10]Ibid., pp. 24–25.

tics described by Albert Cohen in our review of subcultural theory:[11] "The exaggerated, unsocial, stubborn bluntness of some violators of the law corresponds to the unyielding persistence of infantile anal spite. The characteristic self-centered stubbornness of the anal character acquires in the majority of criminals the form of proud, inaccessible spite, which is directed against all humanity." The authors delimit three large classes of criminals:[12]

1. *Neurotic Criminal*—hostile activity against society is a result of an intrapsychic conflict between the social and antisocial components of his personality; this conflict, like that of a psychoneurosis, comes from impressions of earliest childhood and from circumstances of later life (psychological etiology);
2. *Normal Criminal*—psychic organization is similar to that of the normal individual, except that he identified himself with criminal prototypes (sociological etiology); and
3. *Organic Criminal*—criminality is conditioned by some pathological process of an organic nature (biological etiology).

The authors note that these classes of criminality fall between two extreme theoretical types:

(a) the pure criminal who has not formed any superego to represent the demands of society within him; any control over id instincts is the result of fear of consequences—punishment—from agencies of social control; and

(b) the perfectly adjusted social individual, who without any inner conflict considers the interests of the community before he considers his own; his superego and ego are fused into one.

It is impossible to find such "pure" forms in real life, e.g., conflict free individuals; only intermediary types can be found.

Abrahamsen presents three ways in which a person may be led into criminal behavior:[13]

1. His criminalistic tendencies are exposed to antisocial influences all of which, under the impact of precipitating events, may lead him to commit antisocial acts;

[11]Ibid., p. 34.
[12]Ibid., pp. 45–46.
[13]David Abrahamsen, *Who are the Guilty?* (Westport, Conn.: Greenwood Press, 1952), p. 58.

2. Feelings of guilt of which he is unaware and for which he unconsciously wants to be punished; and

3. In reacting to his surroundings a person may express his aggression in a criminal manner.

Abrahamsen states:[14]

The peculiar phenomenon is that the Superego in a person criticizes not only a criminal act he has committed, it also censors his mere intention or desire to commit it. The proof of this is that conscious or unconscious fantasies or thoughts about committing a crime may give rise to a sense of guilt. We can thus see that the Superego has been interposed between the Id and the Ego in order to help out the ego, thereby serving as a defense against unwelcome desires which otherwise would reach the Ego and possibly destroy it. The Ego has to be assisted and the Superego does that by frequently posing the question whether the former should follow its desires.

Resistance to committing a crime, states Abrahamsen, "is to a large extent located in the Superego and depends upon its development." The lack, or overcoming, of resistance is based on "an overwhelming amount of unconscious emotions," and concerns the phenomenon of *aggression*:[15]

All criminal behavior is a direct or indirect manifestation of aggression. This aggression whatever form it may take, may be an expression of sexual or other drives. Everyone has aggressive tendencies; thus the inclination toward crime is present in everyone. That a man does not commit a crime does not mean that he is void of antisocial tendencies. It simply means that he is able to cope with these inclinations, sometimes by sublimating them, at other times by turning them against himself, thereby producing emotional symptoms or both. Sometimes again he is able to overcome his criminal tendencies and lead them into constructive channels.

Bromberg states that "Every crime represents the resolution of an inner struggle between instinctual [id] desire and the residue of moral and ethical ideas seated uneasily in the conscience [superego]."[16] Antisocial behavior often relates to superego defects in one of three forms:

[14]Ibid., p. 63.
[15]Ibid., pp. 64–65.
[16]W. Bromberg, *Crime and the Mind* (New York: Macmillan, 1965), p. 91.

1. poorly developed (lenient)
2. overdeveloped (harsh)
3. counter-valued (parasitic)

In the first form, persons have a paucity of feelings of guilt and submit to impulses that run counter to acceptable behavior. This socio- or psychopathic behavior is diagnosed as a personality disorder and has been estimated to account for anywhere from 9 to 24 percent of the (convicted) criminal population.[17] In the second form, antisocial behavior results from a sense of guilt and an unconscious desire for punishment. These criminals are driven by feelings of guilt and they "constantly experience stress in situations which would not be defined as stressful by others." Halleck notes that these persons "will suffer without knowing why," and "they may engage in antisocial behavior which inevitably invites detection, apprehension, and the desired punishment—punishment for a forbidden unconscious desire."[18] Halleck and Bromberg state that "Crimes which have an apparent unreasonable quality are often an unconscious effort to resolve some type of familial or interpersonal conflict."[19] About persons in category three, Fenichel states:[20]

> It may also be that an unsocial childhood milieu has formed a superego whose valuations are contrary to those of the average superego in a given society; and it may also be that after a 'normal' superego has been established subsequent circumstances create a contradictory 'parasitic' or double of this superego.

Abrahamsen refers to these persons as *environmental sociopaths*: persons who are brought up in a criminal environment that adversely affects the superego resulting in acts directed against society.[21] These aspects of psychoanalytic theory obviously are similar to certain items discussed in differential association and subcultural theory.

Schoenfeld notes the connecting link between parental deprivation and delinquent behavior:[22] "the lack of sufficient parental—

---

[17]Ibid., p. 86.

[18]Halleck, *Psychiatry and the Dilemmas of Crime*, p. 77. Reprinted by permission of the publisher.

[19]Seymour L. Halleck and Walter Bromberg, *Psychiatric Aspects of Criminology* (Springfield, Ill.: Charles C Thomas, 1968), p. 20.

[20]Fenichel, p. 504.

[21]David Abrahamsen, *Crime and the Human Mind* (Montclair, N.J.: Patterson Smith, 1969), p. 93.

[22]C. G. Schoenfeld, "A Psychonalytic Theory of Delinquency," *Crime and Delinquency* 17 (October 1971): 475.

particularly motherly—affection during childhood is likely to result in the development of a superego unable to control the antisocial impulses that appear during infancy and are revived just before puberty begins." This is consistent with the sociological view presented by Hirschi:[23]

> In other words, we take the view that definitions favorable to violation of law are rooted in the absence or weakness of intimate relations with other persons, especially in most cases the parents. The person closely attached to his parents is rewarded for conformity by the approval and esteem of those he admires. If such attachments are absent, there is no reward for conformity and only weak punishment for deviation. Lack of concern for the reactions of such persons as parents generalizes as a lack of concern for the approval of persons in positions of impersonal authority. The child who does not need the love and approval of impersonal others, will thus be free to reject the normative pattern "they" attempt to impose. The beliefs that arise or are adopted under these conditions will tend to reflect and in some sense to rationalize the position of the unattached: the only reason to obey the rules is to avoid punishment.

According to psychoanalytic theory, whether or not a crime will occur depends on how the ego is able to accomodate id impulses: "the weaker the ego is, and the less differentiated it is from the id, the more it will be at the mercy of the blind forces of instinct."[24] Nuttin notes that the ego is that psychic mechanism which enables the id instincts to be accomodated within the context of reality:[25]

> Knowledge, and conscious activity of the human mind, are simply a "buffer" between the blind instinct and external reality. Without this "buffer" the "id," in its urge toward satisfaction would be shattered against reality. This is the reason why life raises up the conscious "ego" to make contact with the external world.

Halleck emphasizes that crime has considerable psychological advantages for the offender: During the planning and execution of a criminal act the offender is a free man, free from the oppressive dictates of others since he has temporarily broken out of control. "The value of

---

[23]Travis Hirschi, *Causes of Delinquency* (Berkely: University of California Press, 1972), p. 200.
[24]Joseph Nuttin, *Psychoanalysis and Personality* (New York: New American Library, 1962), p. 57.
[25]Ibid., p. 66.

this brief taste of freedom cannot be overstated. Many of the criminals' apparently unreasonable actions are efforts to find a moment of autonomy, of reassurance that he is 'his own man.' ''[26]

Psychoanalytic theory denies some of the obvious conclusions about crime causation, for example, that it is based on simple economics. Instead, a particular criminal act may be interpreted on a symbolic-unconscious level. This can be illustrated in the case of a burglary, which Bromberg describes as breaking and entering a forbidden space—symbolic for a phallic penetration. Arguing against a simple economic or sociological explanation he states: burglary, and other "passive-aggressive" crimes, are motivated by deep unconscious drives for revenge on the orally depriving mother or the denying father.[27]

Antisocial activities are usually associated with the onset of adolescence, a period of particular stress—social, biological, and psychological. Halleck notes that stressful experiences during adolescence reinforce "criminogenic" tendencies in those strongly predisposed and may precipitate criminal behavior in those whose predisposition is less intense.[28] One psychoanalytically based theory of adolescent delinquency relates to vicarious participation. Slavson states that the delinquent act "is frequently a means of fulfilling an unconscious wish of a parent, or a demonstration to denigrating parents of a child's ability for achievement, in this case by flouting authority."[29] He notes the "unmistakable jealousy and envy on the part of adults toward younger people;" in addition to which parents are likely to remember their own adolescence vividly—the suppressions and prohibitions to which they were subjected and the guilt they felt at that period of their lives as a result of committing "prohibited" acts or entertaining "bad" thoughts. Some pass on their confused feelings to their children, while others seek to deny those feelings by repressive measures against their offspring.[30] Johnson and Szurek note that many parents "unwittingly seduce the child into acting out the parents' own poorly integrated forbidden impulses, thereby achieving vicarious gratification."[31]

Eissler[32] concludes that insofar as the delinquent is concerned his

---

[26]Halleck, *Psychiatry and the Dilemmas of Crime*, p. 77. This coincides with Miller's subcultural theory.

[27]Bromberg, p. 231.

[28]Halleck, *Psychiatry and the Dilemmas of Crime*, p. 117. Reprinted by permission of the publisher.

[29]S. R. Slavson, *Reclaiming the Delinquent* (New York: Free Press, 1965), pp. 7–8.

[30]Ibid., p. 15.

[31]Adelaide M. Johnson and S. A. Szurek, "The Genesis of Antisocial Acting Out In Children and Adults," *Psychoanalytic Quarterly*, 1952, p. 342.

[32]Eissler, p. 24.

value representations are a composite structure—some integrated, some not, some represented with full awareness, while others are unconscious. It is from these value representations that the delinquent's ego withdraws and this withdrawal of the delinquent's ego from normative representations corresponds to the withdrawal from reality as it occurs in psychoses. The assault against reality is the analogue of the process of restitution in psychoses. Since this mechanism of assault against reality does not lead to a gratification of the original id impulse, the mechanism is similar in this respect to that of the neurotic. Although the delinquent withdraws partially from the original demands of the id, especially as they are directed against his parents, his gratification of id demands is far more satisfactory and less disguised than any the neurotic achieves.

However, we should remember that even the "normal" adolescent exhibits neurotic-psychotic type behavior, at times, and of course many, if not most, adolescents commit delinquent acts of some type for which they may or may not become the subject of official attention.

There is a strong deterministic base in psychoanalytic theory as characterized by the following quote attributed to August Aichhorn:[33] "the therapist must accept the fact that the delinquent is always right in his behavior, in the sense that he could not have behaved otherwise."

In 1959, Guze and his colleagues, with the cooperation of the Missouri Board of Probation and Parole, began an extensive, perhaps the most extensive, long term and systematic psychiatric study of offenders. In a recent book based on his findings, Dr. Guze reports that convicted felons tend to come from severely disordered families and backgrounds characterized by poverty, broken homes, parental criminality and alcoholism. Guze points out, however, that most people raised under these conditions do not become felons. Furthermore, the people who commit so-called white collar crimes, "crime in the suites," have not been systematically studied. One might add, nor have they been systematically prosecuted and punished.

Guze found that the great majority of the male felons studied (78%) were diagnosed as *sociopathic*: "early onset of delinquency, frequent school difficulties, frequent fights, a poor job history, poor marital adjustment, frequent wunderlust, a bad military history with recurrent troubles, excessive drinking and drug abuse, and recurrent trouble with the police."[34] In contrast, Guze's study of psychiatric patients

[33]Hyman S. Lippman, "Difficulties Encountered in the Psychiatric Treatment of Chronic Juvenile Delinquents." In *Searchlights on Delinquency*, p. 160.

[34]Samuel B. Guze, *Criminality and Psychiatric Disorders* (New York: Oxford University Press, 1976), p. 42. This contrasts with Bromberg's estimates (9–25%).

indicated that it is not often that individuals with psychiatric problems are linked to serious crime. These findings have policy implications with respect to preventing crime: a societal response geared to dealing with poverty and the causes of family disorder.

Falk notes that psychoanalytic theories cannot be tested empirically: "They cannot be proved or disproved since the variables cannot be measured and the relationships between the symbols of psychoanalytic interpretation and the emotions they represent cannot be understood by laymen." Falk also notes the tautological aspect of psychoanalytic theory: "If a sex conflict is found, it proves the theory. If not, then hidden resistance is the cause and that also proves the theory. Any criticism is called an emotional conflict so that no valid critique can ever be accepted."[35]

This author is reminded of an explanation given to tardiness by his fellow classmates in graduate school who were enmeshed in psychoanlytic theory and who also recognized some of its absurdities:

The student arrives early to class is
*anxious*
The student who is late to class is
*resistant* or *hostile*
The student who is on time—he or she is
*compulsive*

Briar and Piliavin take issue with *motivational theories* of crime causation, which include both subcultural and psychoanalytic theory: "motivational theories of delinquency do not account for the well-documented fact that the vast majority of boys engage in delinquent behavior to some degree."[36] They note that although many boys are subjected to experiences which, according to motivational theories, should produce delinquency, it does not; while "many boys who exhibit these dispositions do not appear among the identified delinquents." They argue that delinquent behavior is both episodic and confined to certain situations:[37]

we assume that the motives for such behavior are frequently episodic, oriented to short-term ends, and confined to certain situations. That is, rather than considering delinquent acts as solely the product of long-term motives deriving from conflicts or frustrations whose genesis is far removed from the arenas in

[35]Gerhard Falk, "The Psychoanalytic Theories of Crime Causation," *Criminologica* 4 (May 1966): 9–10.

[36]Scott Briar and Irving Piliavin, "Delinquency, Situational Inducements, and Commitment to Conformity," *Social Problems* 13, 1965, p. 35.

[37]Ibid., p. 36.

which the illegal behavior occurs, we assume these acts are prompted by short-term situationally induced desires experienced by all boys to obtain valued goods, to portray courage in the presence of, or be loyal to peer, to strike out at someone who is disliked, or simply to "get kicks."

In what appears to be a combination of sociological, psychoanalytic, and learning theory the authors explain the cause of delinquency: These actions occur because of an insufficient commitment to conformity as a result of a dysfunction between the youth and his parents affecting parental authority. Those youths whose "behavior is not governed by parental evaluations lack an important basis for developing concern about the consequences of arrest."[38]

## PSYCHOANALYTIC THEORY AND THE CRIMINAL JUSTICE PRACTITIONER

Criminal, like noncriminal, acts are often the result of unconscious motivations, which according to psychoanalytic theory are to be dealt with by insight therapy or psychoanalysis. This is usually beyond the scope of the criminal justice practitioner in most settings. However, Halleck argues that even intellectually understanding these motivations can be therapeutic for the client: "Having an explanatory model upon which one can lean during times of stress is comforting and could bolster efforts to find noncriminal adaptations." Thus, if, with the help of the criminal justice practitioner, the offender is able to discover the motivations underlying his/her behavior "he may come to feel that they are no longer important."[39] Smart states that psychoanalytic explanations of client behavior provide a level of self-awareness which enables the client to make more rational choices.[40] Federico notes that psychoanalytic theory "can be helpful in understanding those problems that are strongly related to personal feelings and personality characteristics and may be especially helpful in trying to understand how the problem occurred."[41]

Social service practice often focuses on ego concerns in the form of the client's day-to-day functioning. The theoretical basis has its origins in psychoanalytic theory and its current representation is referred to as *ego psychology*. Freed notes that ego psychology is the core of

[38]Ibid., p. 42.
[39]Halleck, *Psychiatry and the Dilemma of Crime*, p. 326.
[40]B. Curtis Brown, ed., *Frances Smart: Neurosis and Crime* (New York: Barnes & Noble, 1970), p. 89.
[41]Ronald C. Federico, *The Social Welfare Institution* (Lexington, Mass.: Heath, 1973), p. 69.

current personality theory in social casework,[42] and she explains why Freudian theory was transfigured:[43]

> Freudian theory overemphasized internal, instinctual forces and psychic conflicts and underemphasized the significance of the social, cultural, and interpersonal environment in molding personality. Ego psychology, in contrast, deals with both the internal and external forces that impinge on the growing human personality. It stresses the adaptive and coping mechanisms of the individual and the individual's efforts to change and grow. In ego psychology, the human being is seen as an open system that interacts with the various systems around it. It reflects a shift away from the view that man is a conflict-ridden internal system struggling to contain his instincts. Instead, it assumes that people are born with a conflict-free autonomous ego sphere.

Using ego theory, the worker evaluates the client's social functioning: the "nature and efficacy of the individual's conscious and just preconscious behaviors. . . . the mechanisms by which he protests, adapts, or copes with both the internal and external stresses he encounters."[44] The worker assesses the client's ego strengths, i.e., memory, frustration tolerance, ability to relate to others—in general, his/her capacity to deal with the environment. Through the use of ego support, the worker helps the client "maintain himself at his present balance, where changes in his level of ego functioning are either unnecessary, or beyond the help of available skill or current knowledge."[45] While ego functioning is primarily rational, under great stress perceptions are distorted and behavior may become irrational. The irrational behavior of the criminal justice client is often of a criminal nature. The criminal justice practitioner works to enable the client to better deal with stress, providing what Freed calls an "auxiliary ego."[46] Thus, by clarification and information-giving (using role play, for example), the criminal justice practitioner strengthens the ego-ability of his/her client. Smart notes that the showing of respect by the criminal justice practitioner to the client is ego-supportive.[47]

[42]Anne O. Freed, "Social Casework: More Than a Modality," *Social Casework* 58 (April 1977): 216.

[43]Ibid., p. 217.

[44]Robert W. Klenk and Robert M. Ryan, *The Practice of Social Work* (Belmont, Calif.: Wadsworth, 1970), p. 58.

[45]Henry S. Maas, "Social Work With Individuals and Families." In *Concepts and Methods of Social Work*, ed. Walter A. Friedlander (Englewood Cliffs, N.J.: Prentice-Hall, 1976), p. 78.

[46]Freed, p. 218.

[47]Brown, p. 87.

There are two basic concepts in using ego-related methods that are especially important for the criminal justice practitioner. The first is not to do anything for clients that they are capable of doing for themselves, thus avoiding an action that can undermine ego strength. Widen reminds us of the second concept: begin where the client is. Work with the client at his own level, and do not try to change him immediately. "This maxim warns us that the ego cannot immediately be assaulted, with few exceptions, by demands for abrupt change without mobilizing anxiety that may impair the relationship."[48]

As we have noted, psychoanalytic theory delineates between three types of superego-related developments that can manifest themselves in antisocial behavior: 1) a poorly developed superego; 2) an overly restrictive superego; and 3) an environmentally distorted superego. In working with clients of the first type, the criminal justice practitioner must be the firm "father-figure" that was absent during the formative years of personality development. The sound use of controls must be emphasized, at first to provide real limits to potentially harmful behavior, and hopefully, later to enable the client to internalize controls and to develop his conscience-like mechanism to the degree necessary to control antisocial impulses. In dealing with type two clients, the criminal justice practitioner helps offenders to understand the unconscious motivation for their behavior as suggested above, assisting in finding alternative, noncriminal, means of coping. Type three clients, sometimes referred to as "environmental sociopaths," (Bromberg refers to them as counter-valued/parasitic)[49], can be, from a psychoanalytic viewpoint, quite "healthy." As such, psychoanalytic theory does not offer a method for altering their behavior. Indeed, as Halleck points out, one of the problematic aspects of psychoanalytic theory for the criminal justice practitioner, is that refraining from crime is not a necessary indication of effective treatment.[50]

## Behavior/Learning Theory[51]

The general behaviorist response to psychoanalytic theory is that "there is no scientific proof of the existence of a functional system correspond-

[48]Paul Widen, "Some Dimensions of Ego Continuity in Social Casework," *Social Work* 11 (October 1966): 52.

[49]Bromberg, p. 91.

[50]Halleck, *Psychiatry and the Dilemma of Crime*, p. 234.

[51]It should be noted that some behaviorists eschew theory, B. F. Skinner, for example. Thus, the concepts that relate to behavior and learning are often presented in descriptive as opposed to explanatory forms. Meyer and Chesser note that operant conditioning "is defined operationally because of the difficulty in formulating a theoretical definition," Victor Meyer and Edward S. Chesser, *Behavior Therapy in Clinical Psychiatry* (New York: Science House, 1970), p. 35.

ing to the 'dynamic unconscious' postulated by Freud."[52] Behaviorists often dismiss "as irrelevant, if not fraudulent, the traditional psycho-personality theories and the treatment approaches based on these theories."[53] The behaviorist rejects the determinism of Freud and psycho-analytic theory—the individual is not at the mercy of unconscious forces, he is merely the sum behavioral product of his learning. Accordingly, "abnormal" behavior is not the result of unconscious conflicts, but is caused by inappropriate learning: "The behavior therapist believes that whatever has been improperly learned can be unlearned and replaced by a more suitable behavior pattern."[54]

Bachrach presents some of the points of agreement between psychoanalysis and behaviorism:[55]

1. Importance of observing behavior
2. Acceptance of cause-effect relationship (behavior not whimsical)
3. Behavior is determined according to laws
4. Importance of understanding the history of the individual and his learning experiences
5. From this history, relation of past events to current behavior
6. Acceptance of genetic, constitutional factors as relevant

The noted behaviorist, Neal Miller, states his intention to cast the first rope of a slender bridge across the chasm that separates psychoanalytic and behavior theory.[56] He states: "The ultimate goal toward which we aimed was to combine the vitality of psychoanalysis, the rigor of the natural science laboratory, and the facts of culture."[57] Shectman also stresses the need for an integration of psychoanalysis and learning theory.[58]

Behaviorism proceeds on the theory that all forms of behavior are the result of responses to certain stimuli. Behavior theory, like

[52]Percival Bailey, "Sigmund Freud: Scientific Period (1873–1897)." In *The Conditioning Therapies*, ed. J. Wolpe, A. Salter, and L. J. Reyna (New York: Holt, Rinehart & Winston, 1964), p. 95.

[53]Max Bruck, "Behavior Modification Theory and Practice: A Critical Review," *Social Work* 13 (April 1968): 43.

[54]Herbert Fensterheim, *Help Without Psychoanalysis* (New York: Stein and Day, 1971), p. 12.

[55]Arthur J. Bachrach, "Some Applications of Operant Conditioning to Behavior Therapy." In *The Conditioning Therapies*, pp. 62–63.

[56]Neal E. Miller, *Selected Papers on Conflict, Displacement, Learned Drives and Theory* (Chicago: Aldine-Atherton, 1971), p. 74.

[57]Ibid., p. 348.

[58]Frederick A. Shectman, "Operant Conditioning and Psychoanalysis: Contrasts, Similarities, and Some Thoughts About Integration," *American Journal of Psychotherapy* 29 (January 1975): 72–77.

psychoanalytic theory, does not draw a distinction between criminal and noncriminal behavior—that distinction is drawn by the legal authorities. As distinct from psychoanalytic theory, however, behaviorists do not make a distinction between normal and neurotic behavior: "They regard behavior as simply adaptive or maladaptive (undesirable) and both types are developed and maintained by reward (positive reinforcement) from the environment in ways that are immediate and observable."[59] Criminal behavior is thus the result of inappropriate reinforcement that supports its continuance. The behavior modifier looks for the reinforcers which maintain maladaptive behavior and design strategies which change environmental conditions so that contingencies are placed on behavior patterns which are accepted by society. "Behavior modification is an approach that is concerned with *how* to change behavior, not *which* behaviors should be changed."[60] As opposed to other forms of therapy which require the cooperation of the client, behavior modification can be accomplished without even the knowledge of the subject. Behavior modification is, in and of itself, amoral and politically neutral, while "undesirable" behavior is obviously quite subjective. This is one reason why behavior modification is a controversial method of treatment.[61]

A second reason for controversy has to do with behavior modification's origins, and the charge that behavior/learning techniques conceive of (and treat) human beings as if they were animals. Behavior therapy developed out of the work of experimental psychologists working with animals in laboratories. One of the most noted pioneers in this area is the Soviet physiologist Ivan Petrovich Pavlov (1849–1936), who received the Nobel Prize in 1904. Franks notes that a Pavlovian orientation permeates almost every branch of medicine and medical research in the Soviet Union.[62] Salter states that one aspect of behavior modification, the *conditioned reflex*, is based completely on the work of Pavlov and Bechterev.[63] Because of the basic importance of Pavlov and his associates in behavior theory, we will present some Soviet materials on the subject.[64]

[59]Bruck, p. 44.

[60]Beth Sulzer and G. Roy Mayer, *Behavior Modification Procedures for School Personnel* (Hinsdale, Ill.: Dryden, 1972), p. 7.

[61]For a discussion of the social, moral, and political implications of behavior modification, see: Harvey Wheeler, ed., *Beyond the Punitive Society* (San Francisco: W. H. Freeman, 1973).

[62]Cyril M. Franks, "Individual Differences in Conditioning and Associated Techniques." In *The Conditioning Therapies*, pp. 161–62.

[63]Andrew Salter, "The Theory and Practice of Conditioned Reflex Therapy." In *The Conditioning Therapies*, p. 21.

[64]Adapted from V. V. Shelyag, A. D. Glotochkin, and K. K. Platonov, *Military Psychology: A Soviet View* (Washington, D.C.: U.S. Government Printing Office, 1976), pp. 80–84.

# The Reflex Theory of the Psyche

*The reflex.* The concept of a reflex (in Latin, reflection) was introduced into science by the French scientist René Descartes (1596–1650). But his views were still naive and contradictory. At the beginning of the last century, physiology had sufficiently sudied the cerebro-spinal reflexes. The honor of creating the reflex theory of the psyche belongs to I. M. Sechenov (1829–1905) and I. P. Pavlov (1849–1936). Materialistic psychology rests on it.

I. M. Sechenov in his book *Refleksy golovnogo mozga* (Reflexes of the Brain) (1863) pointed out that "all acts of conscious and unconscious life, in terms of their origin, are reflexes."[65] He isolated three components in reflexes:

The initial component, that is, the external stimulus and the conversion of it by the sense organs into the process of nervous excitation transmitted to the brain;

the middle component, that is, the central processes in the brain (the processes of excitation and inhibition) and the occurrence of mental states (sensations, thoughts, feelings, and so forth) on this basis;

the end component or an external movement.

In Sechenov's opinion, brain reflexes "start by sensory excitation, they are continued by a certain mental act and terminate in muscular movement."[66] To the degree that the middle component cannot be separated from the first and the third, so all mental phenomena are an inseparable part of the entire reflex process which has its cause in the effects of the real world which are external to the brain.

This was the first and successful attempt to create a reflex theory of the psyche. . . .However, the honor of an extensive experimental elaboration of the reflex theory of the psyche belongs to I. P. Pavlov who created a new area of science, the study of higher nervous activity.

*Higher nervous activity* is a concept which generalizes both the psychology and physiology of higher nervous activity, but in no way means that they are identical. A conditioned reflex, which is simultaneously both a physiological and psychological phenomenon, lies at the basis of nervous activity.

Here is how I. P. Pavlov himself, in an article entitled "The Conditioned Reflex" written in 1934, described his classical experiment: ". . . Let us make two simple experiments which will succeed for everyone. Let us rinse the mouth of a dog with a mild solution of a certain acid. It will cause the usual defensive reac-

---

[65]I. M. Sechenov, *Izbrannyye filosofskiye i psikhologicheskiye proizvedeniya* (Selected Philsolophical and Psychological Works) (Moscow, Gospolitizdat, 1947), p. 176.
[66]Ibid., p. 111.

tion of an animal, that is, by energetic movements of the mouth the solution will be ejected, and at the same time in the mouth, (and later externally) saliva will begin to flow heavily, diluting the administered acid and washing it off of the mucous membrane of the mouth. Now, another experiment. Several times, by using any external agent, for example, a certain sound, let us use this noise on the dog just before putting the same solution into his mouth. What happens? It is enough to repeat just this sound and the same reaction will occur in the dog, that is, the same movements of the mouth and the same secretion of saliva.

"Both these facts are equally accurate and constant. They both should be designated by the same physiological term 're-flex' . . .

". . . A permanent link between the external agent and the response activity to it by the organism is legitimately called an unconditioned reflex, while a temporary link is a conditioned reflex. . . . A temporary nervous link is a universal physiological phenomenon in the animal world and in ourselves. At the same time this pheonomenon is also mental, it is what the psychologists have called an association, be it the formation of combinations from all sorts of actions and impressions, or from letters, words, and ideas."[67]

Consequently, mental functions are carried out by conditioned reflexes (Fig. 2-1) from which higher nervous activity is formed, while the simpler functions are by unconditioned reflexes which comprise lower nervous activity. The reflex described in the dog (light-salivation) is a conditioned reflex of the first order. But the significance of conditioned reflex activity is increased by the possibility of forming so-called reflexes of a higher (second, third, and so forth) order. It turns out that if the first conditioned reflex will be sufficiently strong, then under certain circumstances, after a certain period of time, it also can become a conditioned stimulus. In this instance, the "bell-salivation" connection will be a reflex of the second order. There are also more complex reflexes.

A reflex of the second order can be formed only on the basis of a sufficiently sound first-order reflex. Initially, any just formed reflex is not sound and is easily disrupted. Any external stimulus, for example, the same bell given at the same time or immediately after light, causes a stopping of salivation, that is, inhibits the reflex. Such an inhibition of a reflex, under the influence of another stimulus, was called an external inhibition by I. P. Pavlov.

*Cortical neurodynamics.* If in experiments with a dog, which already possesses an elaborated "light-salivation" reflex, the light

---

[67]I. P. Pavlov, *Poln. sobr, soch.*, Vol III, Book 2 (Izd-vo AN SSSR, 1951), pp. 322–325.

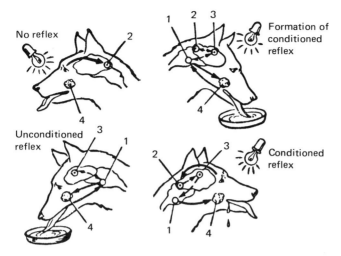

**Figure 2-1.** Diagram of the formation of a conditioned reflex: 1—center of salivation in subcortex; 2—visual center in cerebral cortex; 3—center of salivation in cerebral cortex; 4—salivary gland

is turned on many times without the dog being fed, then less and less saliva will be secreted, and finally the reflex will completely die out. This is the result of *internal extinctive inhibition.* Extinctive inhibition occurs, for example, in the process of the loss of the skills of firing a gun without practice.

Extreme inhibition, caused by an extreme stimulus of a conditioned reflex, is a unique form of external inhibition. For example, if in the experiment with a dog, in which a reflex has formed to the turning on of the light, a very bright light in given, then salivation cannot only decline, but disappear completely. With such *extreme inhibition,* excitation in certain centers is so intensified that it changes over to its opposite, inhibition.

For a man, the strength of the stimulus is determined not only by its physical features (brightness, loudness, and so forth), but also by its individual significance for any given person. In this regard, extreme inhibition plays a great and very complex role in the area of emotions and, in particular, in the manifestation of tension. Sometimes the "dressing down" of a soldier has no pedagogical effect precisely because it causes extreme inhibition in him.

Let us turn to that stage of the experiment when the turning on of the light without feeding has just begun to cause salivation in the dog. Instead of an ordinary light, let us use a blue or red one. It turns out that at first the conditioned reflex salivation will occur in turning on any color of light. This first stage, in forming the reflex, is due to the *irradiation* (propagation) of the nervous

excitation through the cerebral cortex. However, with further reinforcing of any one stimulus, for example, only red light, all the
other stimuli will cause the so-called *differentiated inhibition,*
that is, the conditioned reflex will be differentiated, and nervous
excitation will be concentrated. At a certain stage of reflex dif-
ferentiation, not only other colors, but even different shades of red
will not cause salivation.

The formation of the inhibition of conditioned reflexes is
complicated by the process of *inductio..* The nervous process of
excitation, which has formed in a certain area of the cerebral cortex, spreads or irradiates to adjacent areas. But when a certain
area of the cerebral cortex reaches a state of excitation, then in its
other areas, due to *negative induction,* the process of inhibition
occurs. Conversely, an area of excitation arises around an inhib-
ited area due to *positive induction.* Due to *sequential induction,*
the halting of excitation in a certain area of the cerebral cortex
leads to its temporary inhibition, while the halting of inhibition
leads, respectively, to its increased excitability.

The irradiation, concentration, and reciprocal induction of
nervous processes form that alternation of excitation and inhibition which I. P. Pavlov called the *functional mosaic* of the cerebral
cortex, or *cortical neurodynamics.* The latter concept makes it
possible to more clearly distinguish the objective material process
of cortical neurodynamics and its product, consciousness.

The system of conditioned reflexes connected into a single
whole and manifested as a result of a single *trigger signal* was
called by I. P. Pavlov a *dynamic stereotype* which is a physiological mechanism of skills and habits. A person who has fallen under
new conditions must break his previously formed stereotype, and
create a new one. This is a process which sometimes necessitates
great "nervous effort," and this must not be forgotten in working
with young soldiers.

At the end of his life, I. P. Pavlov established the basis for the
study of a *second signal system of reality.* . . .

In observing the intelligent behavior of the higher apes, I. P.
Pavlov concluded that in addition to unconditioned and conditioned reflexes, there is a third type which he called a *causal*
reflex. ". . . When an ape builds a tower in order to reach fruit, this
cannot be called a 'conditioned reflex,' " he said. "This is an instance of forming knowledge and comprehending a normal relationship of things. This is another case."[68] Thus, the founder of
the study of conditioned reflexes further deepened the reflex
theory of the psyche.

[68]*Pavlovskiye sredy* (Pavlovian Surroundings), Vol III (Moscow: Leningrad,
Izd vo AN SSSR, 1949), p. 262.

P. K. Anokhin most creatively developed the ideas of his teacher. Anokhin was the first in our nation to begin working out the feedback idea, having shown here that the reflex arch is a reflex ring which closes a series of reflexes into a spiral. Of even greater significance is the theory elaborated by P. K. Anokhin of the acceptor of action. The *acceptor of action* is a physiological nervous appratus in the cerebral cortex. It carries out the functions of programing necessary actions under certain conditions and evaluating the acutally executed action. Connected with the working organ (for example, the muscles of the hand) not only by a direct link (in our example, by the impulses to the muscles causing their contraction), but also by feedback which signals the result of these contractions, the acceptor of action not only sets the program of action and controls it, but also corrects it. P. K. Anokhin has linked the concept of *anticipatory reflection*, a unique form of biological reflection which prepares the organism for future and still unoccurred events, to the theory of the acceptor of action. The studies concerning higher nervous activity and the development of the psyche are the natural scientific basis for all psychological sciences, including military psychology.

The American Psychiatric Task Force notes that behavior therapy is most appropately defined in operational terms:[69]

> The behavior therapist begins with a detailed and objective description of the patient's problem behavior. In the empirical tradition of the laboratory from which the approach is derived, the focus of this functional analysis is on observable and quantifiable behavior, rather than on inferred unconscious conflicts. In developing this analysis, the therapist looks for particular situations in which the behavior typcially occurs or fails to occur, as well as for current maintaining conditions.

The Task Force notes that "emphasis is placed on modification of the principal presenting symptoms, rather than on analysis or understanding of the character structure or unconscious conflicts presumed to underlie the behavior pattern."[70] This raises the question of *symptom substitution*: the belief (in psychoanalytic theory) that any reduction in symptoms achieved without treating the underlying causes will result in new symptoms replacing the old. The Task Force responds:[71]

[69]American Psychiatric Association Task Force on Behavior Therapy, *Behavior Therapy in Psychiatry* (New York: Jason Aronson, 1974), p. 2.

[70]Ibid., p. 3.

[71]Ibid., pp. 52–55.

1. Cognitive changes (insights) may catalyze behavioral changes (a basic principle in psychoanalysis), but, the Task Force notes, insight can develop after successful behavior change.
2. Symptom substitution appears to occur only infrequently. In some instances the symptoms, maladaptive behavior, may be so dysfunctional—in certain cases of schizophrenia, for example—that psychoanalytically based therapy is not practical. Behavior therapy offers a system for reducing symptoms to (at least) a level where other therapeutic techniques can be applied.

In an explanation of symptom substitution that is analogous to the scientific principle that nature abhors a vacuum, O'Leary and Wilson state that the removal of one behavior automatically results in the appearance of another. Thus, they argue: "In this sense there is always behavior substitution."[72] Bandura states that symptom substitution should relate only to the appearance of undesirable behavior, and he argues that[73]

> there exists no reliable criteria for determining whether the occurrence of so-called symptomatic behaviors after completion of treatment represents emergent substitute byproducts of a psychic pathology, the development of new modes of maladaptive response to environmental pressure, or the persistence of old modes of maladaptive behavior which had gone unnoticed until even worse behavior was eliminated.

Behavior therapy begins with a functional analysis in order to develop a treatment program designed to deal with specific *target behaviors*. The analysis deals with the day-to-day functioning of the subject in order to discern the independent variables causing maladaptations (the dependent variables):[74] "the behavior analyst attempts to elicit a specific description of the actual events that constitute a problem so that he can evaluate which of the many components of the situation are amenable to change by known methods." The specific description, whenever possible, is based on direct observation or interviews with the client and/or significant others (e.g., parents, spouse),

[72]K. Daniel O'Leary and G. Terrence Wilson, *Behavior Therapy: Application and Outcome* (Englewood Cliffs, N.J.: Prentice-Hall, 1975), p. 448.
[73]A. Bandura *Principles of Behavior Modification* (New York: Holt, Rinehart and Winston, 1969), p. 49.
[74]Frederick H. Kanfer and Laurence G. Grimm, "Behavioral Analysis: Selecting Target Behaviors in the Interview," *Behavior Modification* 1 (January 1977): 8.

and a review of any relevant records. Maladaptive behavior is analyzed in terms of intensity and/or frequency, and is often presented in the form of graphs.

Kanfer and Grimm state that problematic behavior can often be broken down into one of three components: response classes, stimulus classes, and contingency relationships. Presenting problems, or complaints, can be formulated as belonging to one or a combination of five categories derived from the above (three) components:[75]

1. deficiencies in information or required (socially acceptable, for example) behaviors;
2. behavioral excesses;
3. inappropriate environmental stimulus control;
4. inappropriate self-generated stimulus control; and
5. problematic reinforcement contingencies.

The authors indicate a behavior modification technique to deal with each category. For example, a person may be deficient with respect to category one: "lack information concerning social norms and expectations, available sources of satisfaction, or behavioral standards appropriate for his milieu." Category four can often be seen to be a problem with criminal justice clients: "frequently engage in behaviors that are controlled by immediate pay-off but have long term negative outcomes." The authors recommend, among a host of techniques, teaching clients to conduct their own functional analysis for subsequent self-produced modification of the environmental contingencies that are reinforcing their maladaptive behavior.[76]

Fensterheim divides "irrational" or "undesirable" behavior into four general groups for therapy purposes:[77]

1. *phobias*—person has learned to associate an emotion, e.g., fear or anger, with an object, situation, or action. Treated by *systematic desensitization*.
2. *lack of assertion*—person cannot express innermost thoughts and feelings openly and honestly, and is easily dominated by persons and situations. Treated by *behavior rehearsal* for assertive actions.
3. *persistance of undesirable habits*—these "habits" include such

---

[75]Ibid., p. 10.
[76]Ibid., pp. 11–17.
[77]Fensterheim, pp. 13–14.

items as alcoholism, drug addiction, sexual deviances, etc. Treated by *aversive conditioning.*

4. *lack of desirable hiabits*—Treated by modifying behavior by positive reinforcement of "desirable" behavior—operant conditioning.

After the functional analysis has been completed (it is never really ended, but is constantly subject to revision based on new observations) behavioral goals are set. These goals are always related to specific items of behavior that can be subjected to empirical measurement. Sulzer and Meyer note: "Some goals are practical; others are not. A goal is practical only if it can be achieved. Therefore, those involved in behavior modification prefer to work with a series of easily achievable goals, rather than a single long-term goal."[78] By using only items that can be subjected to empirical validation, the therapist can demonstrate a functional relationship between the dependent behavior and the independent (reinforcement) behavior.

The stress on observable behavior and measurement is highlighted by Ayllon and Huges:[79]

> the basic principles of measurement must be retained. There is no substitute for objective assessments of observable behavior, whether these be obtained through electronic recordings or through tally marks charted by well-trained humans observers. This kind of an assessment and behavioral engineering must meet several requirements of which the following are examples. There must be specification and unequivocal definition of an observable behavior, such as entering the ward dining room. An objective record must be kept of the frequency with which the behavior was exhibited during a given time period, for example, the patient entered the dining room for 25 out of 42 consecutive meals. The empirical determination of an effective reinforcer must be made which will, for example, isolate either social reinforcement or food to determine whether they control the patients' frequency of entering the dining room to eat. There must also be a mechanical or human agent which will deliver the reinforcer as an immediate consequence of the specified response according to defined schedules.

[78]Sulzer and Mayer, p. 4.
[79]T. Ayllon and Heidi B. Hughes, "Behavioral Engineering." In *Operant Conditioning in the Classroom,* ed. Carl E. Pitts (New York: Thomas Y. Crowell, 1971), p. 98.

Social service practitioners are primarily concerned with operant conditioning for two reasons: first, it is clearly the most useful method for dealing with the behavior symptoms of most offenders, and two, "social workers are not trained or oriented to intervene directly at an organic level so that it would be inappropriate for them to use certain techniques such as those involving drug administration, muscular relaxation, or physical aversive stimulation."[80] In addition, such techniques as aversive conditioning can be "easily misused and misunderstood and can become a cruel form of punishment." Silber explains, for example, that "in aversive conditioning, the object is to associate ('condition') the unpleasant feeling coming from the drug or the shock with the pleasant stimulus so that eventually the stimulus becomes unattractive."[81] This technique was dramatically portrayed in the popular film *A Clockwork Orange*.

Operant conditioning is associated with the work of B. F. Skinner who observed that when some aspect of behavior is followed by a certain type of consequence—a reward—it is more likely to be repeated. The reward is a *positive reinforcer*. When punishment is used to decrease the likelihood that some aspect of behavior will be repeated, it is called a *negative reinforcer*. The use of reinforcement results in *shaping* behavior. As we noted earlier, much of behavior modification was developed in the laboratory using rats, cats, dogs and monkeys, and the "animal" origins of the techniques have been retained in some of the nomenclature used. Note the use of the term "organism" (as opposed to client, person, subject or patient) in the description of operant conditioning provided by Bachrach:[82]

> If the operant conditioner, approaching an organism in an experimental space, specifies the response he desires from the organism and the frequency with which he wishes this response emitted, he is in a position to shape the organism's behavior.

Bachrach also reminds us of an important principle in operant conditioning, one which makes its application in noninstitutional or outside

[80]Derek Jehu, "The Role of Social Workers in Behavior Therapy," *Journal of Behavior Therapy and Experimental Psychiatry* 1, 1970, p. 18.

[81]David E. Silber, "The Place of Behavior Therapy in Correction," *Crime and Delinquency* 22 (April 1976): 215.

[82]Arthur J. Bachrach, "Some Applications of Operant Conditioning to Behavior Therapy." In *The Conditioning Therapies*, p. 68.

of laboratory settings very difficult: "A basic rule is to reinforce the behavior immediately."[83]

In operant conditioning the tendency is to focus on a specific observable condition, the *target behavior*, and the environmental events which follow the behavior and thus reinforce and maintain it. "Therapeutic intervention involves the manipulation of reinforcements so that the behavior is extinguished and replaced by more adaptive responses. Reinforcement is given when desired responses are made and withheld when there are undesired responses. When the appropriate behavior is lacking, successive approximations to the required response are reinforced until the new response is established."[84] Hosford and Moss (in a discussion of a correctional counselor training program based on behavior therapy) note that antisocial criminal behavior is learned the *same way* that socially accepted behavior is.[85] Thus, criminal behavior is the result of "learning principles rather than disease-oriented internal constructs." They note that many criminals are proud of being good at their criminal activities "because there are so few other behaviors they have learned in life for which they receive any reinforcement." Thus, they argue, the role of the counselor involves working "with those significant persons and those institutional and societal practices which have control over and shape the inmate's behavior."[86]

The use of the term *shape* is deliberate, since shaping is a basic device in operant conditioning. Ayllon and Hughes state:[87]

> This differential reinforcement of the "correct" or appropriate response—the one that the experimenter desires to shape—along with simultaneous extinction of all other responses through lack of reinforcement, is a vital aspect of the shaping process. Since extinction of inappropriate or irrelevant responses is involved in any shaping procedure it is easy to lose the behavior altogether and special care must be taken in planning the successive steps in shaping a response. The steps must not be too large and the experimenter must make certain that each approximation to the final response is well established before moving on to the next.

Sulzer and Mayer provide an operational definition of shaping:[88]

---

[83]Ibid.

[84]Meyer and Chesser, pp. 111–12.

[85]Ray E. Hosford and C. Scott Moss, *The Crumbling Walls* (Urbana, Ill.: University of Illinois Press, 1975), pp. 91–104.

[86]Ibid., p. 96.

[87]Ayllon and Hughes, p. 96.

[88]Sulzer and Mayer, pp. 69–70.

The procedure for shaping a new behavior begins with a behavior as it exists and involves reinforcing slight changes in the behavior as it gradually approaches the target behavior. Thus, rather than selecting and reinforcing a subset of behaviors that is in fact the desired goal, elements, or subset, of a behavior which *resemble* the desired behavior are selectively reinforced.... At the same time, old or inappropriately directed changes (curvier lines) will not be reinforced. The series of slight changes, or subsets, that are reinforced are referred to, technically, as *successive approximations*. *Shaping, then, is a procedure in which successive approximations to a goal behavior are reinforced.*

### BEHAVIOR MODIFICATION

Eysenck states that we should ask, not why some people are criminals, but, "how does it come about that so many people are, in fact, law-abiding citizens who do not go counter to the rules of our society..."[89] He concludes that whether or not a particular behavior, an antisocial act, will occur depends on the strength of a "fear-anxiety reaction" which develops as a result of "the conditioned avoidance reaction which has been built into him, as it were, through a process of conditioning."[90] This process is not dependent on structural or external constraints such as the police, but rather on the training an individual receives as a child. Eysenck notes that crime is not followed immediately by punishment, even in those cases where the perpetrator is apprehended. However, the "fear-anxiety," an autonomic reaction, is immediate and it is an inhibiting factor that accounts for why most people are not criminals.[91] The resemblence of this mechanism to the superego is obvious.

A review of claims and counter-claims about behavior modification indicate conflicting results. Wolpe reviews a series of studies which claim that behavior therapy was successful and its effects long-lasting.[92] Bruck questions the Wolpe findings because of an alleged lack of adequate control groups and the failure to account for "dropouts."[93] Carter and Stuart reply to Bruck's criticism and expound on the success of behavior therapy.[94]

[89]Hans J. Eysenck, *Crime and Personality* (London: Routeledge and Kegan Paul, 1964), p. 100.
[90]Ibid., p. 108.
[91]Ibid., p. 110.
[92]Joseph Wolpe, "The Comparative Clinical Status of Conditioning Therapies and Psychoanalysis," *The Conditioning Therapies*, pp. 5–20.
[93]Bruck, p. 46.
[94]Robert D. Carter and Richard E. Stuart, "Behavior Modification Theory and Practice: A Reply," *Social Work* 15 (January 1970): 37–50.

Hilts, in a book for general audiences, relates some of the rather impressive claims of the behaviorists, especially those working in mental hospitals.[95] However, based on a five-month study, Biklen questions the effectiveness of behavior techniques used in a state hospital: it is unlikely, he concludes, "that an outside agent can promote changes on the part of any group of people, in this case patients, when the group to be changed does not share, develop, or desire a common perspective with the change agent."[96]

Behavior modification has been reported effective in institutional settings, e.g., prisons and hospitals, since it is in such "total institutions"[97] that the greatest amount of environmental variables can be subjected to control and manipulation by those in charge. Cohen and Filipezak report on the use of behavior therapy in the National Training School. While the program was apparently successful in promoting institutional harmony and academic learning, the rate of recidivism, while delayed for those in the program, was the same as the norm for those treated by other methods.[98] Indeed, there is a paucity of reports on the effective use of behavior modification with offenders in noninstitutional settings. Shah, an advocate of the behavior approach, provides an explanation, the lack of control over environmental factors:[99]

> To take a more specific aspect of the relationship between social and environmental factors and deviant behavior, it seems evident that the form and frequency of certain criminal acts bears some connection to the environmental structure and opportunities provided. Thus, the relative ease with which checks may be obtained and also cashed in the United States is undoubtedly related to the frequency of bad checks and various related offenses. The relative ease with which cars may be broken into and be started without the use of ignition keys, clearly affects the frequency of offenses involving "joyriding" and automobile theft. Similarly, the facility with which firearms may be obtained by almost all segments of

[95]Phillip J. Hilts, *Behavior Mod* (New York: Harpers Magazine Press, 1974).

[96]Douglas P. Biklen, "Behavior Modification in a State Hospital: A Participant-Observer's Critique," *American Journal of Orthopsychiatry* 46 (January 1976): 61.

[97]A term used by Erving Goffman in his classic work *Asylums* (Garden City: Doubleday, 1961).

[98]Harold L. Cohen and James Filipczak, *A New Learning Environment* (San Francisco: Jossey-Bass, 1971).

[99]Saleem A. Shah, "Treatment of Offenders: Some Behavioral Concepts, Principles, and Approaches," *Federal Probation* 30 (June 1966): 37.

the population would appear to have a definite bearing on the numerous offenses involving such weapons.

Shah suggests an approach that deals with the control of crime-producing variables:[100]

It seems obvious that certain changes in community practices, the requirements that the vast technological skills available in the country be utilized more adequately in the manufacturing of automobiles with better door locks and less vulnerable ignition systems, the enactment of other appropriate legislation, etc., could do much to influence the frequency of certain law violations and other undesirable social situations.

Fox questions the effectiveness of behavior techniques in changing the behavior of delinquents and adult criminals, and he argues that results have been "consistantly disappointing." Fox states that eighty-one percent of the experimental studies fail to show any realistic follow-up and other studies with follow-ups are disappointing. Close scrutiny must be given to behavior modification approaches in the future," Fox states, because in the past "the observation has been that those subjected to behavior modification techniques will 'play the game' as long as they are in the behavior modification situation and will revert to previous behavior when returned to their original setting."[101]

However, Schwitzgebel argues:[102]

Some of the difficulties in the criminal justice system, such as the inconsistent definition of offenders, cannot be corrected merely by an increased use of behavior modification techniques. On the other hand, behavior modification techniques are remarkably well suited for integration into the criminal justice system because they, and their underlying theories, focus upon behavior, and most offenses involve observable behavior. Unlike treatment orientations that focus upon goals such as mental health, which are diffuse and difficult to define, behavior modification goals are readily measurable. Thus, questions about the effectiveness of the

---

[100]Ibid. See also C. Ray Jeffery, *Crime Prevention through Environmental Design.* (Beverly Hills, Ca.: Sage Publications, 1978).

[101]Vernon Fox, *Introduction to Criminology* (Englewood Cliffs, N.J.: Prentice-Hall, 1976), p. 167.

[102]Ralph K. Schwitzgebel, "Behavior Modification Programs." in *Deviance,* ed. Simon Dinitz et al. (New York: Oxford University Press, 1975), p. 500.

approach and its influence on the criminal justice system can be answered by empirical study rather than by speculation unsupported by data.

## BEHAVIOR MODIFICATION AND
## THE CRIMINAL JUSTICE PRACTITIONER

It was previously suggested that the use of behavior therapy in social service be limited to operant conditioning. The token economy, a form of operant conditioning, has proven popular in institutional settings. The token economy, however, requires rather extensive programming which is beyond the scope of this book. Instead, we will review two behaviorist approaches which can be applied by the criminal justice practitioner in any setting: *self-monitering* and *behavioral contracting*.

The *self-monitering* technique requires a highly motivated client and a specific target behavior. The client maintains a daily log of the specific problem, e.g., lack of temper control. The client records the number of times he or she exhibits the specific manifestations of a lack of temper control. This technique is often used in conjunction with other forms of therapy, although Bootzin notes that this method alone has proven effective in certain cases. Why does self-monitering change behavior?[103]

> One possibility is that it increases awareness and makes the response sequence less automatic. This may provide the opportunity for the person to suppress the response or engage in some incompatible behavior. Additionally, self-monitering may encourage the person to reward or punish himself depending upon whether appropriate gains have been made. Investigators have shown that self-reinforcing statements such as "I am doing well" are important in maintaining one's own behavior. A recording system which facilitates this process undoubtedly will be effective in helping people to change their own behavior as well.

Bootzin also notes that client-improvement may have been the result of the worker's attention to the targeted behavior.[104]

*Behavioral contracting* is "a means of scheduling the exchange of positive reinforcements between two or more people."[105] The contract establishes goals and assigns responsibilities for which privileges (re-

---

[103]Richard R. Bootzin, *Behavior Modification and Therapy: An Introduction* (Cambridge Mass.: Winthrop Publishers, 1975), p. 11.
[104]Ibid., p. 12.
[105]O'Leary and Wilson, p. 205.

wards) are exchanged. Stuart, in an article on behavior contracts within families of delinquents, lists the elements of a behavioral contract:[106]

1. Details the privileges which each expects to gain after fulfilling his/her responsibilities, e.g., allowance, use of car, TV.
2. Details the responsibilities essential to securing each privilege, e.g., performance at school, adhering to a curfew. Every effort is made to restrict privileges to prosocial behavior in order that the family can serve as an agent of social control. Of course the responsibilities must be moniterable by parents.
3. Contains a system of sanctions for failure to meet responsibilities, e.g., shortening curfew hours, TV time.
4. Provides a *bonus clause* which assures positive reinforcement for compliance with the terms of the contract.

Based on Stuart's model the University of Illinois used behavioral contracting in their Adolescent Diversion Project which is discussed in Chapter 5.

Weathers and Liberman caution against using behavioral contracts as *the* mode of treatment: "Contracting should not be viewed as an effective intervention strategy or 'treatment package' in itself, but rather as a supplementary aid in a wider range of interventions."[107]

## Reality Therapy

Reality Therapy, unlike psychoanalytic and behavior theory, does not have an extensive body of professional literature. Indeed, the major work on the subject has only 166 pages in the paper edition.[108] Reality Therapy, although it does not present a distinct body of theoretical knowledge with respect to crime causation, is popular among criminal justice practitioners. In Maryland, for example, Reality Therapy is the only method of treatment that is part of that state's training program for probation and parole agents. According to the Maryland Correctional Training Academy, Reality Therapy is emphasized because it provides a treatment base for

[106]Richard B. Stuart, "Behavioral Contracting Within the Families of Delinquents," *Journal of Behavior Therapy and Experimental Psychiatry* 2, 1971, pp. 1–11.

[107]Lawrence Weathers and Robert Paul Liberman, "Contingency Contracting With Families of Delinquent Adolescents," *Behavior Therapy* 6 (May 1975): 356–66.

[108]William Glasser, *Reality Therapy* (New York: Harper & Row, 1975).

the need to enforce administrative limits and standards of socially acceptable behavior established by the law, the society, the courts, and the parole board, in an attempt to stimulate the movement of the offender toward responsible and productive citizenship.[109]

The Academy states that Reality Therapy is "a practical, meaningful and systematic *alternative* to traditional counseling approaches to parole and probation work."[110]

Reality Therapy was developed by William Glasser while he was a psychiatrist at the Ventura School for (Delinquent) Girls in California. This sets it apart from psychoanalysis and behavior modification which were developed in clinical or laboratory settings. Reality Therapy bears a strong likeness to behavior modification, and it is of some interest that the forward to Glasser's book was written by a noted behaviorist, O. H. Mowrer. Reality Therapy's stress on learning and the use of reinforcement through the medium of a relationship with the client, point up the similarity with operant conditioning.

Reality Therapy is concerned with those persons who have not learned or who have lost the ability to lead responsible lives, criminal offenders for example. Such persons are not "sick" or "psychotic," they are *irresponsible.* It is the task of the practitioner to teach responsibility through the medium of involvement:[111]

the therapist must become so involved with the patient that the patient can begin to face reality and see how his behavior is unrealistic. Second, the therapist must reject the behavior which is unrealistic but still accept the patient and maintain his involvement with him. Last, and necessary in varying degrees depending upon the patient, the therapist must teach the patient better ways to fulfill his needs within the confines of reality.

Reality Therapy focuses on three areas of "human need:"[112]

1. the need to love
2. the need to be loved
3. the need to feel worthwhile

It is the result of deficiencies in these areas that criminal, and other irresponsible, behaviors emanate. Glasser states that one who is

---

[109]Quoted from *The Revised Entrance Level Training Program for Parole and Probation Agents*, Maryland Correctional Training Academy, 1976.
[110]Ibid.
[111]Glasser, p. 21.
[112]Ibid., p. 10.

worthwhile is usually someone who is loved and who can love in return, but he notes that "whether we are loved or not, to be worthwhile we must maintain a satisfactory standard of behavior."[113]

Without denying psychoanalytic theory with respect to personality development, Glasser rejects the belief that the person can "change his attitude and ultimately his behavior through gaining insight into his unconscious conflicts and inadequacies."[114] Schmideberg states, moreover, that "by dwelling on the past the person is encouraged to disregard present problems which is a relief at times, but often—undesirably—the person feels that having provided so many interesting memories he is now entitled to rest on his laurels and make no effort to change his attitude or to plan for the future."[115] The nonjudgmental basis for psychoanalytically oriented therapy is seen by the Reality Therapist as permitting the client to "cop out"—blame his behavior on such uncontrollable variables such as parents and "upbringing." Reality Therapy, on the other hand, is concerned, and deals, exclusively with the present and the future—the past is just that.

In a more recent book Glasser lists the principles of Reality Therapy:[116]

1. *Involvement*—The therapist must become involved with the person he is trying to help. The therapist must therefore be warm, personal, and friendly. Involvement is the foundation of therapy, and all other principles build on and add to it.

2. *Current Behavior*—Accompanying the consistant warmth and involvement in principle one, is a constant effort by the therapist to help the person become aware, consciously and in detail, of his/her own behavior at the present time. It is necessary for the therapist to judge the capacity of the client to become increasingly aware of his/her irresponsible behavior.

3. *Self-Evaluation*—The therapist does not judge the behavior; he leads the person to evaluate his/her own behavior through the medium of involvement, and by bringing the actual behavior out in the open.

4. *Planning Responsible Behavior*—The therapist assists the

---

[113]Ibid.

[114]Ibid., p. 51.

[115]Melitta Schmideberg, "Some Basic Principles of Offender Therapy: Two," *International Journal of Offender Therapy and Comparative Criminology*, no. 1, 1975, p. 29.

[116]Adaptation of pp. 74–98 from *The Identity Society*, Revised Edition by William Glasser. Copyright © 1972, 1975 by William Glasser. By permission of Harper & Row Publishers, Inc.

client in developing realistic plans for action based on decisions about current behavior and self-evaluation. Such planning may include referrals to other specialists for specific problem areas. Most importantly, the plan should be realistic and in reach of the client—failure should not be reinforced.

5. *Commitment*—A verbal or, preferably, written contractual agreement to carry out the plan.

6. *No Excuses*—We do not ask "Why?" since that implies that we accept excuses for not carrying out the commitment. Glasser notes: "If the therapist accepts his excuses the man may never be able to handle future situations of stress."[117]

7. *No Punishment*—This principle is as important as "no excuses," although Glasser also states: "Mild punishment is sometimes effective when it serves to remind people that better options are open than their present choice."[118] He concludes: "Giving praise for a job well done instead of rejection for a job below expectations will motivate people toward success."[119]

Reality Therapy's greatest advantage may be its simplicity.[120]

---

[117]Ibid., p. 93.
[118]Ibid., p. 96.
[119]Ibid., p. 98.
[120]For a rather complete review of the literature on Reality Therapy see *The Reality Therapy Reader*, ed. Alexander Bassin, Thomas E. Bratter, and Richard L. Rachin (New York: Harper & Row, 1976).

# 3

# Criminal Justice
# Sequence and Agencies

## The Path of Criminal Justice

This chapter will review the criminal justice sequence,[1] focusing on areas of discretion and on that information most relevant to the social service practitioner who must learn to maneuver through this maze-like conglomeration in order to provide social services.

### STEPS IN THE CRIMINAL JUSTICE SEQUENCE

The criminal justice sequence (Figure 3-1) begins at that point where an act constituting a criminal offense (or in the case of a juvenile, a delinquent act[2] or status offense[3]) comes to the attention of a law enforcement agency. The sequence ends with the involvement of a correctional agency. Let us review the sequence, noting that what is

[1]The term *sequence* is preferable to *system* since criminal justice agencies are part of a vast network of independent, and frequently overlapping, jurisdictions administered by counties, cities, states, and the federal government. This highly fragmented network hardly constitutes a system.

[2]An act committed by a juvenile for which an adult could be prosecuted in a criminal court, but for which a juvenile can be adjudicated in a juvenile court, or prosecuted in a criminal court if the juvenile court transfers jurisdiction.

[3]A status offense is an act or conduct which is declared by statute to be an offense only when committed or engaged in by a juvenile, e.g., truancy.

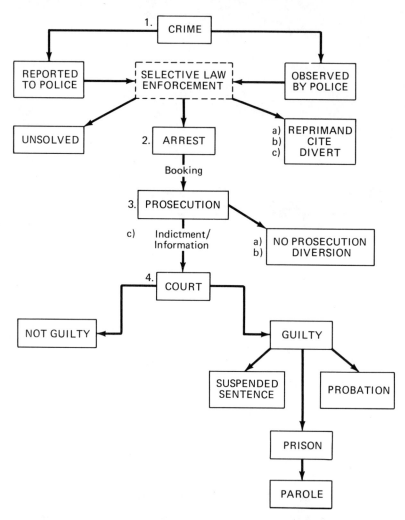

**Figure 3-1.** Criminal justice sequence

described here is of a general nature, approximating the process in all jurisdictions while, possibly, not accurately reflecting any one of them.

1. *Crime.* A crime is an "act committed or omitted in violation of a law forbidding or commanding it for which an adult can be punished, upon conviction, by incarceration and other penalties or a corporation penalized, or for which a juvenile can be brought under the jurisdiction of a juvenile court and adjudicated a delinquent or trans-

ferred to an adult court."[4] Crimes can usually be distinguished as felonies, misdemeanors, or offenses. In order for a crime to become, at least statistically, part of the criminal justice sequence it must be *known* to a criminal justice agency, usually the police. However, criminal victimization studies in the United States consistently report that most victims of crime do not make a report to the police. For example, a survey of five large cities indicated that, on the average, less than 38 percent of the victims of crime reported the incidents to the police.[5]

The fact that a crime comes to the attention of the police does not necessarily result in a particular action, but a number of options arise. The police may

(a) issue reprimand/warning: the police officer may determine that a warning or reprimand is sufficient in a particular situation. This option is seen frequently in motor vehicle-related infractions.

(b) cite/issue summons: certain offenses may be handled without an arrest, by issuing a citation, which will subsequently be adjudicated in a court or at an administrative hearing. The use of the summons procedure has greatly expanded in recent years and may now include various misdemeanors and even certain felonies.

(c) divert/referral: the official halting or suspension of processing, after a recorded justice sequence entry, against an alleged offender and possibly a referral of that person to a treatment or care program.

2. *Arrest.*[6] Criminal prosecutions usually begin with the summary arrest of a defendant by a police officer, or by the filing of a formal action in court and the issuance of an arrest warrant or summons. A person who is arrested is taken to a police station for processing and detention. The processing of an arrested individual consists of taking personal data and, where required, the individual is fingerprinted. The word "booked" has entered common parlance as the thing done to arrested persons, although the "booking" is actually an entry in an arrest record and a minor part of the processing.

---

[4]*Dictionary of Criminal Justice Data Terminology* (Washington, D.C.: United States Government Printing Office, 1976).

[5]*Criminal Victimization Surveys in Chicago, Detroit, Los Angeles, New York and Philadelphia* (Washington, D.C.: United States Government Printing Office, 1976).

[6]Some of this material has been adapted from an informational pamphlet provided by the Office of the District Attorney, Nassau County, New York.

Accusatory instruments, including informations, misdemeanor complaints, and felony complaints, may be prepared in the police station or at another location, e.g., the courthouse, by police personnel or staff from the prosecutor's office.

---

### ACCUSATORY INSTRUMENTS[7]
#### NEW YORK STATE

*Informations* are sworn statements charging offenses of less than felony grade. The Information of supporting depositions annexed to it supply allegations to each element of the crime on personal knowledge, (for example an Information charging unauthorized use of an automobile, will have statement sworn to by a policeman indicating the defendant operated a motor vehicle). Attached will be a supporting deposition of the vehicle's owner indicating that no person had permission to so use the vehicle.

*Misdemeanor Complaint* is simply an allegation made on hearsay (Example—the information alluded to above would be a misdemeanor complaint if the deposition of the vehicle's owner was not attached). A person may only be held five days on such a misdemeanor complaint, and unless he waives, he cannot be forced to trial on such an instrument.

*Simplified Information* is a very short Information charging a misdemeanor offense or less, for example: a traffic ticket.

*Prosecutor's Information* is a written accusation filed by the District Attorney, either at the direction of a Grand Jury, the direction of a local criminal court, or at the District Attorney's own instance.

*Felony Complaint* is a complaint charging a felony. It commences the proceeding, but no person may be tried for a felony except by the indictment of a Grand Jury or Superior Court Information (if the defendant waives indictment).

---

A detective will usually be assigned to cases in which an investigation is needed. The detective will gather evidence and help to prepare the case for trial. He/she will interview and interrogate arrested persons, complainants, and witnesses in order to procure statements concerning the criminal incident.

After processing, a person is either detained or released on bond or

[7]Ibid.

appearance ticket for a court appearance that day or the next, depending upon the time processing is completed.

3. *Prosecution.* After arrest processing has been completed the defendent has entered the prosecutorial phase of the criminal justice sequence. Sometime during this phase the prosecutor's office will decide upon one of several options:

(a) no prosecution: the prosecutor can decide not to prosecute a case, usually due to lack of sufficient evidence, because of tained (illegally secured) evidence, or because the defendant has agreed to cooperate (e.g., inform) on matters of concern to law enforcement.

(b) divert: suspend prosecution with the proviso that the defendant enter a specific treatment or care program often attached to the office of the prosecutor.

(c) indictment/bill of information: move the case into the next phase of processing by way of a bill of information or presentation to a grand jury. The use of a grand jury varies with the jurisdiction:

While most jurisdictions have a grand jury, the extent of its use varies. In most of the Eastern states, the common practice is to process all felonies and even some indictable misdemeanors through a grand jury. Since the use of grand juries is derived from the English system of justice, this practice is most prevalent in those states which formed the original thirteen colonies. Rhode Island, for example, until 1975 processed all felony cases through the grand jury. In fact their first examination by the Assistant Attorneys General was at this processing stage. In 1975, Rhode Island made a major change in its felony processing, substituting the use of grand jury to obtain indictments with filing by information based on probable cause. As one moves westward, the use of grand jury indictments to begin felony prosecutions diminishes while the practice of filing by information increases.*** In the far West, the use of the grand jury is reserved almost solely for investigations of corruption of public officials.[8]

4. *Court.* The first time a defendant appears before a judge is usually for arraignment—merely a formal reading of the accusatory instrument, together with a setting of bail. The defendant is given an opportunity to get a lawyer or one may be appointed if he cannot afford

[8]Joan Jacoby, *The Prosecutor's Charging Decision: A Policy Perspective* (Washington, D. C.: United States Government Printing Office, 1977), p. 14.

counsel. At arraignment the defendant sometimes pleads guilty to petty crimes or has the case against him dismissed, but usually the case is adjourned pending further court action or referral of the case to the grand jury.

   After arraignment and usually prior to a trial, plea bargaining commences. Plea bargaining usually involves the defense attorney and the prosecutor's office. In some jurisdictions the judge may also be involved directly in this process at some stage. If an agreement is reached between the prosecutor and the defense counsel, acting on behalf of the defendant, the latter will plead guilty to a lesser crime than the one he/she has been accused of committing. In return, the defendant will receive a lesser sentence than the one he/she could have been sentenced if the case went to trial on the original charges. If plea bargaining fails, which is rather infrequent, the case will go to trial, a procedure which we will only outline here.

---

### TRIAL[9]

1. The People* examine prospective jurors.
2. The Defendant examines prospective jurors.
3. People exercise challenges to excuse jurors. (each side has three Peremptory challenges).
4. Defendant exercises challenges to excuse jurors.
5. The Jury is sworn.
6. People open. (Outline case they intend to prove).
7. Defendant open, if he wishes.
8. People call witnesses—defendant cross examines them.
9. People rest case.
10. Defendant calls witnesses, if he wishes—People cross examine.
11. Defendant sums up.
12. People sum up.
13. The judge charges the jury—(Explains the legalities of the case).
14. Jury deliberates and returns verdict.

---

*In criminal cases the complainant is "The People." The prosecutor always represents the people in a criminal case.*

   If there is a finding of guilt, following a trial or plea of guilty, the probation department conducts a presentence investigation on the de-

   [9]Information adapted from pamphlet provided by the Office of the District Attorney, Nassau County, New York.

fendant and submits a report, usually with a recommendation, to the sentencing judge. After reviewing the presentence report, the judge imposes a sentence of incarceration or probation (or perhaps a fine or suspended sentence), which means that the offender will be sent to a correctional facility or returned directly to the community under the supervision of the probation department. If the offender is imprisoned, sometime during his incarceration, he will become eligible for release on parole. If he is paroled, the offender will be under the supervision of a parole agency.

## HUMAN REACTION TO THE
## CRIMINAL JUSTICE SEQUENCE

What this overview fails to provide is the human dynamic—the degradation that often accompanies an arrest. Upon being arrested the (alleged) offender ("perpetrator" in police parlance) is taken to be "booked." He is placed in a "lock-up"—a small cell in a police station or city jail—while fingerprinting and clerical chores are completed. Irwin notes:[10]

> The booking-room officers who are working in close proximity process scores of incoming prisoners daily and, therefore, tend to maintain an insulation of formality or ferocity to withstand the frequent supplications from the mass of incoming prisoners. To gain permission to make a single telephone call, as is his legal right, often takes considerable persistance on the part of the prisoner.

The offender is brought to court for arraignment, transported in a van, handcuffed to other prisoners, and placed in a holding pen in the court building. (In some jurisdictions booking and arraignment take place in the same building.) In the holding pen are an assortment of persons: drunks, addicts (possibly suffering from withdrawal), misdemeanants and felons, first offenders and "hardened felons." In New York, where this writer worked, the pens are overcrowded, hot, and odoriferous. There is no furniture, and the defendants awaiting arraignment or transportation back to jail must either stand or sit on the cement floor.

Arraignments often take only a few minutes as the judge sets bail and determines if the defendant can afford an attorney or if one will be appointed to represent him. The court setting in the arraignment part is filled with activity, and for the uninitiated it presents a confusing array

---

[10]John Irwin, *The Felon* (Englewood Ciffs, N.J.: Prentice-Hall, 1970), p. 38.

of faceless people and legal papers. After arraignment the defendant is transported to a jail where, if he is unable to post bail, he will await futher court action. Local jails, as opposed to state prisons, are notoriously inhospitable places. Recreation facilities are often limited or nonexistent, and the high rate of inmate turnover makes any meaningful individualization impossible—it is a truly dehumanizing experience. Although at this stage of the criminal process the defendant, under our system of law, is presumed innocent, he is already being subjected to punishment. In addition, the defendant is separated from family and friends, and his job may be in jeopardy or already lost. Irwin notes:[11]

> These experiences—arrest, trial, and conviction—threaten the structure of his personal life in two ways. First, the disjointed experience of suddenly being extracted from a relatively orderly and familiar routine and cast into a completely unfamiliar and seemingly chaotic one where the ordering of events is completely out of his control has a shattering impact upon his personality. One's identity, one's personality system, one's coherent thinking about himself depend upon a relatively familiar and continuous, and predictable stream of events.

In this new world, "the boundaries of the self collapse." Previous social relationships are strained or degenerate; bills are not paid; obligations are not met. Under these conditions a defendant will often seek the easiest—earliest—way out, even if it means pleading guilty and waiving his right to a trial.

## Juvenile Process

The juvenile process differs from that of adults both in substance and philosophy. At the center of the process is the juvenile court, an institution which took root and rapidly expanded at the end of the nineteenth and beginning of the twentieth century. The court was established through the efforts of feminist reformers who wanted to remove children from the adult criminal process. The underlying concept of the juvenile court and process is *parens patriae*, the state acting in the capacity of a substitute father. Until the *Gault Decision* in 1967, little or no due process safeguards were provided to juveniles. The Gault Decision[12] provided due process guarantees to juveniles facing juvenile

[11]Ibid., p. 39.
[12]*Gault v. Arizona*, 387 U.S. 1 (1967).

court proceedings. These guarantees include:

(a) written notification of charges
(b) right to legal counsel
(c) protection against self-incrimination
(d) right to confront and cross-examine witnesses
(e) right to appeal

The juvenile court will deal with three basic types of cases:

1. *Delinquency*—where an act which could be prosecuted in a criminal court is handled in juvenile court because the offender is a minor.[13]
2. *Status Offense*—conduct by a minor which would not constitute an offense if the subject was an adult, e.g., truancy, incorrigibility. These youngsters are sometimes referred to as CHINS, JINS, PINS, and MINS.[14] The inclusion of status offenders under the jurisdiction of the juvenile court is a matter of some controversy.[15]
3. *Neglect/Dependency*—where care by parent or guardian falls short of a legal standard of proper care. This could be the result of willful or unintentional neglect or abuse.

There is a lack of uniformity among juvenile (sometimes called "Family") courts throughout the United States. In some jurisdictions, certain violations of law are handled by the adult criminal courts no matter what the age of the offender (for example, murder, kidnapping, and armed robbery). The juvenile court is usually closed to the general public and its records are confidential. In most jurisdictions a juvenile is not routinely fingerprinted or photographed by the police. Hearings in juvenile court are less formal than in adult courts. Judges usually do not wear robes and they sit at a desk instead of the high bench that is characteristic of the adult courts.

We shall briefly review the juvenile process in general, with the

---

[13]In six states the age is fifteen or younger; in twelve states it is sixteen or younger; and in thirty-two states and the District of Columbia it is seventeen or younger. Source: Aurora Gallagher, *Juvenile Delinquency: A Basic Manual for County Officials* (Washington, D.C.: National Association of Counties Research Foundation, 1976).

[14]Children in Need of Supervision; Juveniles in Need of Supervision; Persons in Need of Supervision; and Minors in Need of Supervision.

[15]For a discussion of this issue see Howard Abadinsky, "The Status Offense Dilemma: Coercion and Treatment," *Crime and Delinquency* 22 (October 1976): 456–60.

caveat that what is described may not exactly mirror any specific jurisdiction. Throughout this section you may wish to refer to Figure 3-2,
which outlines the entire juvenile court sequence.

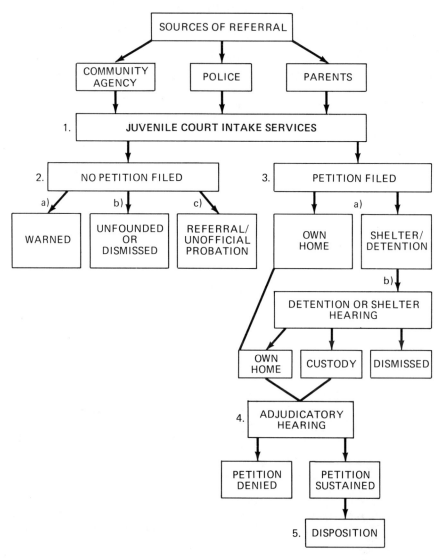

Adapted from: Jay Olson, Intake Screening Guides: Improving Justice for Juveniles
(Washington, D.C.: U.S. Department of Health, Education and Welfare, 1975), p. 18.

**Figure 3-2.**    Juvenile court sequence

1. *Intake Screening.*   Cases are referred to the juvenile court by parents, police, private and public agencies and school officials. The case is first reviewed by an intake officer, usually a member of the probation staff. This officer interviews the young person, the policeman or agency representative, and the child's parent(s) in an effort to determine if the juvenile court has jurisdiction. If the answer is in the affirmative, the officer must determine if the case is appropriate for formal court processing or can be handled without a *petition,* which parallels the complaint in the adult criminal court. This responsibility is similar to that exercised in adult criminal courts by the prosecutor who decides which cases are to be presented to the court for prosecution. Roughly one-half of all cases are disposed of without the filing of a petition.

2. *No Petition Filed.*   During the intake phase several options are available: a) the child may be warned about the consequences of future misbehavior and contact is terminated; b) the basis for the complaint may be determined as unfounded or of a trivial nature; c) the child, with the consent of his/her parents or guardians, may be placed on unofficial probation, usually not to exceed ninety days. If at the end of this period, further action is indicated a petition can be filed. Dawson states that this process of informal adjustment at intake has important legal implications: "The sole sanction to secure acceptance of the disposition by the juvenile and his family is the threat to file a formal court petition. Yet, because that sanction is, in effect, a delay in the adjudication of the case, it presents difficult problems of conformity to the juvenile's right to a speedy trial."[16] During this phase the child and his/her family may be referred to a treatment or care agency.

3. *Petition Filed.*   The decision to file a petition is based on the following:

1. The child or his/her parents deny the allegations
2. Unofficial handling does not seem appropriate in view of the seriousness of the case
3. Informal probation has failed

After the decision is made to file a petition, the first concern is where the child will remain pending court action. There are several options:

[16]Robert Dawson, "Legal Norms and the Juvenile Correctional Process." In *Contempory Corrections: A Concept in Search of Content,* Benjamin Frank, ed. (Reston, Va.: Reston Publishing, 1973), p. 57.

(a) all possible attempts are usually made to keep a child at home during this period. In neglect cases, a child may be in need of immediate substitute care; emergency homemaker or caretaker services may be called for. Homemakers act as temporary guardians when the parent is not at home. Caretakers help care for the child when parents are unable to perform their routine parental responsibilities. If the probation officer believes the situation to be too threatening for the child to remain at home, immediate steps are taken to place the juvenile in a resident program or under temporary foster care. In cases of delinquency or status offenses, detention or shelter may be deemed appropriate.

(b) continued custody, beyond the immediate emergency, requires a detention hearing to determine if the child, called a *respondent* (instead of a defendant), should be held in a shelter or juvenile detention facility pending further court action. If the judge determines that the respondant's behavior is a danger to himself or the safety of others, or is in need of protection/care, or that the respondant will probably not return to court voluntarily, the young person can be held in detention or shelter/foster care. If continued custody is not necessary, the child may be sent home. The case may also be dismissed during this hearing in appropriate cases.

4. *Adjudicatory Hearing.* During this phase the allegations in the petition are tried in the first stage of a bifurcated hearing process. If the allegations are sustained, the judge makes a *finding of fact* (which parallels the verdict in adult criminal court), then orders a predisposition report (which parallels the presentence report). Afterwards, at the *dispositional hearing* the judge reviews the report and decides on a disposition.

5. *Disposition.* Based on the probation officer's social investigation, or predisposition report, there are four basic possibilities:[17]

(a) *commitment to an institution*—the child is removed from his/her home and committed to the custody of a correctional institution, community treatment facility, or residential school or treatment center. The youth can also be placed in a group home or foster care.

(b) *probation*—the child remains at home, or in foster care, but is supervised by a court probation officer and must meet certain

[17]Jackwell Susman, "Juvenile Justice: Evenhanded or Many-handed?" *Crime and Delinquency* 19 (October 1973): 499.

conditions such as continuing in school, finding a job, or attending a narcotic treatment clinc, etc.

(c) *suspended sentence*—a sentence of probation or institutionalization is imposed, but its execution is suspended, often for a fixed time at the end of which the child's behavior is reviewed.

(d) *dismissal*—the court does not impose a sentence or supervise the child or commit the youth to the custody of a public agency.

## Criminal Justice Agency Operations

A criminal justice agency is defined as:[18]

Any court with criminal jurisdiction and any other government agency or subunit, which defends indigents, or of which the principal functions or activities consist of the prevention, detection and prosecution of alleged offenders; the confinement or official correctional supervision of accused or convicted persons, or the administrative or technical support of the above functions.

The five major classes of criminal justice agencies are:[19]

1. *Law Enforcement*—a criminal justice agency of which the principal functions are the prevention, detection, investigation of crime and the apprehension of alleged offenders. Examples include police departments, sheriffs' departments, federal enforcement agencies, e.g., Federal Bureau of Investigation.

2. *Prosecutorial*—a criminal justice agency of which the principal function is the prosecution of alleged offenders. Examples include district attorney's officers, state's attorney, United States Attorney.

3. *Public Defender*—a criminal justice agency or subunit of which the principal function is to represent defendants unable to hire private counsel.

4. *Court*—an agency of the judicial branch of government, authorized or established by statute or constitution, and consisting of one or more judicial officers, which has the authority to decide matters of controversy in law and disputed matters of

[18]*Dictionary of Criminal Justice Data Terminology.*
[19]Ibid.

fact brought before it. There are three basic levels of court jurisdiction:

   (a) *court of limited jurisdication:* These courts are where the vast majority of legal actions, predominantly misdemeanor and traffic (and possibly juvenile) cases begin and end.

   (b) *court of general jurisdiction:* A court which has jurisdiction to try all criminal offenses, misdemeanors and felonies, and which may or may not hear appeals from courts of limited jurisdiction.

   (c) *court of appellate jurisdiction:*  A court which does not try criminal cases, but which hears appeals. The highest appellate court is the United States Supreme Court.

5. *Correctional*—a criminal justice agency under a single administrative authority, of which the principal functions are the investigation, intake, screening, supervision, custody, confinement, or treatment of alleged or adjudicated adult offenders, delinquents or status offenders.

The social service worker in criminal justice often plays a direct or indirect part in the discretionary[20] system. These workers may have cases referred by a criminal justice agency, or they may be employed by the referring agency. These referrals may be for evaluation and/or service. In either case, the criminal justice practitioner must often make recommendations to a criminal justice agency which can be a major factor in determining if an offender is to continue through the sequence—be incarcerated, for example. In some situations the criminal justice practitioner will intervene at some stage in the sequence in order to prevent further processing—to keep a person from becoming involved further in criminal justice. As a general rule, the earlier the intervention, the easier it is to extricate the offender from the sequence. Currently there is a trend toward diverting persons out of the criminal justice system, and this diversion can take place at a number of junctures in the sequence.[21] (See Appendix J for a review of diversion programs and glossary of terms.)

[20]"Discretion is an authority conferred by law to act in certain conditions or situations in accordance with an official's or an official agency's own considered judgment and conscience. It is an idea of morals, belonging to the twilight zones between law and morals." From Roscoe Pound, "Discretion, Dispensation and Mitigation: The Problem of the Individual; Special Case," *New York University Law Review* 35 (1960): 925–26.

[21]"Diversion: discretionary acts directed at forestalling adjudication which terminate official intervention and/or refer the person to a program outside of the justice sequence." From Andrew Rutherford and Robert McDermott, *Juvenile Diversion* (Washington, D.C.: United States Government Printing Office, 1976).

Mullen provides the rationale for the proliferation of diversion programs:[22]

> In recent years, a great deal of public and professional attention has been focused on the congestion and delay in criminal courts, on the harsh and often unnecessary restrictions placed on defendants awaiting trial, and for many of those defendants, the social and economic consequences of full criminal prosecution. These problems have generated a number of strategies to reform traditional methods of dealing with the accused during the period between arrest and adjudication.

Of the three strategies listed by Mullen, the last is of particular concern to the criminal justice practitioner:[23]

> To use the arrest incident itself as a means of identifying defendants in need of treatment (or at the very least, those not in need of criminal prosectuion), intervention and diversion schemes evolved. No longer simply a means of securing the release of appropriate defendants, these alternatives added the goals of case screening and rehabilitation to the pretrial process.

*Criticism of Diversion.* Howlett states that juvenile diversion programs, "provide police officers (potentially the most influential 'social workers' on the contemporary scene) with an easy way to avoid exercising their discretion. Whereas policemen previously returned most errant children to their homes—a procedure which to some extent required the parents to deal with them—they are now sending them to the youth service bureau. Such children immediately become the subject of a file and, in the more sophisticated Youth Service Bureau's (those with diagnostic or clinical services immediately available), become labeled as some sort of mild deviate, but deviate nonetheless."[24] Dunford argues: "The police in their diversionary zeal succeeded, in this instance, in increasing rather than reducing the number of youth falling under their jurisdiction."[25] Thus, "youth who would have been free of the system and related stigma by virtue of a screening procedure

---

[22]Joan Mullen, *The Dilemma of Diversion* (Washington, D. C.: United States Government Printing Office, 1975), p. 5.

[23]Ibid.

[24]Frederick W. Howlett, "Is the YSB All It's Cracked Up To Be?" *Crime and Delinquency* 19 (October): 491.

[25]Franklyn W. Dunford, "Police Diversion: An Illusion?" Criminology 15 (November): 344.

were, under the banner of diversion, kept in a condition with considerable potential for negative labeling."[26] Dunford is particularly critical of the coercive element: "Coerced participation potentially leads youth to view diversion programs as extensions of the justice system." He argues: "To force a youngster to participate in a diversion program under the threat of adjudication has most of the elements of the formal justice system save due process."[27]

Mullen points out that the economics of diversion is questionable, and she declares that diversion is a rather expensive alternative to regular processing. "If they were truly functioning as alternatives to incarceration, justifying the expense would not be difficult. The evidence available indicates, however, that in the absence of a diversion alternative, few project participants would have faced a jail sentence."[28] She concludes:[29]

> in attempting to circumvent these basic system deficiencies, a new system with its own attractions and deficiencies has begun to mature without furnishing convincing evidence that it has seriously affected the basic problems that attend the pre-trial criminal process.

Diversion has had an effect that is realized only later in the criminal justice system. Insofar as diversion is successful in screening out "lesser" offenders, it leaves a residue of serious offenders at the end of the sequence, particularly in prison and parole settings. A not uncommon concern of correctional officials is the greater percentage of "hardened" offenders who now make up prison populations in the United States. As one official expressed it, the "boy scouts" have been filtered out of the system.

## Police[30]

### OBJECTIVES OF THE POLICE FORCE

Fundamentally, the police mediate between the community and the legal system. The police are the major representatives of the legal system in their transactions with citizens. They are re-

[26]Dunford, p. 341.
[27]Dunford, p. 350.
[28]Mullen, p. 24.
[29]Mullen, p. 29.
[30]Parts of this section have been adapted from: Task Force on Policing in Ontario, *The Police Are the Public and the Public Are the Police* (Ontario: Office of the Solicitor General, 1974).

sponsible for enforcing all criminal laws, regardless of the willingness of the citizenry to be policed. Given their small numbers relative to the magnitude of their task, the police regard themselves as the "thin blue line" maintaining law and order in the community.[31]

The police have three primary objectives:

1. crime control
2. protection of life and property
3. maintenance of peace and order

Within the context of these objectives, the police have six principal functions:

1. *Response.* The automobile and two-way radio have given the police the primary response capability—citizens know that the police are as far away as the nearest telephone. Many of the calls are only peripheral to "real police work" insofar as they do not involve crime. However, the response function is central to all three primary objectives and is a fundamental police service.

2. *Referral.* Although this function would seem more appropriate to social service practitioners, the police are called upon in virtually any emergency because of their availability. They are often faced with situations in which other community resources are required. The police provide a twenty-four-hour-a-day service, and, therefore, they are most often in the key position to ensure that appropriate referrals are made. The way in which this referral function is carried out may be critical to finding a lasting solution for the immediate problem. Unfortunately, the referral function suffers from the fact that many agencies and resources are not available outside of the 9 A.M. to 5 P.M. working day.

3. *Prevention.* This function includes a range of activities some of which are aimed at alleviating social conditions which are closely associated with crime. Others have to do with improvements in the detection and apprehension of criminals and with using such techniques as "hardening of the site" in order to make criminal activity more difficult. Crime prevention implies a longer-term orientation for the police.

[31]Albert J. Reiss, Jr., *The Police and the Public* (New Haven, Conn.: Yale University Press, 1972), p. 1.

4. *Public Education.*   This function, which entails educating the public about the law and its application, as well as about criminal activity, is an essential component of a balanced police role. It may be utilized in several ways: (a) a broad public relations program, and (b) sharply focused programs to bring police officers into close contact with students in primary and secondary schools.

5. *Crime Solving.*   Crime-solving or investigation is at the core of the popular conception of "real police work." It is a central function.

6. *Law Enforcement.*   This function is basic—the laws and their infraction are why the police exist.

### DISCRETION BY THE POLICE

Of all of the official agencies in the criminal justice sequence, the police exercise discretion over the largest number of persons. From enforcing traffic laws to arresting serious felons, the police are the most visible segment of criminal justice. As a para-military organizaion, the police constitute a small army whose soldiers tend to concentrate in areas of high crime—areas which also tend to contain the most poor and discriminated-against populations. As a consequence of this concentration, among a number of important variables, most persons arrested by the police tend to be poor and/or from minority groups. The police do not usually have the opportunity, nor are they organized and trained, to investigate white-collar and other similar types of crime. Because of the *class-specific* nature of much of their law enforcement activities, the police may be viewed as an "army of occupation" by ghetto residents. Reports of abuse of power, brutality, or corruption provide a negative frame of reference.

The use of discretion is perhaps the most salient feature of a policemen's responsibility. Research indicates that there is a disparity in the way policemen treat different persons with whom they come into official contact. Katz states:[32]

> Even though the community disowns the police when they react imprudently, the attitudes and actions of the police reflect, on the whole, how the majority in the community wants blacks and young people treated.... discretionary power is also used in reverse to deny full police protection in the inner-city areas. Conduct that would warrant police action elsewhere may be ignored or dismissed by the police officer. An assault between ghetto

[32]Lewis Katz, *Justice is the Crime* (Cleveland, Ohio: Press of Case Western Reserve, 1972), p. 102.

blacks, even where there is knifing involved, may be dismissed by the beat officer as a normal part of the subculture of the black ghetto. Within our memory is hearing a policeman say that there is no such thing as rape in the ghetto. Such notions offer little comfort to the victims of assault or rape.

The police are basically a reactive force and they respond to requests for assistance or to activities which they view as needing their intervention. As part of this response, a policeman must often decide whether an offense has been committed and, if so, whether or not to invoke the criminal process. Citizen requests for help may in fact be more appropriately handled as private or civil matters. It is often a policeman's discretion that determines whether a particular situation is handled as a civil or criminal matter, or whether an arrest is made, a summons issued, or a warning or reprimand delivered. Reiss notes that "many citizens have only a vague understanding of the difference between civil, private, and criminal matters."[33]

The Task Force (on Policing in Ontario) points out the importance of discretion in the role of a policeman:[34]

> The real police role is the summation of many thousands of judgments of individual officers. The framework within which these judgments are made is the key to a police role which is in tune with the needs of a modern society.

The Task Force suggests the following principles:[35]

(a) *The police officer's role is firmly rooted in law, and the law is applied with discretion and judgment.* It is the sworn duty of all police officers to maintain and enforce the law. This requirement, and the statutory powers granted him to do so, are what distinguish the police officer from his fellow citizens. However, it has long been recognized that a police officer has the authority *not* to invoke the criminal law process even when elements of an offense may be proven. It is a fact of life that police officers are daily called upon to decide whether or not to invoke the criminal law process.

Law is not intended for rigid and mindless uniform application. It, in itself, is designed to serve the larger purposes of the community. Police judgments not to invoke the criminal law process, therefore, must relate to the intention of the legislature in enacting a particular law. The larger purposes of the community must be kept in mind.

[33]Reiss, p. 77.
[34]Task Force on Policing, p. 13.
[35]Ibid., pp. 13–15.

Law, viewed from a functional perspective, is the process of compelling individuals to act in accordance with rules, so that all may live, if not in harmony, at least with a minimum of discord. The criminal law is one device which our society has employed to ensure that at least the minimum standards of human behavior in society are observed. It was never intended by the legislating authorities that all laws should be enforced with the same rigidity. Some rules, as for example the prohibition of murder, are so fundamental to society (*mala in se*) that failure to enforce them would lead to the complete disintegration of the community. Other rules, such as the ones regulating driving, are merely designed to achieve a safe and rapid flow of traffic through the community (*mala probibita*). Some legislation, that pertaining to liquor control, for example, provides a police officer with alternatives. He may arrest an intoxicated person if there is a disturbance of the peace, or he may caution or refer the person for help. At times, the police officer must decide whether to arrest or issue a summons to a suspected offender. While most legislation does not provide alternatives, our society has come to expect police officers to exercise some degree of judgment in deciding when to invoke the criminal law process. However, the judgment must be related to the objectives of the particular law and how those objectives relate to the situation within his community. If it is related to the personality of the offender, his race, religion or economic status, it creates one law for the privileged and another for the helpless.

(b) *The more serious the offense, the less leeway for judgment.* This principle suggests a greater latitude for offenses which, in the contemporary view, are more regulatory than seriously criminal in nature. It suggests very little, if any, latitude for serious crime. A concept which emphasizes this elastic relationship with the law is essential to providing the individual officers with the ability to judge how the law should be applied in any particular situation. Latitude in the use of judgment is both appropriate and necessary for those offenses which society in its contemporary mood regards with some tolerance. This principle also takes into account cultural differences which makes certain conduct acceptable in one community while it may be a breach of the peace in another. Offenses which the community regards as serious or grave, however, permit less judgment and require the letter of the law to be enforced.

In a paper on the problems inherent in the use of police discretion, Herman Goldstein, a former Chicago police official, asks:[36]

---

[36]Herman Goldstein, "Police Discretion: The Ideal Versus the Real," *Public Administration Review* 23 (September 1963): 141.

How often have law enforcement personnel released a drunk and disorderly person without charging him? released a juvenile offender to his parents? warned a driver who had clearly committed a violation? ignored the enforcement of some city ordinances? arrested an individual known to have committed fornication or adultery? arranged for the release of a narcotic addict in exchange for information? dropped charges against an assailant when the victim failed to cooperate in the prosecution? ignored Sunday blue laws or simply been instructed not to enforce a specific law?

Goldstein provides a further insight into police behavior:[37]

> Police officials too often fail to recognize that there are many persons in the communities which they serve who have an inherent distaste for authority—and especially police authority. Joining with others of the same view and those whose beliefs are more firmly grounded in a support for our democratic processes, these people closely guard against the improper use of authority by the police. It behooves law enforcement officials to refrain from unnecessarily creating a situation which annoys such individuals. Such situations can often be avoided through the exercise of proper discretion.

### DIVERSION

As noted above, when the police have probable cause to believe that a crime has been committed by a particular person, they may choose not to arrest him for potential prosecution. As McCall notes, the police may "choose to halt any further police proceedings against the suspect; such a choice represents police screening of offenders from the criminal justice system." However, in other cases the police may "halt or suspend any further formal police proceedings against the suspect on the condition that he does something in return: participate in some specified program or activity; such a choice represents police diversion of offenders from the criminal justice system. If a diverted offender does not satisfy the police that the condition has been fulfilled, they may resume formal police proceedings against him."[38] The range of programs or activities to which the police may divert offenders is quite extensive, as is the range of offenders who may be diverted. The types of cases most frequently diverted by the police include juvenile offend-

[37]Ibid., p. 147.

[38]George J. McCall, *Observing the Law: Applications of Field Methods to the Study of the Criminal Justice System* (Rockville, Md.: National Institute of Mental Health, 1975), p. 66. Reprinted by permission of the U.S. Department of Health, Education and Welfare, and George J. McCall.

ers, domestic dispute offenders, mentally ill offenders, drunkeness offenders, and drug abuse offenders.

Diversion alternatives for juveniles range from the informal remanding of the offender to his own family, to formal social, educational, vocational, or medical programs offered by community-based youth service bureaus. Special family intervention services or units are sometimes available for diverting domestic disputants, emergency psychiatric programs are increasingly available for police diversion of mentally ill offenders, and detoxification centers represent alternative dispositions for drunkeness and drug abuse offenders.[39]

Bloch and Specht note that "Diverting individuals into treatment has the same advantages for the criminal justice system as does exercising police discretion by not making an arrest. It unclogs court calenders. It also makes space available in prisons to house hardened offenders. The officer who funnels these serious cases out of the criminal justice system in appropriate ways has made a contribution to the effectiveness of the whole system."[40] Rutherford and McDermott state that the police "have always engaged in 'traditional diversion' because of the high level of discretion inherent in the police function." They note that it "is the officer in the street who typically first exercises the discretion to divert or to 'further process' a juvenile. He/she may ignore an incident, do 'something' short of formal processing or may institute such formal processing. Police diversion occurs when 'something' is done short of formal processing. A typical dispositional option is cite, warn, and release ('kick in the pants')." The authors also note that many police departments have special units for handling juveniles, and that the patrolman may refer the dispositional decision to officers in these units. They also note that officers in these units "infringe upon the role of the probation intake officer."[41]

## SERVICE ROLE

The anomaly of the policeman's role is that most of his work has nothing to do directly with crime fighting.

Policemen, in large numbers, direct and control traffic. Policemen watch the polls on election day, escort important visitors in and out of town, license taxicabs and bicycles, and operate animal

---

[39]Ibid., pp. 66–67.
[40]Peter B. Bloch and David Specht, *Neighborhood Team Policing* (Washington, D.C.: United States Government Printing Office, 1973), p. 101.
[41]Rutherford and McDermott, p. 27.

shelters. Policemen assist stranded motorists, give directions to travelers, rescue lost children, respond to medical emergencies, help people who have lost their keys unlock their apartments.[42]

Studies have indicated "that by far the greatest part of a policeman's time is spent performing his social service and order maintenance functions."[43]

The police are often called upon to deal with problems which appear quite removed from law enforcement. In his extensive and detailed look at the *City Police*, Rubinstein describes one of these situations, the paramedical role.[44]

> Sometimes an old person will fall out of bed. If his aging companions are too weak to lift him off the floor, the police are called to help put the person back in bed. On one occasion, a sick assist occupied a patrolman and his partner for almost four hours on a New Year's Eve. They arrived at a dreary apartment building to find a terrified old woman in fear for her aged husband's life. Their electricity had gone out and the refrigerator containing his medicine was getting warm. The patrolmen found the basement locked and they were unable to get to the fuse box. The landlord could not be reached; his babysitter said he was at a party. They scavenged some wire and extension cord from the apartment and returned to their station to pick up some more, in order to run a live-wire from the refrigerator into a hallway where they had located a live socket. When the refrigerator was working again, they bid the couple good night and returned to work.

A situation that is always fraught with difficulty, if not danger, for the police is the domestic dispute. Katz states:[45]

> When responding to a call for help arising out of a family dispute, the officer must determine what is necessary to restore order. Since often no other social agency is available when the disputes occur, the beat officer bears the burden of decision. If he arrests the belligerent family member, the officer knows that invariably the next day cooler heads will prevail and the family will elect not to pursue the matter.

[42]President's Commission on Law Enforcement and Administration of Justice, *The Challenge of Crime in a Free Society* (New York: Avon Books, 1968), p. 252.

[43]G. Douglas Gourley, in the Forward to Louis A. Radelet, *The Police and the Community* (Beverly Hills, Calif.: Glencoe Press, 1973), p. viii.

[44]Jonathan Rubinstein, *City Police* (New York: Ballantine, 1973), p. 93.

[45]Katz, p. 100.

Katz observes that as both peace-keeper and marriage counselor the officer must constantly keep in mind that most homocides are committed among people who know each other and often within a family. A recent report by the Police Foundation stated that homicides and aggravated assaults are often preceded by a series of requests for police intervention in domestic disputes. The report states: "Surveys consistantly show that disputes and disturbances are the largest single category of calls that most police departments receive. Also, as potential homocide and assault producers, these situations are dangerous not only to the participants; more assaults on police officers occur during response to disturbance calls than in any other area of police work."[46]

## Prosecution

In 1966 the President's Commission observed that there is a gross disparity between the number of cases sent to court and the personnel and facilities available to deal with them.[47] The situation has not improved to any significant extent—indeed, in some jurisdictions it has become more acute. The President's Commission noted in 1966, that "for most defendants in the criminal process, there is scant regard for them as individuals," and they have become numbers on dockets, "faceless ones to be processed and sent on their way."[48] This continues to be relevant today. Thus, the role of the criminal justice practitioner in this part of the criminal justice sequence is two-fold:

1. to bring individualization to the process by providing information that will permit agency personnel to focus on the person who is the defendant; and
2. to provide expertise in order to help screen out or divert cases that are more appropriately handled outside of the criminal justice process.

McCall provides some insight into the prosecutory process:[49]

Upon arrest, the offender enters the lawyers' segment of the

---

[46]See "Domestic Assault Linked to Prior Dispute Calls to Police," *Law Enforcement News,* June 7, 1977, p. 5.

[47]President's Commission on Law Enforcement and Administration of Justice, *The Challenge of Crime in a Free Society* (New York: Avon Books, 1968), p. 318.

[48]Ibid., p. 319.

[49]McCall, *Observing the Law,* pp. 75–77. References in the original have been deleted.

criminal justice system. Immediately upon arrest, and prior to police interrogation, the offender has the right to demand legal counsel on his behalf. At the same time (in most jurisdictions), if the police wish to continue criminal processing of the offender they must prevail upon the local prosecutor to file formal criminal charges against the offender.

In any community, relatively few lawyers regularly practice in the criminal courts. Criminal practice is less remunerative and is regarded as the low status "dirty work" of the legal profession. As a consequence, prosecution and defense attorneys (together with the small number of criminal court judges) effectively form a local criminal law community, characterized by intimate acquaintance, close working relations, and mutual concern for the problems of the marginal legal practitioner.

According to judicial ideology, in the processing of a criminal case, prosecution and defense attorneys are to play adversary roles in a clash of evidence before an impartial referee in order to determine the guilt or innocence of the accused. Several field studies of criminal lawyers have shown that these adversarial roles are sharply tempered by the organizational demands of the local criminal law community. Conflict must be muted, since defendants come and go, while lawyers must continue to rely on one another to make their work less than impossibly difficult. Thus, under certain conditions bargaining roles tend to displace the adversarial roles.*

A fact of central importance in understanding the work of the prosecutor is that the prosecutor functions as a double-agent in the criminal justice system. He is the chief law enforcement agent in his jurisdiction, charged with enforcing all laws, and he is also an officer of the court, charged with obtaining justice for all people in his jurisdiction. This position, while generating the ethical "prosecutor's dilemma," underlies the great power of the prosecutor's office. As the link between the enforcement and adjudicative functions, the prosecutor may be the most powerful individual in the criminal justice system. If he does not act, the judge and the jury are helpless and the policeman's word is meaningless.

Given the considerable power of the prosecutor as vital link between police and courts, yet responsible only to the electorate, the office is a valuable political prize (the office is appointive only in the States of Connecticut, Delaware, Rhode Island and New Jersey). Numerous studies have investigated the extent of effect of political partisanship on local justice, as exerted through the prosecutor's office. These studies have seldom detected any sweeping effects on systematic law enforcement; rather, the political

---

*For an extensive review of bargaining roles, see Suzanne R. and Leonard Buckle, *Bargaining for Justice* (New York: Praeger, 1977).

utility of the office seems to lie primarily in the capability to prevent occasional political harm to the party and in the substantial patronage involved in staffing the office.

The prosecutor's office has also been thought of as a political prize, in the sense of a stepping stone toward higher political office. Although research seems to indicate that most prosecutors do not go on to hold higher offices, most of them perceive that holding the office is beneficial to a political career and most of them do have political ambitions. This perception probably does have an impact on the prosecutor's role orientation. For example, one study found that prosecutor's with political ambitions preferred an "officer of the court" role orientation and those without ambitions tended to prefer a "law enforcement" orientation and higher conviction rates.

Numerous deputy prosecutors and clerks are necessary in even moderately large communities to handle all of the work of the prosecutor's office. Partisan and ethnic politics are important considerations in staffing. Deputy prosecutors are generally new law graduates or older lawyers who had difficulty maintaining an adequate practice. Remuneration and promotion possibilities are not impressive, so that few deputies remain more than three or four years. Although the prosecutor's office ordinarily handles some civilian and domestic matters, the bulk of the work is in criminal law, so that experience as a deputy prosecutor is little valued by most law firms. Former deputies do tend to enter partnerships or solo practices which involve some criminal practice.

### DISCRETION BY THE PROSECUTOR

As was noted, the prosecutor's central role, that which gives him/her enormous power, is determining whether or not to bring charges. Leonard and Saxe outline some of the factors which determine if charges will be brought:[50]

1. Does the prosecutor think the individual is guilty?
2. Will it result in a conviction?
3. Will the time and effort which will have to be spent on this case be justified if a conviction is obtained?
4. Is there pressure from another agency or division of government?

[50]Robert F. Leonard and Joel B. Saxe, *Screening of Criminal Cases* (Chicago: National District Attorneys Association, 1973), p. 2. Reprinted by permission of the Publisher.

5. Will a conviction make it appear that the prosecutor is being heartless?

6. Is the prospective defendant someone well-known in the community so that the resulting publicity would impose a more severe penalty than justified?

7. Would the resulting sentence be too severe for the crime committed?

8. Is this an area in which juries are loath to convict?

9. Would it be better to wait until he commits another offense with a stronger set of facts for the prosecution?

10. Would he be valuable as a witness in another trial or against parties involved with him?

11. Will the probable judge who will be hearing this case be favorable?

12. Even though the possibility of a conviction is slim, should it be undertaken because the defendant appears to be guilty of other offenses for which he was not charged?

13. Should the case be prosecuted, in spite of a doubtful outcome, since civil rights are involved?

14. What are the prosecutor's personal feelings?

15. Can this case be transferred to another Court or to another agency for civil penalties?

The authors also present some of the "outside" influences which can effect the prosecutor's discretion:[51]

1. *Police.* Police arrests set the outer limits of prosecution. The prosecutor is generally limited by those cases which are actually presented to him by the law enforcement agencies within his jurisdiction. Since the police practice discretion in their arrests, the cases which come to the prosecutor's attention have been selectively determined by the police. Therefore, it is important that the prosecutor's office establish rapport with the law enforcement agencies, particularly with regard to arrest policies. The quantity and quality of the evidence in a case will normally depend upon the police as well as the procedures used to obtain it. A decision not to prosecute is often based on shortcomings in this area. Also, the charging decision is usually relegated to the police for most minor offenses.

[51]Ibid.

**Figure 3-3.** Bronx Case Evaluation Form

| A. NATURE OF CASE | check if applicable | pts. |
|---|---|---|
| VICTIM | | |
| one or more persons | — | 2.0 |
| VICTIM INJURY | | |
| received minor injury | — | 2.4 |
| treated and released | — | 3.0 |
| hospitalized | — | 4.2 |
| INTIMIDATION | | |
| one or more persons | — | 1.3 |
| WEAPON | | |
| defendant armed | — | 7.4 |
| defendant fired shot or carried gun, or carried explosives | — | 15.7 |
| STOLEN PROPERTY | | |
| any value | — | 7.5 |
| PRIOR RELATIONSHIP | | |
| victim and defendant-same family | — | -2.8 |
| ARREST | | |
| at scene | — | 4.6 |
| within 24 hours | — | 2.9 |
| EVIDENCE | | |
| admission or statement | — | 1.4 |
| additional witnesses | — | 3.1 |

C. REFER TO M.O.B. IF ANY OF THE FOLLOWING CONDITIONS APPLY: (check those applicable-offense is most serious charge)

— FORCIBLE SEXUAL OFFENSES BETWEEN UNRELATED PARTIES

— ARSON WITH SUBSTANTIAL DAMAGE OR HIGH POTENTIAL FOR INJURY

— CHILD ABUSE, CHILD SEVEN OR UNDER

— MULTIPLE ROBBERIES OR BURGLARIES

D. SUMMARY INFORMATION

NO. OF VICTIMS____
— received minor injury
— treated and hospitalized
— hospitalized and/or permanent injury
— law officer
— attempted murder of officer

WEAPON
— gun
— knife
— bomb or explosive
— other____

BURGLARY
— night-time
— evidence of forcible entry
— Church, School, Public Bldg.
— no. of premises burglarized

IDENTIFICATION
line-up — 3.3

TOTAL CASE SCORE _____

B. NATURE OF DEFENDANT

FELONY CONVICTIONS
— one — 9.7
— more than one — 18.7

MISDEMEANOR CONVICTIONS
— one — 6.6
— more than one — 8.3

PRIOR ARRESTS—SAME CHARGE
— one — 4.5
— more than — 7.2

PRIOR ARRESTS
— one — 2.2
— more than one — 4.2

PRIOR ARREST-WEAPONS TOP CHARGE
— more than one — 6.4

STATUS WHEN ARRESTED
— state parole — 7.1
— wanted — 4.2

TOTAL DEFENDANT SCORE _____

| VALUE OF STOLEN PROPERTY | recovered | not |
|---|---|---|
| — under $250 | — | — |
| — $250 to $1499 | — | — |
| — $1500 to $25,000 | — | — |
| — over $25,000 | — | — |

PRIOR RELATIONSHIP
— other family
— neighbor
— friend
— acquaintance
— other

IDENTIFICATION
— photograph
— on or nearby scene
— other
— no. of persons making I.D. _____
— time delay of I.D. _____

SUPPORTING EVIDENCE
— crime observed by police officer
— fingerprints recovered

E. DISTRICT ATTORNEY'S EVALUATION
TOTAL SCORE _____
RANKING CLERK _____
A.D.A. NOTICED    yes —    no —
ACTION BY A.D.A.:
— accepted    — furthered
— rejected    — referred to M.O.B.

reasons: _____

2. *The Trial Court.*    The attitudes of the court affect the decision to prosecute. The prosecutor's decisions have a strong tendency to conform to the court's predispositions.
3. *The Defense Counsel.*    Oftentimes the defense counsel influences the decision of the prosecutor by indicating weaknesses in the case and possible mitigating circumstances. "Negotiations" between the defense counsel and the prosecutor determine whether a charge will be reduced, dropped, or not initiated.
4. *Public Opinion.*    The press and other news media, civic organizations, individuals, and political groups exercise influence on the policies of the prosecutor.

The role of the prosecutor's office usually begins with pretrial screening:[52]

> Pretrial screening is an intake and review procedure, whereby the prosecutor or his assistants attempts to determine, based upon information given them by law enforcement agencies, what type of action should be taken with regard to a particular case.

Joan Jacoby notes that the process extends over a period of time and operates in conjunction with other elements in the criminal justice system such as law enforcement agencies, judges, and correctional agencies. Among the persons who may be involved in the process are social service workers who may be asked to evaluate the rehabilitation potential or to recommend in favor or against diversion. Jacoby reviews a screening method used by the Bronx County (New York) District Attorney's Office (as well as other prosecutor's):[53]

> Case evaluation systems are based on the adaption of the scaling techniques developed by Sellin and Wolfgang[54] and by Don Gottfredson.[55] The Sellin and Wolfgang scales measure the seriousness of the offense primarily in terms of the amount of personal injury or property loss sustained. Gottfredson's Base Expectation scales are directed to predicting recidivism from California correctional institutions. These scales have been modified to measure the seriousness of the defendant's prior criminal

---

[52]Joan Jacoby, *The Prosecutor's Charging Decision,* p. 3.

[53]Joan Jacoby, *Pre-Trial Screening in Perspective* (Washington, D.C.: United States Government Printing Office, 1976), pp. 37–39.

[54]Thorsten Sellin and Marvin Wolfgang, *The Measurement of Delinquency* (New York: Wiley, 1964).

[55]D. M. Gottfredson and K. Ballard, Jr., "Differences in Parole Decisions Associated with Decision Makers," *Journal of Research in Crime and Delinquency,* July 1966.

behavior. This scale weights the amount, character and density of previous arrests and the mobility of the defendant. In addition, new scales were recently derived for the Bronx District Attorney to gauge the evidentiary strength of the case.[56]

Figure 3-3 shows the form used by the District Attorney's office in the Bronx to rate the cases coming into the system according to his policy. The items with numbers are those factors which were found to be statistically significant for the prosecutor's policy. All cases with scores higher than a predetermined cut off point are referred to the Major Offense Bureau for review.

The advantage of these types of case evaluation systems lies in their inherent objectivity. Since each case presented for prosecution review is scored on the basis of the *same* factors, the evaluation is uniform and consistent. Objectivity is also achieved because the factors used for the evaluation are statistically derived (quantifiable) and require only minimal subjective interpretation.

Since the priority ranking is a reflection of policy and can be applied to the case at intake, it not only measures the seriousness of the case for prosecution but it permits the analysis of uniformity of charging. In addition, it offers a means of comparing the expected outcome of the case with the actual outcome relative to the policy of the prosecutor. For example, one would expect that a case scoring high on the urgency scale should result in a disposition favorable to the prosecutor (conviction) and even receive a longer sentence or harsher punishment than a case scoring low on the scale. Where deviations occur in the actual outcome as compared to the expected, this technique provides a means of identifying such results. However, it does not pinpoint the reasons for the discrepancies in outcomes.

## Defense

McCall discusses the role of the defense counsel in the criminal process:[57]

> Like the prosecutor, the defense attorney, too, serves as a double-agent in the criminal justice system. He is, on one hand, advocate of the defendant and, on the other, an officer of the court. Given the general tendency for the adversarial model to be subordinated to the bargaining model of criminal justice, most defense lawyers function as "agent-mediators" of the court, seeking to persuade the defendant to eschew adversarial proceedings and to accept negotiated justice. Some few defense lawyers, generally

---

[56]Joan E. Jacoby, "Case Evaluation: Quantifying Prosecutorial Policy," *Judicature* 58 (May 1975), p. 10.

[57]McCall, pp. 82–83.

with exceptional trial abilities, choose to function primarily as advocates in the adversarial model.*

In every court, nonindigent defendants are represented by privately retained counsel, if any. Private practitioners frequently obtain paying clients through referrals from brokers elsewhere in the criminal justice system (e.g., police, bondsmen), supplementing such practice by seeking fees for serving as court-appointed counsel. The central problem in private practice is making money; clients are generally poor to begin with, unreliable in paying their fees, and facing a possible protracted incarceration. The criminal lawyer is constrained to act rather ruthlessly in order to obtain payment for his services and is, in any case, compelled to rely on volume of business to survive.

In large metropolitan courts, the majority of criminal defendants are now represented by a public defender, a full-time salaried official charged with the responsibility of representing indigent defendants. The office of the public defender, though more insulated from partisan politics than the prosecutor's office, likewise involves a sizeable number of deputies and clerks. Characteristics of personnel and of internal organization of the office closely parallel those of the prosecutor's office. In smaller courts, indigent defendants are typically represented by court-appointed private practitioners occasionally receiving a set fee from the state to represent a designated defendant.

Casper discusses some of the shortcomings of the public defender:[58]

In many jurisdictions the public defender's office is greatly overburdened, handling a volume of cases far beyond their capacity to give any one sufficient personal attention. Most defendants reported spending about five to ten minutes with "their" public defender. He typically sees the defendant in the bullpen (lock-up) of the courthouse, in the corridor, or in the courtroom. The conversations are brief; they center not around the circumstances and motives of the crime, potential legal defenses, the defendant's needs and desires, but around the "deal"—what can be obtained in return for a guilty plea.

---

*For a detailed look at the role of defense counsel see: Lynn M. Mather, "Some Determinants of the Method of Case Disposition: Decision-Making by Public Defenders in Los Angeles." *Law and Society Review* 8 (Winter 1973): 187–211; Albert W. Alschuler, "The Defense Attorney's Role in Plea Bargaining." *The Yale Law Journal* 84 (May 1975): 1179–1314.

[58]Adapted from Jonathan D. Casper, *American Criminal Justice: The Defendant's Perspective* (Englewood Cliffs, N.J.: Prentice-Hall, 1972), pp. 16–17.

Casper states that the defendant often wonders whether the attorney is on their side:[59]

> He doesn't spend much time with them; he doesn't seem concerned with them as persons; rather, he is concerned with the disposition. Most conclude that he is not on their side. Contributing to this view is an institutional factor: the public defender is *paid* by the state.

Blumberg has stated that the criminal defendant is a secondary figure in the court system: "The accused's lawyer has far greater professional, economic, intellectual and other ties to various elements of the court system than he does to his own client."[60] McCall states:[61]

> For opposite reasons, then, the typical private criminal practitioner and the public defender are necessarily involved in high volume of cases. Cooperation and regularity are conducive to processing large numbers of cases; the individualization of adversarial combat is not. It is only the unusual private practitioner who can depend on obtaining very large fees, who can afford to function as an adversary advocate. Most criminal lawyers, private or public, are constrained by the organizational realities of their practice to function primarily as bureaucratic negotiators.

Thus, "Organizational goals and discipline impose a set of demands and conditions of practice on the respective professions in the criminal court to which they respond by abandoning their ideological and professional commitments to the accused client in the service of these higher claims of the court organization."[62] Blumberg concludes: All court personnel, including the defense attorney, "tend to be coopted to become agent-mediators who help the accused redefine his situation and restructure his perceptions concomitant with a plea of guilty."[63]

A criminal defendant with an attorney who has certain "connections" based on, for example, political activities or status as a former district attorney, may be in a more advantageous position than a defendant without such representation. A "connected" attorney is better equipped to navigate and negotiate through what Blumberg refers to as the *bureaucratic due process* "characterized by superficial ceremonies and formal niceties of traditional due process, but not its substance."[64]

[59]Ibid. p. 17.

[60]Abraham S. Blumberg, "The Practice of Law As Confidence Game: Organizational Cooptation of a Profession," *Law and Society Review* 1 (1967): 21.

[61]McCall, p. 83.

[62]Blumberg, "The Practice of Law," p. 19.

[63]Ibid., pp. 19–20.

[64]A. Blumberg, *Criminal Justice* (Chicago: Quadrangle Books, 1970), p. 4.

He is referring to the fact that most, as high as 85 to 95 percent, of the criminal cases are resolved in the judicial process without a trial, through plea bargaining.

## Plea Bargaining*

McCall observes:[65]

> The overwhelming majority of convictions in most metropolitan courts result not from trials but from pleas of guilty by the defendants, typically on the assurance of defense counsel that pleading guilty will obtain more lenient disposition than the maximum which might be levied upon trial conviction. The assurance of the defense lawyers in these cases is well founded, since the general disposition has been explicitly negotiated and agreed upon between the defense and the prosecutor, based upon their thorough knowledge of the sentencing patterns of the particular judge. (In some jurisdictions, the judge directly participates in these plea negotiations.) . . . Indeed, given the oppressive workloads of these courts, the time-consuming and expensive character of trial proceedings, and the shared administrative presumption that virtually all defendants are guilty of some crime, the functioning of the court system rather openly depends on nearly every case being settled through plea negotiation.

Olson makes this observation about plea bargaining:[66]

> the pragmatic utility of plea bargaining accounts for a good deal of its vitality. In addition, the continued use of out-of-court negotiation also flows from the moral vagueness surrounding plea bargaining. Once again, we find the criminal justice system caught in a dilemma: regularized procedures which guard against arbitrary and "discriminatory" outcomes confront the possibility of rigid, archaic, and irrelevant legalism; discretionary justice, which allows the fashioning of decisions to fit situations, confronts the possibility of capricious, arbitrary behavior governed by the passions or contingencies of the moment.

McCall raises the specter of so-called normal crimes:[67]

---

*For a detailed look at plea bargaining see the widely-acclaimed paper by Albert W. Alschuler, "The Prosecutor's Role in Plea Bargaining." *University of Chicago Law Review* 36 (1968): 50–112.

[65]McCall, pp. 83–85. References in the original have been deleted.
[66]Sheldon R. Olson, *Issues in the Sociology of Criminal Justice* (Indianapolis, Ind.: Bobbs-Merrill, 1975), p. 24.
[67]McCall, p. 85.

The administrative regularities employed by the local criminal law community include concepts of "normal crimes,"[68] the statistical regularity of certain offenses being committed in standard manner and location-type of offenders of a specific social character. For such normal crimes, the prosecution and defense lawyers have informally developed normatively standard bargains. Crimes departing in some way from the cultural stereotypes held by the local criminal law community must be negotiated over in less patterned fashion, with now the prosecutor and now the defense lawyer receiving a break. Both parties maintain careful account of the distribution of such breaks, striving to preserve a rather precise balance of exchange of these credits and favors.

Casper provides a look at plea bargaining from the defendant's perspective:[69]

in most cases the defendant will, at some point, be offered a deal—some charge reduction, sentence agreement, or both in return for a plea of guilty. The prosecutor holds most of the cards in the plea-bargaining game—at least as most defendants see it, for he is viewed as having the power to determine the sentence. Although technically he can only make a recommendation to the judge, his recommendations are usually followed. Occasionally a judge may intervene and impose a higher or lower sentence than is recommended, but usually he will go along. Most defendants believed that the judge is a hidden partner to the agreement; and in many cases the prosecutor does clear the deal with the judge before commiting himself to it.

Katz notes:[70]

The etiquette of plea bargaining differs from city to city. It may occupy several months, if the practice of the attorneys is to become involved in a series of offers and counteroffers. Or it may be a one-time effort by the prosecutor to reduce the charge or recommend a lenient sentence, in return for a plea of guilty, or a single offer by the defense attorney to plead his client guilty, in return for reduction. In some situations, it may be done prior to the schueduled trial date; in others, it may normally occur on the first date set for trial. Occasionally it happens before the defendant in the courtroom, but more often the lawyers negotiate out of the defendant's presence. Although the absence of the judge during the negotiations avoids undue pressures upon the attorneys, often

---

[68]See David Sudnow, "Normal Crimes: Sociological Features of the Penal Code in a Public Defender's Office," *Social Problems* 12 (1965): 255–76.
[69]Casper, p. 78.
[70]Katz, p. 194.

the judge is present and serves as an outside factor forcing attorneys to come to terms.*

Wilson goes so far as to suggest that, since determining guilt is largely a myth (most arrestees are guilty), perhaps the court system should be organized around sentencing. Thus, sentencing would be administrative, and the use of judges and due process safeguards would be reserved for those cases "where the issue of guilt is in doubt."[71]

## Judiciary/Courts

A good starting point for understanding the courts is a statement by McCall: "The terms 'courthouse' and 'politics' are practically inseparable in American usage."[72] The criminal justice practitioner, if he is to be effective in a court setting, must understand the political nature of this part ot the criminal justice sequence. Control of the judicial system translates politically into control of a vast array of posititons—clerks, aides, law secretaries, and judgeships. A judgeship is often used to repay political obligations, or to reward party service. The bench provides a prestigious position for mediocre politicians who are tired of the arena or who have failed at their jobs or reelection. It is the isolated exception that did not come up through the political ranks to gain a judgeship.

Since virtually all judicial candidates and sitting judges aspire to a high court, the lower courts tend to be staffed by those either waiting for a promotion or who are not considered deserving enough, politically or based on competence, to secure a higher bench. This situation is particularly acute in the juvenile court. Rubin and Smith note that judges in juvenile court tend to know little about the court's treatment philosophy and procedures, usually have little knowledge of child wel-

---

*Blumberg, and other critics, approach criminal justice administration with an emphasis on "system pathology." For a criticism of this see: Lief H. Carter, *The Limits of Order* (Lexington, Mass.: D.C. Heath & Co, 1974); David Neubauer, *Criminal Justice in Middle America* (Morristown, N.J.: General Learning Press, 1974).

Neubauer, for example, points out that the fact that the defense attorney and the prosecutor are on good terms "does not mean the adversary process has broken down. It may be only a reflection of the normal rules of conduct expected of lawyers. The 'cooperation' of defense and prosecution is a product of such general expectations about how lawyers should conduct themselves." (p. 78)

[71]James Q. Wilson, *Thinking About Crime* (New York: Basic Books, 1975), pp. 179–80.

[72]McCall, p. 91.

shall be imprisoned, the exact length of imprisonment and parole supervision is afterwards fixed within statutory limits by a parole authority.

In most jurisdictions, the court selects a particular maximum and sometimes a minimum limit for the particular person being sentenced, within a given statutory range. In others, the parole authority may set any length of period of confinement and parole within the statutory limits for the offense. The relative discretion granted by statute to the court and the parole authority varies greatly among different states.

The exact duration of the *penalty* is supposed to be fixed in consideration of the previous record of the convicted person, his behavior while in prison or while out on parole, the apparent prospect of reformation, and other such matters.

Those who support indeterminate sentencing note that no two criminals are alike, and therefore judges and parole boards should be able to weigh the particular circumstances surrounding each offense and each offender: the punishment should fit the criminal, not merely the crime. The basis for this position dates back to the *Positive School* of the nineteenth century in contrast with the *Classical School* of a century earlier.[78] Critics of the indeterminate sentence maintain that its basic premise is that offenders can be treated, or rehabiliated, and that they should be released to the community after this is effected. However, offenders do not necessarily need treatment; society often generates crime; and those who need or can benefit from treatment often do not receive such help in a prison setting. Some critics contend that there is no known way of effectively treating offenders.[79]

Some states have limited judicial discretion by adopting *determinate* or *presumptive* sentencing. The former, sometimes referred to as "fixed" or "flat time" sentencing, calls for specific legislatively imposed terms for each category of offense. Presumptive sentencing establishes a "typical" sentence to be served for each offense, unless the judge finds aggravating or mitigating circumstances that would raise or lower the sentence according to a fixed formula. California has adopted this method. Under their system most felonies are divided into four classes and the court is required to pick the middle of the three terms

[78]For a discussion and analysis of these two schools of thought see Ian Taylor et al., *The New Criminology* (New York: Harper & Row, 1973), pp. 1–30.

[79]Those interested in a fuller discussion and criticism of indeterminate sentencing are advised to see David Fogel, *We Are the Living Proof: The Justice Model for Corrections* (Cincinnati, Ohio: W. H. Anderson, 1975); Norval Morris, *The Future of Imprisonment* (Chicago: University of Chicago Press, 1974); Andrew von Hirsch, *Doing Justice* (New York: Hill & Wang, 1976).

(mitigating, typical, aggravating) in the absence of a motion and supporting evidence in mitigation or aggravation.

Pope presents a review of the problem of differential sentencing:[80]

> For years, many critics have charged that the criminal justice
> system operates in a biased manner toward certain disadvantaged
> members of society. According to this perspective, those under-
> privileged segments of society such as the poor, the black, and
> other minorities are overrepresented in official crime records and
> receive more severe treatment than other similarly situated offen-
> ders.... While such observations invoke intuitive reactions,
> adequate empirical data bearing on the issue is sparse at best.
> Although a number of social researchers have attempted to mea-
> sure the degree to which discrimination is operative in sentence
> dispositions, the findings of these endeavors have often proven to
> be contradictory....
>
> A partial explanation for contradictory findings may lie in
> the nature of the data and the strategy often used to explore the
> issue of differential sentencing. A major shortcoming of many
> studies in this area is that generally only one indicator of possible
> severity is employed—that most often being the length of con-
> finement imposed by the trial judge (or jury). Keeping in mind,
> however, the fact that criminal processing is dynamic rather than
> static, it would seem worthwhile to employ additional indicators
> of severity. Decisions made at one stage, for example, may be
> strengthened, diluted, or left unchanged by those occurring at a
> later point in time. For example, sentence lengths imposed by trial
> judges may later be altered by decisions or parole boards. Further,
> it is quite possible that although certain groups of offenders are
> more likely to receive longer sentences than others when con-
> fined, it may also be the case that these groups are less likely to
> actually be confined. The failure of many previous research efforts
> to incorporate this dynamic perspective into their designs is prob-
> ably more a reflection of the inadequacy of available data than
> poor methodological strategy.
>
> A corollary point is the fact that most studies have focused
> on offenses of a very serious nature (e.g., homocide) in which
> offenders were thought likely to receive prison commitments. As
> a result, the focus of inquiry was on those offenders adjudicated in
> superior court or its equivalent (e.g., Federal district court), thus
> omitting analysis at the lower or municipal court level, where a
> substantial proportion of all felony cases is actually adjudicated. It
> is true that superior court convictions and resulting sentences are

---

[80]Adapted from Carl E. Pope, *Sentencing of California Felony Offenders*
(Washington, D.C.: United States Government Printing Office, 1975), pp. 10–11,
23–24.

generally more severe than those occuring at the lower court level, but it would seem worthwhile to investigate sentencing patterns at both stages. Again, data reflecting both stages of processing have not been widely available. . . .

Pope provides a synthesis of his major findings with regard to sentence outcome:[81]

1. At both the municipal and superior court levels, bivariate relationships generally showed that female defendants were more likely to receive less severe sentences than were male defendants. This trend was stronger in urban than in rural areas. When we controlled for prior criminal history, however, substantial relationships disappeared for those defendants adjudicated by the superior court. For those defendants handled at the lower court level, standardized tables showed females to fare better than their male counterparts.

(a) Urban female offenders sentenced by the lower court were substantially more likely to obtain a probation disposition and, further, more likely to avoid a jail sentence than their male counterparts at both the bivariate and standardized levels. No differences were observed in the percentage of males and females accorded "other" dispositions. Similarly, for rural areas female defendants were substantially more likely than males to receive probation at both levels of analysis. Sex differences for jail and "other" sentences, however, were not substantial at either level. Thus, our findings here suggest that females sentenced at the lower court level generally fare better than males—more so in urban than in rural areas.

(b) For both urban and rural superior courts, in those standardized tables, no substantial relationship was found to exist between severity of disposition and sex. With respect to the most severe disposition available, male and female offenders were equally likely to be setenced to prison.

2. Overall, rural courts tended to sentence blacks more severely than whites at both lower and superior court levels. These differences tended to remain even when control variables were introduced. For urban areas, however, sentence differentials between white and black offenders were negligible at both levels of analysis.

(a) In both urban and rural lower courts, the bivariate tables revealed that black offenders generally received more severe sentences than white offenders, but only the rural difference met our criteria of substantiality. After we standardized for initial charge at arrest, prior record, and criminal status, these differences disappeared in urban areas, but remained relatively unchanged in rural areas. Blacks sentenced by rural courts, for example, were substan-

[81]Ibid. p. 25.

tially more likely to be confined and less likely to obtain probation disposition.

(b) With regard to superior court sentences, bivariate tables again showed whites to be favored over blacks in rural areas, but no substantial differences existed in urban areas. When prior record was statistically controlled, the small urban differences between the percentage of white and black offenders sentenced to prison disappeared. In rural areas, however, blacks were still found to be disproportionately sentenced to prison.

3. Age trends were similar across both urban and rural jurisdictions, but differences were noted in both lower and superior courts.

(a) Age played a minor role at the lower court level, as few differences in sentence outcomes were observed across age categories.

(b) At the superior court level, younger offenders tended to fare better than their older counterparts: they were more likely to obtain less severe sentences, especially with respect to prison dispositions. This relationship was substantial and remained even when we controlled for prior criminal history.

In a study of the New York City Criminal Court, Bernstein et al. found that the likelihood that a convicted defendant will receive a more severe sentence increased when: 1) defendant is charged with robbery; 2) has a heavier record of prior convictions; 3) has been employed for a *longer* rather than a shorter period of time; and 4) is *white*. The likelihood of receiving a less severe sentence is increased when: 1) the defendant is charged with assault; 2) has no prior arrest record; 3) has maintained a "clean record" for a longer period of time; and 4) was released from custody pending his final disposition. The authors offer a possible explanation for the unexpected findings italicized above: judges and prosecutors expect more (better behavior) from whites who usually have better employment records, assuming "that nonwhites commit crimes because the nonwhite subculture accepts such behavior."[82]

## Corrections

"Corrections" is a modern euphemism for the prison system, which, as Parker notes, has a tendency to change words instead of conditions: "The theory of rehabilitation has made some changes in the prison; terminology has changed, there are more programs, sweeping floors is now work therapy. The theory of rehabilitation has merely been im-

[82]Illene Nagel Bernstein, William R. Kelly, and Patricia A. Doyle, "Societal Reaction to Deviants," *American Sociological Review* 42 (October 1977): 743–55.

posed upon the theories of punishment."[83] Ramsey Clark has noted that despite the avowed goal of rehabilitation, approximately 95 percent of all expenditures in the entire corrections effort is for custody, while only 5 percent is for health services, education, and vocational training, and the other aspects of rehabilitative services.[84] Criticism of modern prison systems are easy to find.[85] In part, the goal of "corrections" is unclear, a situation which reflects an ambivalent public: punishment and deterrence, or perhaps expiation and rehabilitation. A confused purpose and the high cost of (even noncorrectional) institutional care, provide a trying setting for the criminal justice practitioner.

Prisons, "total institutions,"[86] are usually large fortress-like places located in rural areas and are administered by a state or federal agency. Jails, as opposed to prisons, serve as sites for pretrial detention of offenders and as short-term incarceration centers for misdemeanants. They are local in location and jurisdication.

There are actually three classes of prisons:[87]

1. *Maximum Security*—an institution characterized by being enclosed by a brick or stone wall from eighteen to twenty-five feet high—fences with barbed wire on top are sometimes substituted for the wall. Armed guards are strategically placed, usually in towers. A large percent of inmates are housed, "Auburn style," in cells equipped with complete plumbing and sanitary facilities. Most of these prisons were built before World War I, and fewer have been built since that time because of their prohibitive cost. The Attica Commission provides a look at that maximum security prison:[88]

[83]William Parker, *Parole* (College Park, Md.: American Correctional Association, 1975), p. 26.

[84]Ramsey Clark, *Crime in America* (New York: Simon & Schuster, 1970), p. 213.

[85]See, for example, Joan Smith and William Fried, *The Uses of the American Prison* (Lexington, Mass.: Heath, 1974); Erik Ohlin Wright, *The Politics of Punishment* (New York: Harper & Row, 1973); American Friends Service Committee, *Struggle for Justice* (New York: Hill & Wang, 1971).

[86]This term is used by Goffman to describe places of residence and work "where a large number of like-situated individuals, cut-off from the wider society for a appreciable period of time, together lead an enclosed, formally administered round of life." For a detailed look at the similarities of all such institutions, mental hospitals, convents, monasteries, boarding schools, and military posts, as well as prisons, see Erving Goffman, *Asylums: Essays on the Social Situation of Mental Patients and Other Inmates* (Garden City, N.Y.: Doubleday, 1961).

[87]Alan Coffey, Edward Edelfonso, and Walter Hartinger, *An Introduction to the Criminal Justice System* (Englewood Cliffs, N.J.: Prentice-Hall, 1974), pp. 246–47.

[88]New York State Special Commission on Attica, *Attica* (New York: Praeger, 1972), pp. 21–23.

Security begins at the gray concrete wall of the prison which is 30 feet high, 2 feet thick and sunk 12 feet into the ground. Spaced along the top are 14 gun towers. The wall encloses 53 acres which hold 18 buildings. Five are cellblocks, the rest house various services for the institution and the more than 2000 inmates who were confined there in September 1971 (the time of the riot). New inmates and visitors enter the prison through a black metal door under a gun tower. The inmates live on three floors in each of the four blocks, and a central hallway divides each floor into two cell areas. Two rows of cells are in each area, and each row houses about 120 inmates. Each cell faces barred windows across an 8-foot-wide corridor, or inmates face one another across a corridor and the back of the cell contains a barred window. There is a gate or locked door on every cell, and a second gate bars the stairway entrance.

2. *Medium Security*—an institution usually having a double fence twelve to fourteen feet high and sixteen to twenty feet apart, both topped with barbed wire. The fence perimeter will have personnel guarding it. A building with about 150 cells is used to house difficult inmates, while other inmates are housed dormitory style. These institutions are less expensive than the maximum security type, and they usually house many more prisoners than maximum security facilities.

3. *Minimum-Security*—these institutions operate without fixed posts or armed guards and may even be devoid of a fence around their perimeter. Smaller institutions in rural areas tend not to be enclosed, while those in heavily populated areas, or larger institutions, are usually fenced in. Living is usually dormitory style. Included in this class of institution are farms and camps in which inmates usually are involved in some productive labor such as road repair or forestry projects.

## Classification

By the time an offender reaches a correctional institution, the various criminal justice agencies through which he has passed have already amassed a quantity of documents and information on him. This information (e.g., the presentence report), and that which may be secured and organized in the institution, is used to classify the offender, now an inmate. The concept of classification refers to the allocation of entities to initially undefined classes in such a way that individuals in a class are in some sense similar or close to each other.[89] In corrections,

[89]Don M. Gottfredson et al., eds. *Decision-Making in the Criminal Justice System: Reviews and Essays* (Rockville, Md.: National Institute of Mental Health, 1975), p. 2.

classification is used for determining the needs and requirements of both the inmate and the agency (i.e., security), and assigning the inmate to institutions and programs according to those needs and existing resources. While classification schemes are usually presented as vehicles for treatment and rehabilitation, the concern for security is usually the prime focus. There are four basic methods of classification:

1. classification within an existing institution
2. classification committees
3. reception-diagnosis centers
4. community classification

The first system, when used within a state prison, usually involves a reception unit whose primary responsibility is to act as a diagnostic section. The professional personnel assigned to the unit make diagnostic studies and treatment recommendations which are submitted to the administrative personnel. The second system is similar to the first, but instead of submitting their information and recommendations to administrative personnel, the committee itself is responsible for converting the information into administrative decisions. In the third method all offenders are sent to a central receiving institution for classification, and a prime responsibility is to determine to which institution an offender is to be sent. The fourth method is used on a limited basis, if at all. It involves probation and parole personnel, who collect social histories, and local practitioners, who provide medical and psychiatric information. Institutional personnel, on a state and local basis, cooperate with the other members of the team in order to complete the classification process.

Gottfredson notes that in correctional systems "with sophisticated treatment resources, program placement alternatives may include a variety of programs"—education, vocational training, individual and group counseling, as well as forestry, road camp and work furlough placements.[90]

Gottfredson notes the importance of a classification system:[91]

> To the extent that criminal justice agencies adopt goals of modifying behavior to reduce the probability of law violations, it is important to have available at each decision point (concerning placement decisions) classification information which will indicate the setting and methods most likely to achieve these goals.

[90]Ibid., p. 83.
[91]Ibid., p. 84.

A prison is usually under the control of an administrator called a warden or superintendent who is assisted by one or more associates or deputies responsible for specific aspects of prison operations—security, administration, treatment.[92] The security/custodial staff, the largest group of employees in a prison, are comprised of correction officers organized along quasi-military lines. Each prison also has support personnel, a business manager, bookkeepers and clerical staff, as well as rehabilitation personnel—teachers, social workers, etc. Gibbons notes that "prison officials are expected to deal with their charges in a humane fashion."[93] This, coupled with the fact that prisoners vastly outnumber the staff, means that prison officials must depend on inmate cooperation. This cooperation often depends on "informal *sub rosa* ties which develop between inmates and administrators and are not defined as legitimate or proper within the formal definitions of prison procedures. Similar relationships exist between guards and inmates— guards, using their discretion, provide special privileges to inmate leaders who keep the other prisoners cool."[94] Burnham states: "All prisons are, in several senses, run by their inmates, and a regular supply of these to essential jobs, such as kitchen and the laundary, must be maintained ."[95]

## Parole

Parole, the last segment of the criminal justice sequence, is 1) a method for releasing inmates sentenced to indeterminate terms: and 2) a method for supervision of released inmates in the community.

Inmates may leave prison in one of three ways:

1. parole—discretionary release by a parole board.
2. conditional release—completion of the entire sentence minus "good time" or "time off for good behavior" while in the institution.
3. maximum expiration—completion of the entire sentence. (Of course there are other possibilities: pardon, escape, and death.)

[92]For a detailed look at classification for treatment from the correctional administrator's perspective, see Leonard J. Hippchen, ed., *Correctional Classification and Treatment* (Cincinnati, Ohio: W. H. Anderson, 1975). This work is illuminating for its uncritical view of classification and treatment in prison.

[93]Don C. Gibbons, *Society, Crime and Criminal Careers* (Englewood Cliffs, N.J.: Prentice-Hall, 1973), p. 469.

[94]Ibid., pp. 70–71.

[95]R. William Burnham, "Modern Decisions and Corrections." *Decision-Making in the Criminal Justice System.* Edited by Don M. Gottfredson et al. (Rockville, Md.: National Institute of Mental Health, 1975) p. 93.

## PAROLE RELEASE

The power of parole boards to release inmates from prison is the subject of a great deal of controversy.[96] Part of this controversy concerns the personnel who sit on these quasi-judicial boards. Parole board members are usually appointed by the governor, and Parker concludes that "the only real qualifications for board members may be the political responsiveness and reliability of the local members to the appointing power."[97] In some states the position is part-time and provides only nominal financial rewards or mere expenses; in other states, particularly the more populous ones, the position is full-time and the compensation may be substantial (for criminal justice positions). In New York, for example, where the only qualification is age (over twenty-one), the eleven members of the board receive over $36,000 annually, while the chairman receives over $43,000. Some states do not have parole boards (e.g., California and Maine), and in some jurisdictions hearing examiners interview inmates for the parole board and recommend for or against release. The usual practice, however, is for an inmate to be interviewed by one or more members of the board.

Another aspect of the controversy surrounding parole boards relates to the criteria used by parole boards in making release decisions. There are often incomplete or extremely general criteria, and critics note that it is not possible to accurately predict individual behavior. (It is not difficult to predict behavior of classes of offender using an actuarial method familiar to insurance companies.) Although no estimate of future behavior can be made with certainty, Gottfredson states that it is possible to make predictions about groups with similar characteristics: "persons are classified; and then statements are made about the expected performances of members of the classes."[98]

As a source of information about the offender, the board may use the presentence investigation report. In addition the board has an institutional record, although experience has indicated that this is not a reliable factor with respect to subsequent community adjustment. The former Chairman of the United States Board of Parole, Maurice H. Sigler, states:[99]

> Anyone who has an extensive experience in working with offenders in prison knows that there are inmates who could achieve

[96]For a more complete discussion of parole release see Howard Abadinsky, *Probation and Parole: Theory and Practice* (Englewood Cliffs, N.J.: Prentice-Hall, 1977), pp. 168–81.

[97]Parker, p. 30.

[98]Don M. Gottfredson, "Diagnosis, Classification, and Prediction." In *Decision-Making in the Criminal Justice System*, p. 5.

[99]Maurice Sigler, "Abolish Parole?" *Federal Probation* 39 (June 1975): 46.

almost any set of goals of this kind, but who would still be totally unready for release. I have known offenders who have picked up a half dozen trades during successive terms in prison, high school diplomas, and even college degrees, and who have participated in group therapy and counseling of various types, but still are dangerous people. When ultimately released, they lose no time in sticking up a bank or returning to their preferred variety of crime.

On the other hand, there are inmates who would not be able to meet such "treatment" goals, but who could be released with the expectation that they would never again get into trouble with the law. Many of them don't really need to meet such goals anyway. Some persons convicted of murder, for example, could be released as soon as they are convicted in court, and never get into trouble again. They remain in prison for a relatively long time because our society wants to demonstrate that it does not regard the taking of human life lightly.

As in the sentencing process, the criminal justice practitioner plays a key role in the parole release process by securing, organizing, and presenting information on the inmate, interpreting this information to the board, and sometimes making a recommendation.

### PAROLE (AND PROBATION) SUPERVISION

If an inmate is released by the board of parole (in some jurisdictions, even when he is released by conditional release), he is placed under the supervision of a parole officer.[100] The supervision process in parole is similar, if not identical, to that in probation.[101] In fact, in some states probation and parole supervision is handled by the same agency, e.g., the Florida Parole and Probation Commission. Typically, after being placed on probation or released on parole, an offender is required to make an in-person report to a probation/parole office within twenty-four hours. During his initial visit, the rules of supervision are discussed and the needs and plans of the offender are reviewed. The degree of probation/parole officer involvement with the client will vary according to the needs of the case and, more often, according to the size of the officer's caseload. The client will be cautioned against certain associations and encouraged to find employment. He will be directed to contact his probation or parole officer in person, by mail or telephone on a specific schedule. Depending on the procedures (and

---

[100]The actual title varies considerably from state to state: for example, parole agent in California; probation/parole supervisor, Georgia; parole counselor, Tennessee and Illinois; correctional program officer, Arizona.

[101]For a more detailed look at the supervision process see Howard Abadinsky, *Probation and Parole*, pp. 266–312.

caseload size) of the agency, the probation or parole officer will period-
ically make field visits to the client's residence or place of employment
as well as collateral visits to the police and other law enforcement
agencies in order to determine if the client is suspected of any new
criminal activity.

### PROBATION OR PAROLE VIOLATION

In the event of a violation of probation or parole, agency process
can vary. Based on the *Morrissey* and *Gagnon* decision,[102] which provided some basic due process guarantees to probationers and parolees,
respectively, a violator is provided with two hearings, a *preliminary*
and *final*, at which determinations are made concerning the alleged violation and the disposition of the offender. Probation determinations are
part of the judicial process, and it is a judge who determines if a violation of probation has occurred. In parole, this determination is made by
the parole board. While probation violation has remained a relatively
stable procedure, parole violation has been subjected to intense litiga-
tion, with the result that parole violation procedures remain in a state
of flux. The criminal justice practitioner, in defending his charges of
probation/parole violation, is often required to assume a prosecutorial
role against an attorney representing the offender. Obviously, the
client-advocate or "objective" stance of the social service worker can be
compromised by these procedures. This conflict is discussed by Peter
Doret, an attorney and former parole officer in New York State.[103]

> The Parole Officer generally must fulfill two separate and
> distinct roles; that of social caseworker and that of rule enforcer.
> In the first instance, he assumes the traditional role of the social
> caseworker, "the helping person," and is supportive, understand-
> ing, and forgiving. He aids his charges in their readjustment prob-
> lems and offers them a wide range of social services from counsel-
> ing to employment referrals to treatment for drug addiciton. At
> the same time, however, in his role of rule enforcer, he enforces
> the rules of parole and the rules of society generally. He can and
> often, indeed, must exercise severe sanctions against parolees
> who substantially violate their proscribed limits.
>     That there is a role conflict here is obvious and that this
> creates problems for the practitioner is equally obvious. Often a
> problem where the social caseworker would ordinarily offer his

[102]*Morrissey* v. *Brewer* 408 U.S. 471, 92 S. Ct. (1972) and *Gagnon* v. *Scar-
pelli* 411 U.S. 778, 93 S. Ct. (1973).

[103]Peter Doret, "The Quasi-Legal Role of a Social Service Worker in a Parole
Setting." Adapted from a longer version of this paper with permission of the
author.

assistance is, in addition, a rules violation with which the rule enforcer must likewise deal. This can cause internal conflicts for the practitioner when he must choose between two diametrically opposed courses of action. Difficulty is also encountered with the parolee/client who, very much aware of this duality of roles, is reluctant to place his trust in his parole officer/practitioner. The entire relationship thereby suffers and the delivery of services is adversely affected.

Internally, conflicts arise between the supporting and helping relationship which the parole officer attempts to develop with his parolees and the duty to closely monitor the activities of his parolees from the standpoint of community protection.

Externally, the parole officer is, with increasing frequency, subjected to criticism from sources without the system. When a parolee engages in improper conduct which precipitates punitive case action, the parole officer may be accused of not being a "helping person" and of working to the detriment of his parolee. When no punitive action is taken, the parole officer is criticized for allowing the offending conduct to go unpunished or unchecked.

Now, the very nature of the parole officer/parolee relationship is changing. The Parole Officer must deal with parolees who have a more heightened awareness of their rights and make increasing demands upon the practitioner based on these rights. The system itself has become more formal, legalistic and technical than heretofore, and, with increasing frequency, attorneys have become involved in the parole process.

Parole violation hearings have clearly become highly technical adversarial proceedings which have placed the parole officer in a unique, if unenviable position. Where, in the past, he has been in the virtually unassailable position of the social caseworker cloaked in "righteous virtue," he now, in a quasi-judicial arena, finds his actions and, indeed, even his motives under scrutiny and attack.

# 4

# Locating Social Services in Criminal Justice

## Juveniles in a Police Setting

### SOCIAL SERVICE PROGRAMS FOR JUVENILES

The police are continually in contact with persons who have a plethora of human problems: legal, financial, social and psychological. Police departments that have recognized their human services role have broadened their responses to include crisis intervention in cases of child abuse, suicide, substance abuse, family disputes, and juvenile problems (See figure 4-1). In addition, there has been an overloading of criminal justice agencies which can also be alleviated, in part, by diverting persons with social and personal problems from criminal justice into social service areas. Rutherford and McDermott note that police programs may vary from simple "education" of youngsters to intensive counseling: "In the past such youths would likely have been referred to probation or private programs or dismissed, but 'new diversion' has made funds available for police-controlled and operated program efforts."[1]

One police social service program is in operation in Dallas.[2] The

---

[1] Andrew Rutherford and Robert McDermott, *Juvenile Diversion* (Washington, D.C.: United States Government Printing Office, 1976), p. 28.

[2] Thomas R. Collingwood, Alex Douds, and Hadley Williams, "Juvenile Diversion: The Dallas Police Department Youth Services Program," *Federal Probation* 40 (September 1976): 23–27.

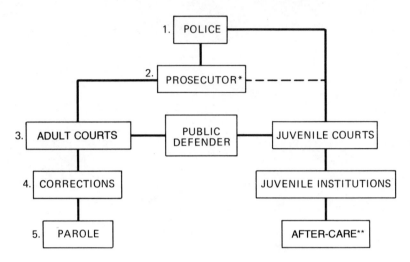

**Figure 4-1.** Locating social services in criminal justice agencies that employ social service workers

Dallas program is based on early identification of youngsters in need of services with two major goals:

1. to divert juveniles from the juvenile justice system; and
2. to reduce recidivism.

The treatment staff are police officers and civilian counselors supervised by a psychologist. Youths who are referred to the program have been involved in both misdemeanors and felonies—but the youth's acceptance of the program is voluntary; the youth and his parents sign a "statement of participation."

When an arrested youth is brought to the Youth Section, a police investigator initiates an interview to determine the needs of the youngster and the most appropriate disposition of the case. The officer has to choose between:

1. sending the youth home
2. referring him/her to juvenile court
3. referring him/her to a First Offender lecture program
4. sending him to the counseling unit

*In some jurisdictions the prosecutor's office determines if a case will be processed into the juvenile court. In other jurisdictions the police (or other agencies) send the case directly to the juvenile court without the involvement of the prosecutor.
**In some jurisdictions the probation department provides after-care services for juveniles.

Established criteria are utilized by the police investigator in making his disposition. First time minor offenders are usually referred to the First Offender lecture program, while the most serious repeat offenders are referred the the juvenile court. The middle range youths who may have committed a moderate to severe offense (theft or burglary) or may have a less serious prior record (one to six previous arrests) are referred to the counseling program. A key determination that the investigator makes in his disposition judgment is whether a youth and the youth's parents could benefit from the relatively short-term counseling alternative. Time is allocated for the investigator to get a more personal view of the youth. The entire Youth Section (sworn officers and civilian personnel) have been given training on Carkhuff's Human Resource Development skills such as interpersonal-counseling and problem-solving skills[3] enabling the police officer to function more effectively as a helper to a youth. If the youth is referred to the lecture, he/she will receive a three-hour "awareness lecture" by police officers on two successive nights within one month of arrest. If a youth is assigned to a counselor, the referring investigator maintains contact with the case throughout the course of the program.

A youth assigned to the Counseling Unit undergoes a systematic three-stage process lasting approximately six months. The first is the intake stage during which the counselor assesses the youth's physical, intellectual, and emotional functioning. The youth next enters the direct treatment phase whereby he/she receives sixteen hours of skills training within a group. The training is provided over a four-week period. Parents also receive training during this period on how to monitor their child's activities and implement behavioral contracts to help their child reach the program goals. After the direct phase, a youth enters followup and is given "homework assignments or behavioral contracts to apply the skills learned to critical outcome areas that relate to avoiding trouble." These include following limits at home, attending school and maintaining certain grades, and participating in constructive activities. Throughout the three-stage process, individual programs, family counseling, and community agency referral programs are also implemented as needed.

The sixteen hours of skills training involves physical fitness, interpersonal skill, and study/learning skills, all designed to help the youth better cope with his environment.

There are both benefits and disadvantages to diversion services being provided directly in a police setting. The advantages include a

---

[3]R. R. Carkhuff, *The Development of Human Resources* (New York: Holt, Rinehart & Winston, 1971).

more expeditious response and police confidence in the program that they administer. Dunford reveals that a typical police diversion program not under police supervision failed to provide any services to 38 percent of the youngsters referred:[4] "over one-third of the youth that the police thought they diverted for services received no services at all." He also suggests that "the quality and quantity of services rendered to diverted youths are often inadequate to meet their needs."[5] In particular, Dunford points out: "Little thought is given to impacting school, home, or community practices and procedures which give rise to so many youth problems."[6] Chwast, in an article written when he was a Lieutenant with the New York City Police Department, notes that the Juvenile Aid Bureau was able to impact on "community" through the use of what he refers to as "aggressive casework:" visits by the police officer-social workers to the client's home, school, community center, etc. He notes that in this regard the police officer has a distinct advantage: he can undertake visits in poorly lighted, high delinquent areas—"as a policeman he is better prepared to deal with any unforseen hazards which may arise."[7]

Another advantage which Chwast notes is the use of authority, something which no other societal control agent symbolizes more than a policeman. In this regard Chwast is critical of what he sees as "the usual permissive casework attitudes" which allow "self-determination" to interfere with help:[8]

> While the family may not interfere with our carrying out the exploratory phase of the contact by our caseworker, they frequently fail to heed our suggestions about going for help. The fact is that many of the more serious delinquent offenders are involved in situations wherein it is necessary to insist that they go for treatment. This is the only sure way of knowing that this will be done. The argument that the client must willingly appear before the treatment resource under his own power is totally unrealistic when it comes to cases of this type.

He provides a case example:[9]

> Robert M. first reported to us when 13 years of age for peeping through windows. He was a handsome and intelligent boy

---

[4]Franklyn W. Dunford, "Police Diversion: An Illustion?" *Criminology* 15 (November 1977): 338.

[5]Ibid.

[6]Ibid., p. 339.

[7]Jacob Chwast, "Casework Treatment in a Police Setting," *Federal Probation* 18 (December 1954): 39.

[8]Ibid., p. 38.

[9]Ibid., pp. 38–39.

who came from a family background that superficially did not appear wanting. A year later repetition of the same offense resulted in our successfully bringing the family into contact with a family casework agency.

Several years later, however, Robert again was accused of voyeurism but the complainant refused to press the charge. The caseworker assigned recognized from the boy's nervous mannerisms, generalized timidity, and inhibition that he was in need of some form of psychiatric assistance. Upon this he contacted an agency specializing in the treatment of the offender which agreed to assume responsibility for the case. Inasmuch as Robert had not accepted opening feelers that he might be willing to receive such assistance, the worker flatly insisted that the boy must go for therapy and told him that he would see to it that he went. Of course our worker appreciated that he could not implement his ultimatum from a legal standpoint. He did, however, skillfully gauge the full psychological impact of authoritarian display at this point in helping the boy make up his mind. In consequence the boy did appear for his initial interview for psychotherapy. Our checkup at the end of 2 months revealed that he was deeply involved in the therapeutic process.

Chwast emphasizes the social use of authority:[10]

Whether he is adult or juvenile, we have found in our considerable experience with delinquents over the course of many years that the vast majority of agency failures in the treatment of the delinquent have resulted from complete inability to understand the role of authoritativeness and the extent to which it should be used for treatment purposes.

### FAMILY CRISIS INTERVENTION

Bard notes that the police role in family crisis intervention derives from their order maintenance function, and he stresses the need for training if such intervention is to be useful.[11] Mann notes that policemen are generally unaware of community resources for assisting with behavior and social problems.[12] Policemen often respond in ways that are familiar to them, and since they are familiar with the "arrest," they often use that tool even when other (e.g., social service) responses may be more appropriate.[13]

[10]Ibid., p. 39.
[11]Morton Bard, "The Role of Law Enforcement in the Helping System," *Community Mental Health Journal* 7 (June 1971): 151–60.
[12]Philip A. Mann, "Establishing a Mental Health Consultation Program with a Police Department," *Community Mental Health Journal* 7 (June 1971): 118–26.
[13]Private conversation with John Ball, Chief of Police, County of Charleston, South Carolina.

Barocas refers to some police activities as *iatrogenic*—in a medical context, an ailment caused by the physicians intervention. He states that it is important to "differentiate between therapeutic intervention in a crisis situation and nontherapeutic interference, especially if a policeman's own tolerance for anxiety is low and does not have sufficient awareness and understanding of interpersonal dynamics and neurotic interaction."[14] The untrained policeman, he notes, will draw upon his own biased notions of family psychodynamics and he may induce tragic reactions. However, the author states: "During a crisis period the potential for change is greatly increased, and police assistance provided at this point can be very effective in stabilizing family relationships." For the intervention to be effective, however, the officers must be well-trained.[15]

In the Illinois communities of Oak Park and River Forest there was concern over the use of the police as a social service since it was felt that they could easily become overburdened in this role, thus diminishing their law enforcement responsibilities. It was noted that the police officer "does not have the time, nor is it his function to break the negative family cycles that lead to such disturbances."[16]

Together with the Family Service and the Mental Health Center, the police departments in those two communities developed the Police-Social Service Project. Among other innovations, the project provides police officers with twenty-four-hour access to social services and monthly progress reports on clients being helped. The project is connected with a community service network which can provide emergency financial aid, homemaking assistance, medical monitering by nurses, home-delivery of meals, psychiatric evaluation in the home, day nursery care, and medical, social, and financial assistance for the aged. Action within the program can be initiated:

1. If a police officer believes that a person with whom he is in contact could benefit from social service intervention, but that such intervention need not be instituted on an emergency basis, he informs the person that he plans to initiate such action and then makes either an oral or written report of the incident to his department's liaison officer. The liaison officer forwards the report to the center liaison worker, who sees that

[14]Harvey A. Barocas, "Urban Policeman: Crisis Mediators or Crisis Creators?" *American Journal of Orthopsychiatry* 43 (July 1973): 633–34.

[15]Ibid., p. 636.

[16]Donald A. Woolf and Marvin Rudman, "A Police-Social Service Cooperative Program," © 1977, National Association of Social Workers, Inc. Reprinted from *Social Work*, vol. 22, No. 1 (January 1977), pp. 62–63.

the case is assigned to a social worker for follow-up. The social worker prepares a monthly progress report which is forwarded to the police department. It is the responsibility of the center's liaison worker to supervise the client's progress through the social service system and to keep the police informed of such progress.
2. If the referring officer desires immediate social service intervention during office hours, he telephones the center and requests that a social worker be sent to the scene. If such a need arises after office hours or on weekends, the officer can reach a social worker by means of a tone-voice paging device. In all cases, the officer has full authority to decide whom he will refer and how.

Burnett et al. stress the need for combining social work and police work so that the two professions can provide help to citizens who look for aid through the police. They describe a police department-social agency project in Pawtucket, Rhode Island, geared to help families who were calling the police although they really needed social service help for a multitude of various family and social problems.[17] The authors note that the domestic dispute usually presents a difficult situation for most police officers—while their ability to deal with the problems is limited, the potential for serious altercations, injury and death, is unlimited. The goal of most policemen in such situations is to "cool" the situation "sufficiently so that no one gets hurt and so that they (the police) are not called back in a few hours." In response to the obvious needs of family crisis intervention, a program was funded in Pawtucket which provides for counselor-officer teams who work in conjunction with the police department and the Family Service Society. Team members are policemen and staff persons and students from the Family Service Society. Burnet et al. describe the program procedures:[18]

> While some of the clients have been seen in the police stations themselves, the Police Crisis teams have made almost all of the contacts in the homes of the clients. To aid confidentiality and in order not to arouse too much neighborhood curiosity, the teams ride in the private cars of the team members and wear no uniforms. The Crisis Teams for the most part do not respond to the

[17]Bruce B. Burnett, John J. Carr, John Sinapi, and Roy Taylor, "Police and Social Workers in a Community Outreach Program," *Social Casework* 57 (January 1976): 41–46. Reprinted by permission of the Family Service Association of America.
[18]Ibid., pp. 44–45.

initial request for police help. For example, in a family disturbance, the squad car is sent to the family initially to insure protection for all involved. The policemen at that time, however, will
suggest to the family a contact with the Police Crisis Team. They
make the referral; the Crisis Team then picks this up at night,
makes an appointment, and follows it through.

Referrals come to the teams from many different sources, but
the bulk of them come from the police themselves. The policemen
on the teams refer many problems to the Crisis Team through their
daytime contacts with clients and through the many normal
police calls in which they might be involved. Sergeants who are at
the front desk in the evening are a valuable source of referrals,
often referring families directly to the Crisis Team. The police
department itself has become more sensitive to the problems
which should appropriately be referred to the teams. The policemen handle most of the calls that come into the station, and as the
teams are connected to the station by radio, many times the teams
are able to respond very soon after or even in the midst of a crisis.
The patrolmen on the beat and others actively involved in police
work have been another valuable source of referrals; referrals from
these sources have thus far been minimal, but are increasing. Also
on the increase are direct calls from people who have seen newspaper articles on the program, or who have heard about the program through friends or neighbors.

The referrals that the teams have experienced have covered
all aspects of social problems. Many of the situations prompting
the calls have been symptomatic of family problems: first time
shoplifting by juveniles, first time incidence of running away,
school problems, alcohol problems, drug-related problems, and
neighborhood disturbances. As the teams have been involved, the
underlying problems have been identified: parent-child personality defects and some psychotic problems have been treated.

The roles of the team members have been varied, depending
on the situation and problems encountered. The police gain the
teams entry into the home, but because they are in plain clothes
and private cars, their arrival is nonthreatening to those seeking
help. Once the teams are interviewing, the social worker carries
the burden, but the policeman has had to be involved where there
is question of criminal behavior or a need to sanction a particular
plan, especially with young people. As the program has pro-
gressed, the police have been able to participate in a more helpful
manner and have become involved in the interviewing process
itself.

With the families who are interviewed, frequently the main
goal is to try to defuse the situation, to help the participants see
that the crisis with which they are coping has perhaps a hidden

message, and that it's probable that it can end soon. There is an attempt to effect some kind of resolution of the crisis as it presents itself, often redefining the problem in terms of ongoing patterns of difficulties within the family. If these patterns can be identified (for example, a marital problem or a situation where the child and the mother simply do not get along), the attempt is to highlight this area and to make a referral to some appropriate community agency. The Family Service Society has been the main receiver of referrals, but other community agencies such as mental health, community action, drug rehabilitation, or children's agencies have been used.

The authors note that caseworkers were concerned about the ability of the police officers to be understanding, while the police officer's previous contacts with social workers had left them with a feeling that social workers are idealistic but have little concrete help to offer those who need it. However, as the program emerged the social worker's role became more positive:[19]

1. He brings with him expertise in counseling skills which often enable him to take the lead in the sessions.

2. Diagnostic skills relevant to crisis and family interaction enable him to set up continuing contact with the families to help them through the days following a crisis.

3. His awareness of the service delivery system is invaluable; in fact, as one officer put it, "the personal relationship of the social worker with the personnel in agencies greatly facilitated referrals, ones we could not utilize before."

4. The social worker brought with him knowledge and experience in working with teams of people, including other professionals.

5. The social worker's presence lent credence to the clients that this was not strictly a police matter, that with a clinician there something different and helpful could happen.

The roles of the policemen are several, and are essential for the functioning of the team:

1. The policemen have afforded a great entree. They know many of the people can relate warmly to them and, if they do not know them, the clients know the badge and seem to view it with a positive attitude. Hostility toward the police has not been apparent.

[19]Ibid., pp. 45–47.

2. The police are authority figures. On entering a volatile situation, their authority seems to quell immediately some of the tense feelings. Also, the police can use their authority to bring someone to the police station or to court if necessary.

3. Knowing the families added much diagnostic understanding to the teams. "Yes, I remember that bad accident she was in, she almost died and she has not been the same since" provides an important note to the understanding of the situation. In addition, diagnostic impression can be verified with knowledge of the background. In one situation, the basis of referral for a man was based on his apparently volatile, uncontrollable temper founded on his anger towards women. The officer later mentioned that he had arrested this man many times; he added that the man's mother had also been known for her carousing and drinking, and habitually left him alone as a child.

4. Police offer the team much backup. They are able to follow up a situation the following day, or can ask to intervene in a situation that the teams know about, so that the crisis handling can continue.

5. Police also know the resources of the community, but usually different service networks from those known to the caseworkers. They can meet people exposed to many potential clients to talk of the program. (During one rather quiet night, the patrolman, social worker, and consultant walked the officer's old beat, and talked to juveniles, bartenders, and others about the program.) The contact between the departments within the state is also invaluable.

6. Police officers may do unusual things to help that caseworkers may not think to do. The second floor was dark and our knocks did not rouse anyone inside, though we had arranged for the appointment just a short time before. The officer hopped up to the third floor to inquire if they knew if the woman was home and we found that she was a bit hard of hearing and that she was in the front of the house. We then went up the front stairs and were admitted. The other social worker and the consultant agreed that with a feeling for confidentiality we would not have done this.

7. The police officer provides security for the social worker. The teams have described their learning a lot from each other and stated that the debriefing that takes place after going into a home is essential for learning and support. The roles outlined are no longer quite so clear; the police officers now take part in the interviews and have become fine counselors. At times, there have been situations where the social workers "thought like a policeman" (in one situation the worker urged the officer to arrest the client, but the officer favored continued discussion, which eventually

worked). Each of the partners has gained respect for the other: one police officer said, "We realize now that we need social workers in the police stations. We have too many decisions to make based on inadequate knowledge." The social workers have all reiterated that without the police officers they would not have gained entry or the clients' cooperation so quickly.

An incident in 1977 highlights the potential dangers involved in the type of cases dealt with by the Pawtucket program. Patrolman James Kareemo, a member of the Family Crisis Team, received the Rhode Island Attorney General's Law Enforcement Award for intervening in a family dispute which resulted in his being stabbed several times. The Patrolman wounded his assailant before losing consciousness.[20]

## In a Juvenile Setting

Agencies responsible for dealing with juveniles usually have a treatment/rehabilitation orientation: when an adult commits an offense he is punished; when a juvenile violates the behavioral norm, he is 'cared for.' Renn notes that "justification for custody of juveniles is care and guidance or therapy."[21] Because of the treatment focus, the social service worker is a central figure in juvenile justice settings. While in the adult court it is the prosecutor who determines if and how a case is to be processed, in the juvenile court there is usually a special intake section staffed by social service personnel (e.g., probation officers) who make these determinations. The best estimates indicate that about half of the juvenile cases that reach intake in the juvenile court are disposed of at that level, that is, without judicial participation. Czajkoski refers to this task as one of the "quasi-judicial" roles of the probation officer.[22]

During the intake stage the worker conducts an investigation, usually interviewing all relevant parties—child, parents, police, complainants—and decides if the case can be handled without a referral to court (unofficial processing). This informal method of handling includes direct counseling by the worker or referral to an appropriate social agency. A youngster may sometimes be placed on informal probation by the intake worker for a period of several months. During this

---

[20]"Crisis Mediation Officer Wins R.I. Attorney General's Award," *Law Enforcement News,* December 6, 1977.

[21]Donna E. Renn, "The Right to Treatment and the Juvenile," *Crime and Delinquency* 19 (October 1973): 481.

[22]Eugene H. Czajkoski, "Exposing the Quasi-Judicial Role of the Probation Officer," *Federal Probation* 37 (September 1973): 9–13.

probationary period, an attempt is made to help the youngster. If this fails, or if the youngster and/or parents are uncooperative, the case can be referred to court for official processing by the filing of a petition. Olson and Shepard note: "A youth's first experience with the juvenile court can have a profound impact on him. As the intake worker for the juvenile court will be the first person at the court with whom the youth has contact, a youth's concept of justice will be influenced by how he is treated at intake."[23] The authors advise: "The worker should be particularly sensitive and skillful in short-term interviewing and should be capable of making important decisions after brief contacts with the complainant, the youth, and the family—together with an examination of the police report."[24]

The Office of Probation, New York Family Intake Branch, provides an outline of the information to be secured by the probation officer at intake. In New York, the intake stage is voluntary; the respondent (or his parents) can insist on the right to a court hearing, thereby avoiding intake. In addition, if the complainant insists, a case must be petitioned (and is thus ineligible for "unofficial" adjustment). The outline notes:[25]

> The Intake Service is the critical point at which a client comes into contact with the judicial process and system. Its purpose is the determination of which cases require court intervention, which require no further action and which require referral to other agencies for treatment without court intervention. The limited period of time alloted the Intake Officer for the decision making process requires a judicious use of the time[26] he spends with clients, and skills in communication to elicit information required for a valid assessment of the case situation, in order to select an appropriate course of action to meet the client's needs.

The intake interview must include an explanation of the voluntary nature of the intake process, both to clients and complainants. The nature of the process and available alternatives should also be explained. Information secured at intakes includes:[27]

---

[23]Jay Olson and George H. Shepard, *Intake Screening Guides: Improving Justice for Juveniles* (Washington, D.C.: United States Government Printing Office, 1975), p. 27.
[24]Ibid.
[25]New York City Family Court instructions to probation personnel (mimeo).
[26]In New York the time limit is sixty days, although, with the approval of the judge, the intake officer may take another sixty days.
[27]New York City Family Court instructions to probation personnel (mimeo).

A. *Allegations:* Nature of the complaint clearly defined.

B. *Circumstances Surrounding Offense:* This area is an expansion of the actual allegations and should include any aggravating or mitigating circumstances, attitude toward the child involved, what the complainant wants. If an arrest was made, what the police officer saw (and/or what was told to him), whether he has any prior knowledge of the child, child's response to him, parents response when contacted. If assault was involved the extent of the injury, treatment required and any hospitalization necessary.

C. *Prior Record:* Previous involvement with the court and an evaluation of any patterns which can be deduced from same.

D. *Child:* His version of what occurred; how he became involved; attitude toward alleged offense (e.g., remorseful, penitent, arrogant or indifferent); attitude toward home and family; school adjustment; any medical problems, or previous placement (hospital or child care agency); his response to his current situation—what he wants—motivation for help.

E. *Parents:* Brief description of family context—if parents separated is there any contact with absent spouse?; parents version of child's behavior and problems he presents; onset of problem; other outstanding family problems, if any; family strengths—has the parent any alternatives to court intervention to offer?; is parent motivated to secure help for child (and/or family)?; was outside help ever sought—where—its effect.

Reports from community agencies having contact with the family should be sought wherever possible.

The report should end with a short evaluation of the situation and a recommendation. If the case is referred to Court a recommendation for interim disposition (prior to fact finding) as well as for disposition following a finding of fact should be made.

If the recommendation is for adjustment without Court intervention, note the nature of the adjustment, the agency to which a referral has been made or whether the case is to be held at the intake level for counseling. On those cases held in intake for counseling the treatment plan should be outlined, and periodic summaries of contacts with the client made.

Referrals to community agencies must be kept open until the Intake Officer learns the service has been initiated and so noted in the record.

At the intake level the child is usually not represented by counsel, and thus any statements made by him are confidential from the court.

### THE COMMUNITY ARBITRATION PROGRAM

A program in Maryland, the *Community Arbitration Program*, attempts to deal with the rapidly escalating number of juvenile referrals which resulted in a delayed delivery of services by the juvenile intake system: "Sound human behavior theory indicates that the most productive time for behavioral and attitudinal changes are prior to, during, and after a crisis. To be most effective, delivery of service should coincide with this span of crisis."[28] The program uses attorneys functioning as intake officers: "to screen more carefully for sufficiency of evidence and to better explain the laws and their philosophy to all involved." Cases reach the intake arbitrators via the police who issue "tickets" similar to those given for traffic violations. Copies of the tickets are given to parents and victims as well as the (child) offender. Social service workers are used in the program to make appropriate referrals, or when services are not available, to attempt to develop them or to provide direct service. The following case examples indicate how approximately 40 percent of the cases are handled.

---

### CASE #1

*The Child and His Offense:* J is a fourteen year old white, middle class high school student who was referred to the Juvenile Arbitrator for a charge of assault and battery.

*The Arbitrator's Decision:* At the time of the initial hearing, J's behavior was marked by loud outbursts which continued during the entire hearing. Due to the nature of the charge against him and his conduct during the hearing, the Arbitrator concluded that J had problems handling his feelings of anger and referred him to a counselor at Arbitration, with the expectation that he would receive some help.

*Informal Supervision:* There were no appropriate community resources near J's home, so the Arbitration counselor assumed the responsibility for counselling. J was attending a special school for students with learning disabilities, and was frequently absent. Additionally, he had been involved in fights on the bus. The counselor arranged a conference with the school principal, school social worker, J's mother and J. During the conference, J expressed his hostility towards the school, jumped up and stormed out of the room.

The next two weeks were filled with the counselor's daily visits to J's home for what J and his mother called "emergencies". The problems ranged from fights between J and his sister to arguments with his mother

[28]Information for this section was received directly from Kay Peacock, Director, Community Arbitration Program.

over money. J's father felt incapable of helping his son, as he had recently suffered a stroke and was quite weak.

A psychological evaluation was requested by the counselor once the family difficulties became apparent. The recommendation was that J be placed in a residential school for emotionally disturbed children. The counselor arranged for financial assistance through a local private agency.

*Establishing Ties Within the Community:* J is now in a special residential school. His relationship to his family is slowly improving as they are receiving counseling from the school. The quality of J's relationships within a school setting are less tenuous, as the school is better suited to meet his needs.

## CASE #2

*The Child and His Offense:* S, a seventeen year old girl, was referred to Community Arbitration following a charge of shoplifting during the Christmas shopping rush at a major department store. She was married and had one child; also, S attended high school regularly. Her husband was attending college during the day and working at night. There was little money available for the family, and S explained that she would not have shoplifted had her economic situation been better. She wanted to make the holidays nice for her family.

*The Arbitrator's Decision:* S admitted to the charges during the Arbitration hearing. The Arbitrator stressed that shoplifting hurt the community, as prices were raised for everyone as a result of loss accrued by the store. The Arbitrator asked S to "pay back the community" by working in a volunteer capacity in some activity that would better others. S understood the effect of shoplifting on prices, and agreed to carry out volunteer work. The Arbitrator also requested that S receive some counseling to help her manage financially.

*Informal Supervision:* A counselor from Arbitration contacted her within one week of the hearing. At that time the counselor learned that the client was interested in working with children, and he suggested that she search for a placement based on her interests. S contacted a center for emotionally disturbed children, and began carrying out her twenty hours of volunteer work.

Also, the field supervisor discovered that there was no appropriate counselling agency in S's community, and began counselling her himself. S expressed confusion over a choice of occupation after high school graduation. The counselor helped her explore social work or occupational therapy as areas where she might acquire special training. Eventually, encouraged by her volunteer work experience, S settled on occupational therapy as a possible career.

*Establishing Ties Within the Community:* At the end of the forty-five day period of informal supervision, S was still actively involved as a volunteer and had completed more than forty-five hours of work. She had also arranged to attend junior college immediately upon graduation from high school. S maintained contact with her counselor from Arbitration, and recently confirmed that she was attending junior college.

**CASE #3**

*The Child and His Offense:* R is a sixteen year old male with no prior record. He was referred to the Department of Juvenile Services for disorderly conduct and interfering with a police officer.

*The Arbitrator's Decision:* During the hearing R explained that he has been with a large group of youths, who were between thirteen and twenty-two years old, at a private community beach. Citizens in the area complained to the police about the loud noise, abusive language and drinking. When police arrived at the beach, R tried to open the door of a police car to free two other youths who had already been arrested.

The Arbitrator stressed that R might have helped his friends in a legal manner by, for example, notifying their parents. R had disrupted the legal process and interferred with the rights of others to use the beach. Therefore the Arbitrator requested R complete fifteen hours of work.

*Informal Supervision:* The counselor from Arbitration discovered that R was the youngest of three children. R's older brother had completed law school, and his sister was in a nursing program. His father was a chemical engineer and his mother a nurse. R's siblings had been achievers in high school, and had been active in school clubs and sports. R was an average 10th grade student with little improvement in school-related activities. He also felt that he had few close friends.

The counselor decided that R would benefit from establishing ties within his community, but there was not an established service which might offer R an opportunity to become involved. A new counseling service was, however, just opening. The counselor arranged for R to assist a social worker in the new service by helping him to set up his office. R made posters, moved furniture, and helped to build room dividers. The social worker supported R's efforts to join a youth football team and become involved in several school activities. Additionally, R began to assist the worker in his work with younger children.

*Establishing Ties Within the Community:* The Arbitration staff member was able to engage R with one person in the community who offered a rather flexible relationship to R. Through that relationship, R gradually developed other ties within his school and neighborhood.

---

In the juvenile court setting, the criminal justice practitioner serves as the source of treatment information and must interpret the youngster to the court. The criminal justice practitioner must be sure to make recommendations that are not only relevant for each case, but are also based on available services. A recommendation for an intensive residential program for psychotherapy, for example, is irrelevant if such a program is simply not available for the youth. A particular problem for social service workers in this setting is the paucity of available resources. Private agencies, although they often receive a great deal of public, tax-supported, funding, usually retain the right to screen youngsters and thus reject any case that they believe does not fit into their program. This often translates into rejecting seriously disturbed or acting-out youngsters. In such situations, where the worker believes the youngster can gain from a particular program, but has been rejected, the practitioner must assume an advocate role. This may involve mobilizing those influences that are available within a court setting in order to pressure the agency to accept the youngster for care.

### AN ADOLESCENT TREATMENT UNIT

The Drenk Memorial Guidance Center in New Jersey is a private agency which receives juvenile court referrals. Richard Quane, the Director of the Adolescent Outpatient Treatment Unit, provides a look at the program, emphasizing the problems encountered by a private agency in dealing with court referred clients. In particular, he notes the problem of client resistance and the complementary problem of agency resistance to treating court referred clientelle.[29]

Our experience and contacts with other private agencies suggests that they are experiencing an increase in the number of referrals from judicial sources, and that they are also experiencing considerable difficulty in servicing these referrals. We believe our experience to be typical.

This problem has two parts, the first part is client resistance. The second part is agency resistance. The typical hostility, resistance, and offensiveness of clients with characterological problems create for many professionals an impasse in the treatment process. It is a common complaint of Judges who refer youngsters to mental health agencies that the agencies involved respond with "the youngster doesn't want to be seen so we can't help him". The Judge's position typically is, "Of course he doesn't want to be seen, he's only there because I referred him, but I want him seen and to receive help whether he's willing and eager or not."

This is the constant dilemma of the community mental health agency. Can and should the agency continue in treatment those youngsters and adults referred by the Court when they are not willing recipients of the services provided? After wrestling with this problem for a number of years, making many minor and major adjustments in our referral procedures and approach to these clients, we at the Drenk Memorial Guidance Center decided to meet the problem head on and to accept the fact of client resistance and hostility and also to accept that the Judge had a legal right to order treatment.

[29]Adapted from Richard M. Quane, "The Court Referred Client: Problem or Opportunity?"—an unpublished paper. Reprinted by permission of the author.

## Adolescent Outpatient Treatment Unit (A.O.T.U.) Operation

We decided to approach these clients, with the thesis, "You are here because you were referred by the Court, whether you wish to be here or not is immaterial at the moment. If you don't attend sessions as scheduled, this will be reported to the Court and it is our understanding that they will take some affirmative action to either assure your attendance or see that there are some negative consequences for you as a result of your nonattendance." We decided then that since this approach was so different from the typical approach taken with voluntary clients referred from other sources, that we would set up a special Unit separated from the regular outpatient clinic in terms of staff, location, and mode of operation. It was our belief at the time that this approach would make it possible to provide a more cohesive, effective, and therapeutically meaningful approach to services for these clients.

The A.O.T.U. utilizes a two part approach to the treatment and rehabilitation of delinquent youngsters. The first part is a treatment program designed to meet the needs of acting out youngsters. The second part is guided supervision from the probation officer or volunteer probation counselor assigned to the youngster. The staff of the Adolescent Outpatient Treatment Unit assists the probation officers by supplying information as to the dynamics and treatment of these youngsters and specific areas that would yield maximum benefits in terms of supervision.

Our major thrust is in the area of a relevant treatment program for the youngster and quite possibly his or her parents.

Our Unit started out with the assumption that you cannot treat clients who are not present. Therefore, our first objective was to insure that the clients attended. Typically noncompliant, these clients very often test the concern and interest of the Court and other agencies involved by failing to keep appointments. Follow up by both the Probation Department and the A.O.T.U. has resulted in good attendance levels.

Once we have the youngsters attending the Unit, it is necessary to have treatment programs geared towards their special needs and to have staff members experienced in dealing with these clients. It is also essential that a close working relationship be developed with the Probation Officers supervising each case and that the youngsters involved be fully aware of this close working relationship. It is our feeling that these two elements of our program are necessary conditions for effective intervention with court referred youngsters.

### Treatment Programs

Eighty to eighty-five percent of our treatment is conducted in a variety of different group modalities. . . .

Regardless of the particular type of group a youngster is in, a concrete, active orientation on the part of the therapist is necessary. The therapists structure and lead the group and set limits all of which are less necessary with adult group populations. The group therapist also provides an atmosphere of caring and concern (nurturing) for the youngster which is a model for the rest of the group. The therapist generally uses more confrontation, explanation, interpretation, and direction in these groups than in more sophisticated voluntary groups. We have found that without this active orientation on the part of the therapist, adolescent groups tend to wither and stagnate.

Initial intake and assessment in the A.O.T.U. takes place in what is called the *Initial Intervention and Screening Group* (IISG). This is a group intake procedure lasting three sessions. . . . This particular intake method allowed the court to set the initial appointment within the two weeks following the youngster's court appearance. Both the rapidity with which the appointment is set, and, setting the appointment at the court at the time of sentencing, are positive factors in assuring compliance.

In the IISG youngsters and parents are seen together while the program is explained, introductions are made and any issues general to both groups, that is parents and youngsters, can be addressed. Following ten or fifteen minutes, the usual procedure is to split the groups into one group of parents and one group of youngsters. One staff member goes with the parents and one with the youngsters. The focus in these sessions is to develop an understanding of the major factors contributing to the youngsters' delinquency. In this way it's possible for us at the unit to gear the treatment program for each youngster to focus on specific areas of conflict which are more likely to yield results.

Following the three sessions we then have an individual recommendation session with the youngster and his parents. In this session we share our assessment. This attempts to answer the question, how come this particular youngster got into trouble? We also share our recommendations to the court for probationary supervision. If we do not feel that our unit's efforts are appropriate for the youngster we will also share this information and make an appropriate referral to another agency.

This information is communicated to the court. Our recommendations, if the court concurs, become a condition of the youngsters probation.

When a youngster remains in the treatment programs of the A.O.T.U. he can be placed in any one of a number of treatment modalities. *Activity Groups:* Youngsters respond positively to treatment groups centering around activities such as playing pool. Activity groups provide a gradual and less frightening introduction to talking about problems for youngsters who find a more verbal mode of treatment too inhibiting. *Drug Dependent Groups:* A very real problem is the reliance of many of the youngsters we see on drug induced highs in order to "feel good" about themselves and their life. We have instituted a group treatment program for drug users designed to help them discover alternative ways of feeling good. *Guided Group Interaction (GGI):* GGI groups are reality oriented and utilize peer pressure to encourage participation and success in socially acceptable enterprises. *Coed Treatment Groups:* For those youngsters able to tolerate more verbal, dynamic and personality change oriented treatment programs, we have experimented with and found effective coed treatment groups. Parents may also participate in either Directive Parent Counseling groups or Parent Therapy groups. A relatively small percentage of youngsters and parents are seen in individual or family therapy.

## THE PRINCIPLE OF LEAST-RESTRICTIVE ACTION

The juvenile system is "governed" by the philosophy of the *least-restrictive action*—"a juvenile should never be locked up when any feasible alternative exists and if no alternative to detention exists, a juvenile should not be locked up any longer than it takes to develop an alternative."[30] This philosophy emphasizes rehabilitation rather than punishment and is the basis for the disposition ordered by the juvenile court.

*Juvenile probation* is used by the juvenile court to provide supervised guidance for adjudicated delinquents and status offenders or to provide services to neglected or abused children. Probation epitomizes the "least-restrictive action," providing service with a minimum of interference with freedom. This freedom, however, is limited, and the juvenile is subject to probation rules. These rules usually "exhort" and "threaten"—e.g., live as a good citizen; do not associate with criminals. In the case of a juvenile there are often specific conditions relating to attending school and/or an employment program. The probationer is required to report in person or maintain telephone or written contact with his/her probation officer. In theory the probation supervision of a juvenile is an intensive casework situation—in practice it is often perfunctory.

*Juvenile institutions* can be either public or private, with the former usually referred to as "training schools" and the latter as "residential treatment facilities/centers." In practice both types of institutions may be government operated or supported. The residential treatment

---

[30]Alan R. Coffey, *Juvenile Corrections*, (Englewood Cliffs, N.J.: Prentice-Hall, 1975), p. 158.

center (rtc) will be characterized by greater freedom as opposed to the strict confinement of the training school. The diagnostic process which determines to what type of institution a youngster will be sent may be accomplished by the probation department, or a diagnostic unit operated by a state agency for youth. Coffey describes the diagnostic process, noting that some states operate institutions (diagnostic or reception centers) which provide this service:[31]

> Diagnostic studies delineate subsequent treatment programs, but the purpose of most reception centers is assessment rather than treatment. The center is staffed with psychologists, psychometricians, psychiatrists, and other physicians. Educational specialists are also frequently used. These institutions do not hold juveniles for long periods—about two and one-half months on the average. Many juveniles are released on parole directly from the reception center. Many more are transferred to training schools.

The use of juvenile institutional care, in particular the training school, is not without controversy. Training schools have been characterized by their failure to provide "meaningful" treatment—educational, vocational and therapeutic services—while maintaining punitive environments. Thus, despite the rather high cost of maintaining such institutions, Ohlin, Coates and Miller state:[32]

> Punishment is a key organizing principle of traditional training schools. There are efforts at vocational and general education in the training schools, but the institutions are basically custodial and authoritarian. Resocialization efforts are commonly reduced to instruments for creating conformity, deference to adult authority, and obedience to rules. Regimented marching formations, shaved heads and close haircuts, omnipresent officials, and punitive disciplinary measures have been authoritative marks of the training school, along with the manipulation of privileges, such as cigarette smoking, television viewing, or release to reward compliance.[33]

The authors point out that the training school is often employed "as a principal means of control and treatment for primarily lower class

[31]Ibid., p. 98.

[32]Lloyd E. Ohlin, Robert B. Coates, and Alden D. Miller, "Radical Correctional Reform: A Case Study of the Massachusetts Youth Correctional System," reprinted in *Juvenile Correctional Reform in Massachusetts*, prepared by Ohlin et al. (Washington, D.C.: United States Government Printing Office, 1977), p. 1.

[33]The manipulation of privileges mentioned here are often part of the "token economy."

offenders," while diversion to privately purchased services has been used extensively for middle-class youths with similar problems. They report on the efforts of Massachusetts to reform its juvenile correctional system by providing privately purchased services for lower-class youngsters as an alternative to training school care.

Between the relative freedom of probation and the relative restrictions of the training school are other types of juvenile care:

(a) *Camp-Ranch-Farm*—a facility characterized by its rural location.

(b) *Group Home*—a nonconfining facility intended to reproduce as closely as possible the circumstances of family life and at a minimum provides access to community activities and services.[34]

(c) *Half-Way House*—a nonconfining residential facility intended to provide an alternative to confinement for persons not suitable for probation or those needing a period of readjustment to the community after confinement.[35]

(d) *Day-Care Centers*—a facility in which programs are conducted for juveniles who are not in residence, but who are assigned to the program. The juvenile usually reports daily for an educational, vocational, and treatment program which may include probation supervision.[36]

(e) *Foster Homes*—used in selective cases, often with neglected and abused children, whose cases do not call for institutionalization but who need to be placed outside of their own homes.

While in any of these programs the youngster may remain under the auspices of the probation department or may be supervised by a probation officer when released to after-care.

*Juvenile after-care* (parole) may be administered by the probation department, the institution from which the youngster was released, a special agency or subunit of an agency set up specifically for that purpose, or after-care may be part of the adult parole supervision agency's responsibilities. The work of the after-care officer is almost identical to that of the supervising juvenile probation officer in the court setting.

---

[34]*Dictionary of Criminal Justice Data Terminology.*
[35]Ibid.
[36]Coffey, p. 202.

## In a Prosecution Setting

The official duty of a prosecutor is to initiate and maintain criminal proceedings on behalf of the government against persons accused of committing criminal offenses. Customary names for these prosecutors include United States Attorney, district attorney, and state's attorney. The work of a social service practitioner in this setting is usually limited to diversion programs. An observation of the President's Commission set the stage for the extensive use of prosecutorial diversion. The Commission recommended:[37]

> Prosecutors should endeavor to make discriminating charge decisions, assuring that offenders who merit criminal sanctions are not released and that other offenders are either released or diverted to noncriminal methods of treatment and control by:
>
> Establishment of explicit policies for the dismissal or informal disposition of the cases of certain marginal offenders.
>
> Early identification and diversion to other community resources of those offenders in need of treatment, for whom full criminal disposition does not appear required.

### PROSECUTORIAL DIVERSION PROGRAMS

*Citizens Probation Authority.* Leonard and Saxe provide a summary of the diversion program used in Genesee County, New York: the Citizens Probation Authority.[38]

In their review, Leonard and Saxe note that the number of defendants placed on probation has declined as the cases placed with the Citizens Probation Authority has increased, and they conclude that adult cases which would have been processed through to probation are being diverted to the Citizens Probation Authority.

Leonard and Saxe state:[39]

> The legal authority for the existence of a program of deferred prosecution is solely constituted in the powers of the prosecuting attorney. All decisions affecting the legal status of the accused are the absolute and final authority of the prosecuting attorney. The

[37]*The Challenge of Crime in a Free Society,* pp. 331–32.

[38]Robert F. Leonard and Joel Saxe, *Screening of Criminal Cases* (Chicago: National District Attorneys Association, 1973), pp. 27–30. Reprinted by permission of the Publisher.

[39]Ibid., p. 27.

prosecutor is guided in policy making by recommendations of the Citizens Probation Authority and a 25-man Advisory Council (in Genesee). The Advisory Council represents a broad cross-section of the community and acts as a "sounding board" of community interests and concerns. It also acts as a liaison with the public.

The program developed in Genesee County began as a function of the Prosecuting Attorney's Office in 1965, utilizing volunteer citizens of social work and related professional backgrounds. In 1967 a professional staff was hired and the program was formally separated from the prosecutor's office. Robert F. Leonard, the Prosecutor, felt that the program should be apart from the formal law enforcement system in order to preserve its value as a voluntary, rehabilitative extra-legal device. Although a separate county department, the program continues to operate under the broad discretionary authority of the prosecuting attorney.

Leonard and Saxe outline the program:[40]

> . . .the Citizens Probation Authority uses very strict screening controls resulting in the selection of only the most rehabilitatable among the offenders for inclusion in its program. One other significant factor in the success of the Citizens Probation Authority is the fact that the offender begins almost immediately after the commission of the offense rather than the delay of four to six to eight months which often occurs between arrest and final sentencing. There is a distinct advantage to being able to deal with the offender at the moment when the magnitude of his offense as an anti-social act is still uppermost in his mind and before he's had an opportunity to spend months making excuses for himself or learning from jailhouse lawyers how to beat the rap or not get caught the next time.
>
> In Genesee County, the probation violation rate for clients of the Citizens Probation Authority has averaged under 5 percent, with many of those being technical violators rather than actual recidivating criminals. Adult probation violation rates often double that figure with many technical and actual criminal violators being continued on probation and not reflected in the recidivism rates.

*Operational Characteristics*

The Citizens Probation Authority is limited to handling adult felony offenders who are residents of the county, who have not committed a crime of violence and who do not have a record

[40]Ibid., p. 28–30.

displaying a continuing pattern of anti-social behavior. All offenders who meet these criteria are referred automatically to the Citizens Probation Authority by the prosecuting attorney. The primary purpose of this automatic referral is to preserve an equitable justice system and avoid any discriminatory practices.

The Citizens Probation Authority interviews the offender, advises him fully of his constitutional rights, describes the program to him, and asks him for permission to conduct a confidential background investigation. If the CPA is satisfied that the offender meets the referral criteria and the offender expresses his desire to continue voluntarily with the program, a thorough investigation into the offender's background, including school and financial records, with interviews of the family, employer and others, is conducted. At all times, participation is voluntary and the offender may withdraw from the program to exercise his constitutional rights to court adjudication.

All of this information is confidential and off the record. It is apparent to the prosecutor that he must preserve such confidentiality for the sake of the continued success of the program. Upon completion of this personal and social history investigation, a 'treatment plan' is recommended to the prosecutor. If the prosecutor believes this to be a realistic plan serving the best interests of the community and the offender, and the offender has agreed to abide by the conditions of the treatment plan for a period of one year, then the prosecutor consents to defer further prosecution pending the offender's successful completion of the probation period. For failure to complete any of the conditions of his probation agreement, the case may be returned to the prosecutor's office and a warrant requested. Upon successful completion of the program, further prosecution is dismissed and the police records are expunged.

It should be noted that the Citizens Probation Authority is not intended to modify criminal behavior. The success of the program, therefore, has not been in preventing recidivism, but in successfully screening out low-risk lawbreakers.

*Dade County Pre-Trial Intervention Project.*    Mullen presents a review of the diversion program used in Dade County, Florida (Miami).[41]

### Dade County Project Design

The Dade County Pre-Trial Intervention Project ... was designed to achieve the dual goals of service to the defendant (through

[41]Joan Mullen, *The Dilemma of Diversion* (Washington, D.C.: United States Government Printing Office, 1975), pp. 105–12.

pre-trial counseling, vocational and educational support, as well as the possibility of a dismissed case) and the criminal justice system (through more responsive pre-trial screening, and relief for overburdened probation caseloads.... Although the relationship with the State Attorney's Office has consistently been a close one, there is no official administrative connection between the project and that office. The State Attorney has provided office space, certain matching monies, the use of official stationary and the time of an administrative assistant to routinely approve project recommendations and terminate the court processing of appropriate project cases.

### Dade County Eligibility Criteria and Participant Characteristics

Based on the project's goal of reaching first-offenders, eligibility criteria are defined as follows:

1. No prior criminal record;
2. Male or female between the ages of 17 and 25;
3. Charged with a misdemeanor or certain third degree felonies such as grand larceny, breaking and entering, or unathorized use of an automobile;
4. Dade County resident;
5. In need of services provided by the project;
6. Not a narcotics addict (experimental users are considered).

A seventh criterion, required of all participants, is the consent of the victim and the arresting officer involved in the case. Although neither party usually objects, project personnel feel that this stipulation has led to a more positive image of the program among police and the general public.[42]

### Dade County Screening and Intake Procedures

Dade County PTI [Pre-trial Intervention] uses bond hearings as the primary method for participant identification. The Project Director or his secretary attend the hearings and scan police and PTR [Pre-trial Referral] reports on all cases. Where the criteria for participation appear to be met, "Pre-trial Intervention Project" is stamped on the court form. That same day, letters go out to the defendant, the victim and arresting police officer. The defendant is advised of the program and his eligibility and is asked to call the project office for an interview. The letter indicates that charges will not be filed if the defendant contacts the project within ten

---

[42]While these criteria are fundamentally followed, in practice they are more broadly and flexibly applied. Some second offenders have been accepted, and certain defendants with more serious felony charges have been accepted.

days. If the defendant does not respond, no outreach is attempted and the case is returned to the court calendar.

## Dade County Service Delivery

Counseling is the primary focus of the program's service delivery strategy. All participants are required to attend one individual and one group counseling session per week. Caseloads are grouped on a geographic basis with a maximum of 20 cases per counselor.

According to the Director, the specific goal of counseling activities is personal growth and development. In addition to dealing with specific individual and family problems, sessions are designed to increase an individual's awareness of him or herself and his or her effect on other people, and to heighten the ability to relate more openly and honestly to individual and group situations.

Apart from the strong emphasis on counseling support, there appeared to be limits on the *coordinated* services staff is able to provide. Vocational training opportunities in the area are limited although the Division of Vocational Rehabilitation has been somewhat helpful. Job placements have been difficult

Outside educational resources have not been used as extensively as had been hoped; in-house educational assistance has been limited; and community health and mental health services have not tended to graciously receive project participants.

Project objectives focus on the defendant of lower economic class, emphasizing the need to provide expanded opportunities, to promote upward mobility and thereby theoretically reduce criminal activity. While this group participates in the project, there is also a substantial group, possibly a more substantial group, of non-economically disadvantaged participants.

## Dade County Termination Procedures

Successful termination of participants is the decision of the case counselor, the assistant administrator, and the project consultant. The Project Director routinely approves termination at an informal conference in his office with the defendant and his or her parents. The defendant does not appear before the court upon successful termination. The Project Director, following routine approval by the administrative assistant to the State Attorney, submits a communication to the court that no criminal information will be filed. Reportedly, this disposition is entered into the criminal justice information system which will reflect successful completion of the program.

Unsuccessful termination may occur by an individual counselor advising the defendant he or she has been deselected, or by a counseling group's decision that the defendant's behavior merits deselection. Termination is usually based on clear evidence of non-cooperation including: a re-offense; dropping out of an educational program without informing the project; not working and not seeking a job; failure to appear for a number of counseling sessions; smoking marijuana out in front of the project office before or after a group meeting. Defendants who are unsuccessfully terminated are not routinely advised of any right to appeal this decision, but if they ask, the counselor may advise them they can appeal to the Project Director. On occasions, the Director has reinstated a defendant.

*Personnel*

*Project Director*: The Project Director maintains an office in the State Attorney's Office. His major duties are to maintain coordination between the project and the State Attorney's Office and to select project participants at bond hearings. Recommendations concerning case dispositions may be made by the Project Director without further validation by the State Attorney's Office.

*Consultants*: Two psychologists are used by the project as professional consultants. One, who works about two-thirds time, supervises all psychological and aptitude testing. In addition, he co-leads group sessions with counselors and provides family counseling services. The second, who gives the project about six hours a week, participates in weekly counseling staff meetings. He leads a therapy group for participants who need a more intensive group experience, leads a parents' group, and is in charge of research and staff training.

*Counselors*: There are presently 9 staff counselors. The Chief counselor assists in the training of new counselors by having them accompany him on home visits and field contacts. He also advises counselors on problem cases.

Counselors generally carry a maximum of 20 cases. Each client must be seen individually once a week either in the office or in the field. Counselors also lead a compulsory group meeting for all their clients once a week. Counselors are required to spend one day a week in the office to meet new clients and schedule appointments. They receive both on-the-job and in-service training from the chief counselor and the two consultants.

*Counselor Aides*: A new position established nine months ago, counselor-aides are students in Dade Community College's New Careers Program. They attend classes two days a week and work in social agencies three days. The project signed a two-year contract with Dade to support three counselor-aides per semester.

One aide has been designated a Job Developer, a role that has been unfilled since the assistant director stopped serving that function. Counselor-aides do initial interviews of new candidates and administer initial tests. Two former project participants, who work at the project office on a part-time basis, also interview new candidates.

*Other Staff:* In addition to project staff described above, an Assistant State Attorney serves part-time to review all potential PTI cases. Another member of the State Attorney's Office is in charge of case dispositions and plea negotiations. Finally, an Assistant Public Defender is assigned to the project to advise potential participants and represent indigent participants at court appearances.

## In a Public Defender Setting

Arrest and trial are traumatic experiences which can affect the ability of a defendant to function properly and be of aid in the preparation of his own defense. In recognition of this, public defender agencies are, increasingly, providing social services as part of their legal defense operations. To a large extent, the social service units are seen as an extension of the advocacy role that is inherent in the practice of law. One such program began in 1973 under the auspices of the New York City Legal Aid Society, an agency that provides counsel for indigent defendants.[43] The program has as its basic purpose to provide social services to clients and enhance the quality of their defense by:

a. on going, long-term, counseling;

b. referral to various community resources;

c. emergency referrals for clients of legal aid attorneys; and

d. verification of information towards the preparation of progress reports for diversion, and also for presentence memoranda.

*Presentence memoranda* are provided for under New York State Law (390.40 CPL) which allows for the inclusion of a report from the defense highlighting positive aspects of the defendant and recommending a disposition favorable to the defendant, e.g., probation. (An example of such a report appears in Appendix F.)

[43]The author wishes to acknowledge the assistance of Rosalind Lichter, Director of the Legal Aid Society Pre-Trial Diversion and Presentence Program who provided the information for most of this section.

In order to be considered for the program, a defendant must meet the following criteria:

1. be charged with a felony, but not have a criminal history which includes a felony conviction, unless there is a reasonable chance that only program intervention could be instrumental in reducing the charge to a misdemeanor; and
2. the client must manifest a degree of willingness to work with the program and be receptive to suggestions and aid. A client who does not cooperate is dropped.

Social services are provided by a social worker and field counselor. The social worker handles the intake interview and determines case acceptability. He/she also prepares all diagnostic reports as well as the presentence memoranda. The field counselor gathers information out in the community, visiting the client's residence and verifying information relative to past employment, education, and community adjustment. He/she may also develop community resources necessary for a defendant's proposed treatment plan.

The diversion aspect of the program attempts "to set forth sociological and psychological factors often so closely related to an individual's court involvement and, in light of these factors, to provide the court with viable alternatives to incarceration." Rosalind Lichter, the program director, explains with respect to the presentence report:[44]

> While the lawyer can contend with the legal aspects of a client's case, he/she is probably not prepared or trained to deal either with sociological and psychological facts relevant to the case or with perceiving and refuting fallacies in these areas that may appear in the probation report. The Diversion teams have the training and the means to delve into a client's background and to use this to effectively supplement a legal defense.

The procedures and goals of the program are described as follows:[45]

> One of the most substantial services our programs can give to clients is that of continual support throughout the ordeal of involvement in the criminal justice system. Oftentimes, having a person, other than an attorney, available to talk to can be of more help than anything else to a client. This section will not attempt to

[44]Program Training Guide (mimeo).
[45]Ibid.

go into specific counselling techniques to be used, but rather will deal with more general information and advice.

The first meeting with the client is generally one that outlines the goals of the Diversion/Presentence Program and the responsibilities of the client within the framework of our mutual goals. At this time the Social Worker should assess the degree of the client's willingness to work with the program and the direction to be followed with the client based on his/her needs.

Basic data on the client's background is also recorded during this first meeting. It is important for the Social Worker to initiate these basic data questions because frequently a much more substantive response from the client can be gleaned through asking the simplest questions, if posed by someone who is more interested in the response the client has than in merely checking off rote categories on the data collection form.

The number of times the Social Worker sees a client depends upon the client's needs, the availability of the client, and the client's relationship to the Social Worker and team. The counselling techniques can be categorized as supportive and/or reality counselling, although the programs consciously avoid using any one form of counselling for all clients and strategies may vary with each person. Basically, counsellors: offer support during the period of court involvement; suggest ways in which a client may be instrumental in helping him/herself; attempt to work through with the client areas of personal tension and problems affecting him/her during this period; attempt to work with family members; and attempt to work with the client in allowing him/her to express any underlying problems leading up to the court involvement. If background problems seem to require more help than we are able to provide, the counsellor should try to make recommendations for more long term or professional treatment.

During counseling the Social Worker should strive to project a sense of honesty and to establish a mutual credibility with the client. A client's involvement in the court and the possibility of doing jail time should not be glossed over, but rather the counsellor should try to focus on the serious consequences this present involvement may have on the client's future. When describing a community program or employment source to a client, the Social Worker and Field Counsellor should present a realistic picture of the program and the services it may or may not provide. If a residential program is being considered, the client should be apprised of its rules and basic treatment philosophy before deciding to enter. In general, a type of reality therapy and overall honesty on the part of the staff appears to be the most effective means to establish our clients' trust and maintain an open relationship. However, this should not be taken as a blanket policy. The Social

Worker's discretion and clinical knowledge should always be employed when formulating the best approach to use with a particular client, especially in an on-going counselling situation. Also, be sure the client knows that we are protected by the lawyer/client privilege and that everything he/she says is completely confidential.

The Social Worker can effectively analyze a client's sociological background and formulate some of the psychological factors that could be operating given the client's background, education, family ties, employment history, medical history, etc. This information is passed on to the sentencing judge in the Presentence Memorandum, when deemed helpful towards effecting a favorable court disposition. It also assists the Social Worker in making an appropriate referral to a community program that can provide longer term treatment if such treatment is necessary.

## In a Court Setting

In 1966 the President's Commission noted that "money bail is an unfair and ineffective device. Its glaring weakness is that it discriminates against poor defendants, thus running directly counter to the law's avowed purpose of treating all defendants equally."[46] Based on its findings the Commission recommended:[47]

Bail projects should be undertaken at the State, county, and local levels to furnish judicial officers with sufficient information to permit the pretrial release without financial condition of all but that small portion who present a high risk of flight or dangerous acts prior to trial.

### PRE-TRIAL SERVICES

One such bail project, *Pre-Trial Services,* is operating is Des Moines.[48] The program has components that resemble, or are identical to, probation investigation and supervision. The purpose of the pretrial release-on-own-recognizance (ROR) component of the community corrections program is to release, without money bond, adult defendants

[46]*The Challenge of Crime in a Free Society,* p. 326.
[47]Ibid., p. 327.
[48]This project is described in David Boorkman, Ernest, J. Fazio, Jr., Noel Day, and David Weinstein, *Community-Based Corrections in Des Moines* (Washington, D.C.: United States Government Printing Office, 1976), pp. 15–26, A-26–29, A-62–68.

whose stable roots in the community indicate that they will appear in court for trial.

Interviews are conducted by law students who work on a part-time basis. They are responsible for conducting and verifying all eligibility interviews with defendants and for preparing recommendations regarding release. In other jurisdictions this function is carried out by social service workers. Interviews are conducted in various jails and lock-ups, and all information provided by the defendant is verified by reference checks. The employer is not, as a rule, contacted since this might jeopardize the defendant's job. A thorough check of his/her police record is conducted. When the verification process is completed, a scoring system is used to determine the recommendation to the court. If the judge accepts the recommendation he authorizes the release of the defendant. For those defendant's who do not qualify for or are denied release on their own recognizance, there is a second component of the program, supervised release.

Supervised release serves those defendants who, because of their lack of community ties and/or their more serious criminal backgrounds, are denied release on their own recognizance. The component seeks to provide a range of services to assist such defendants in rearranging their lives. The purpose of the program is, therefore, not only to release the maximum number of persons consonant with public safety, but also to assist the released defendant to become qualified for probation if convicted. Pre-Trial Services are organized as follows.[49]

> The supervised release unit is staffed by a supervisor, two selection team members (one is also the supervisor of the ROR component and the other is an ex-convict), four counselors, a three-man job development team, and a secretary. The supervisor is responsible for the overall administration of the component. He also makes all counselor assignments, passes on all release bond revocations, and carries a counseling caseload as well.
>
> The two-man selection team is responsible for selecting defendants to participate in the program. They review case files and conduct interviews with all candidates for the program, develop recommendations for release in those instances where their experience and judgment suggest that a defendant will utilize the program's resources, present their recommendations to the court, and obtain the release of those defendants following the approval of the court.
>
> Counselors are responsible for working with defendants on an on-going basis throughout the pretrial period. They administer

[49]Ibid., pp. 15–26.

diagnostic tests and interview defendants to identify other areas of need or problems that might be obstacles to successful participation in the program. Counselors also draw up contracts between the defendant and the program that specify both what the program expects from the defendant in the way of participation, behavior, and attitudes, and what the program can be expected to provide in return. In addition, counselors are responsible for developing a "plan for action"—or treatment plan—with each defendant that defines short- and long-term goals and identifies the resources the counselor proposes to utilize in helping the defendant reach those goals. Each defendant's "plan for action" then serves as the basis for on-going counseling and referral activities.

On the average, each counselor has a caseload of 20–25 defendants. Assignment of clients is made on a random basis with no special considerations given to the respective race or sex of the client or counselor. Problem cases are subject to reassignment, but in such instances revocation of the pre-trial release bond and reincarceration are alternatives also available to the supervisor. Some special assignments are made at the suggestion of the selection team. One selection team member also has, in recent months, been assigned to work with a small caseload consisting of those clients who are deemed to be such high risk defendants that they might otherwise be rejected by the program.

The supervised release component also has access to a consulting psychiatrist who is available to the program on a regular part-time basis. The psychiatrist screens all of the participants in the program through interviews, reviews scores on diagnostic tests, and consults with and advises counselors on referrals and counseling procedures.

The job development team is made up of a job developer, a vocational rehabilitation specialist on loan from the Area Vocation/Rehabilitation Program, and an employment specialist on loan from the Iowa State Employment Service. Functionally, the job development team serves both the supervised release and the probation components.

The vocational rehabilitation specialist is responsible both for assessing the vocational interests, skills, and strengths of those defendants who need assistance in finding jobs or in obtaining better jobs, and for identifying any specific obstacles to employment that might be addressed by the state's Department of Vocational Rehabilitation—such as prosthetic devices, hearing aids, special tools or clothing (helmets, masks, etc.), or manpower training.

The job developer and the employment specialist, on the other hand, are responsible for identifying possible jobs, convincing employers to hire defendants, and for helping the defendant to prepare for the job interview and application process. Following placement, the job. developer is responsible for conducting periodic checks with the employer regarding the defendant's attendance and performance.

*Process.* There are seven basic tasks involved in the supervised release process:

- Selection
- Release
- Intake
- Testing
- Counseling and Referral
- Job Development and Placement
- Termination

Since pre-trial periods vary, the actual duration of defendants' involvement with the supervised release component also varies considerably. On the average, however, the length of time between pre-trial release from jail and sentencing after trial is 110 days in Des Moines.

Once a counselor has been assigned to work with a particular client, he is briefed and introduced to the client. The initial meeting between the counselor and the client usually takes place on the day the client is released—or, at the very latest, the next day. During the first meeting, the client is asked to sign a waiver of privacy granting the program access to any information in the files of other agencies that might otherwise be confidential; the counselor reviews the general rules of the program and any special conditions imposed on the client; and the counselor goes over the provisions of the basic supervised release contract which the client has to make with the program. The contract acknowledges the relationship between the program and the client, details the conditions of release, and specifies the consequences of any breach of the contract by the client. If the client is not willing to sign the contract, the release bond can be revoked immediately and the defendant returned to jail. Finally, during the first meeting with the client, the counselor establishes the schedule for further counseling sessions and for administration of the battery of diagnostic tests which the program utilizes.

*Counseling and referral.* Clients are only in the supervised release program for an average of 110 days prior to trial and during that period the main thrust of the program is aimed at helping clients develop the kind of "track record"—in terms of stability and accomplishment—that will qualify them for probation if they are convicted. To achieve this objective, the supervised release component's counselors utilize an approach to counseling that is reality oriented and directive.

Counselors establish both short-term and long-term counseling goals with the first few sessions with the client. Counseling goals and the approach and methods the counselor intends to utilzie in reaching those goals are specified in a "plan for action"—a treatment plan—for each client. Long-term goals—including goals related to the development of educational and vocational skills—are frequently based on information about the client's needs, interests, and capabilities that is derived from an anlysis of the client's diagnostic test scores. Short-term goals, on the other hand, are most often focused on addressing the kinds of immediate needs and problems that continually disrupt clients' lives on a day-to-day basis and that keep them from dealing with their long-term needs.

Counselors, therefore, devote a great deal of initial attention to identifying those resources in the community that might be called upon to help address clients' pressing need for things like housing, subsistence food supplies, clothing, or family support. The kinds of agencies counselors most frequently contact on behalf of clients are agencies like the local public housing authority, sectarian agencies, public and private welfare agencies, food stamp distribution centers, agencies providing mental health services, family counseling services, or alcohol and drug abuse centers.

In helping clients deal with short-term needs, then, counselors identify the appropriate resources, give the client basic information about those resources, initiate referrals, actively follow up on referrals, and act as the client's advocate in assuring that agencies respond to their request for services.

Counselors draw on a number of resources to help clients achieve long-term goals. Clients who do not have a high school diploma or its equivalent are enrolled in the GED (General Educational Diploma) classes that are held at the supervised release component's office two nights a week. The GED exam—a high school equivalency examination—is administered at regular intervals so that the clients can learn at their own rate and take the exam whenever their achievement justifies it and they feel ready. Teachers from the local community college conduct classes as part of the college's regular program; thus, there is no cost involved for the community corrections program.

Clients who are interested in higher education or some kinds of special vocational training may be referred by the counselor to the local community college's Urban Education Center. Counselors can also call upon the state's Department of Vocational Rehabilitation to help pay the tuition of some clients, to assist them in enrolling in federally funded manpower training programs, or to provide assistance in dealing with job-related disabilities or needs.

There are also a variety of evening activities at the supervised release component's offices that counselors may require clients to attend as part of the treatment plan. Evening activities are frequently cultural or informational in character. For example, various public and private agencies were invited to make presentations and answer questions in a series of evening meetings with clients.

Counselors monitor attendance at the special evening sessions. Extensive absence may result in either admonishment or, in extreme cases, in a decision to revoke the release bond and reincarcerate the client.

A substantial portion of the counselor's time is also spent in documenting the client's progress for use in the pre-sentence investigation conducted by the probation component if the defendant is convicted at trial.

If a client is unemployed at the time of entry into the program, the counselor works with the job development staff to assist the defendant with securing new employment.

There are two ways of terminating a client's relationship with the supervised release component—through revocation of the release bond or through judicial disposition of the case against the client. Revocation of release bond usually occurs in the event of a new arrest or for failure to appear in court. In those cases where the client goes to trial, the relationship between the program and the client ends as soon as a finding of not guilty is entered or as soon as the judge makes a dispositional decision if the defendant is found guilty.

### PRESENTENCE/SOCIAL INVESTIGATION

The presentence report (or social investigation report in the case of juvenile court) is the primary source of information for sentencing or (in the case of juveniles) disposition of cases. The report should provide the judge with information relative to ordering probation or institutionalization, and, with respect to the latter, the recommended length of the term. In addition, the report provides information for correctional authorities. More than a decade ago the President's Commission stated that all courts "should require presentence reports for all offenders, whether these reports result from full field investigations by probation officers, or in the case of minor offenders, from the use of short forms."[50] In 1973, another Presidential Commission, the National

[50]*The Challenge of Crime in a Free Society,* p. 355.

Advisory Commission on Criminal Justice Standards and Goals (NACCSG), made a similar recommendation:[51]

1. A presentence report should be presented to the court in every case where there is a potential sentencing disposition involving incarceration and in all cases involving felonies or minors.
2. Graduations of presentence reports should be developed between a full report and a short-form report for screening offenders to determine whether more information is desirable or for use when a full report is unnecessary.
3. A full presentence report should be prepared where the court determines it to be necessary, and without exception in every case where incarceration for more than five years is a possible disposition. A short-form report should be prepared for all other cases.

However, a study of the inadequacies of state and county probation systems by the Comptroller General's Office (of the United States) indicated that of eleven hundred cases studied in four counties, Maricopa (Arizona), Multnomah (Oregon), Philadelphia (Pennsylvania), and King (Washington), reports were prepared in little more than half of the cases.[52] That report noted that a presentence report should ideally contain:

1. verified information about the person's education, medical history, and previous crimes;
2. estimated chance of rehabilitation;
3. a recommendation for sentencing; and
4. an analysis of the offender's motivations and ambitions.

However this information was often either inadequate or omitted.[53] The report also revealed that although the National Advisory Commission had recommended that presentence reports contain a diagnostic statement and a suggested plan of treatment only 36 percent of the cases reviewed had such information.[54]

The format for a juvenile report is provided by Coffey in Figure

---

[51]National Advisory Commission on Criminal Justice Standards and Goals, *A National Strategy to Reduce Crime* (New York: Avon Books, 1975), p. 489.

[52]Office of the Comptroller General, *State and County Probation: Systems in Crisis* (Washington, D.C.: General Accounting Office, 1976), p. 19.

[53]Ibid., p. 20.

[54]Ibid., p. 21.

4-2.[55] Juvenile hearings are usually bifurcated into a jurisdictional and a dispositional phase when the petition (which parallels the prosecutor's charge in the adult court) is contested. This standard report format is similarly divided into two parts.

---

**FORMAT FOR A STANDARD JUVENILE REPORT FORM**

PART ONE

1. Petition
2. Legal Counsel
3. Reason for Hearing
4. Statement of Witnesses/Victim
5. Statement of Minor
6. Recommendations


PART TWO (Relates to the Needs of the Juvenile)

1. Previous Referrals
2. Present Whereabouts of Minor
3. Additional Circumstances
4. Adjustment Under Supervision
5. Statement of Minor
6. Statement of Parents/Guardian
7. Statement of Relative or Foster Parents
8. School Report
9. Juvenile Hall/Shelter Report
10. Psychological, Psychiatric, or Medical Reports
11. Personal and Family Background
12. Evaluation
13. Dispositional Recommendations

---

For adult cases the format usually is as follows:[56] (An example of a presentence report appears in appendix B)

[55]Alan R. Coffey, pp. 180–82.
[56]From U.S. Probation Presentence Form.

| | |
|---|---|
| OFFENSE | RELIGION |
| Official version | INTERESTS AND LEISURE- |
| Statement of codefendants | TIME ACTIVITIES |
| Statement of witnesses, | HEALTH |
| complainants, and victims | Physical |
| DEFENDANT'S VERSION | Mental and emotional |
| OF OFFENSE | EMPLOYMENT |
| PRIOR RECORD | MILITARY SERVICE |
| FAMILY HISTORY | FINANCIAL CONDITION |
| Defendant | Assets |
| Parents and siblings | Financial obligations |
| MARITAL HISTORY | EVALUATIVE SUMMARY |
| HOME AND NEIGHBORHOOD | RECOMMENDATION |
| EDUCATION | |

While the probation department usually prepares the report subsequent to a plea or finding of guilt, there has been a trend toward preparing the report as part of the plea bargaining process. Thus, in certain cases, with the consent of the defendant, a presentence investigation is conducted prior to sentencing and the resulting report serves as an information basis for negotiating a pleas of guilty. Although it is not uniform, in most jurisdictions the presentence report is usually disclosed to the defense counsel or the defendant. Confidential information, e.g., recommendations, psychiatric evaluations, and certain confidential police reports may be withheld. The disclosure of the contents of the presentence report provides the defendant with an opportunity to challenge information that he/she considers erroneous.

Schrink provides some recommendations for criminal justice practitioner's relative to preparing reports.[57] A great deal of a criminal justice practitioner's time (60 percent or more) is spent with tedious paperwork of one type or another. However, the proper preparation of certain types of "paperwork" (e.g., presentence reports) is an essential part of the duties of the criminal justice practitioners in this setting. Information collected and recorded in one part of the criminal justice system is often passed on to other parts. Misleading, erroneous, or poorly written information produced in one part of the sequence can affect the way other parts view and deal with the criminal justice client.

---

[57]Jeff Schrink, "Strategy For Preparing Correctional Reports," *Federal Probation* 40 (March 1976): 33–40.

Hagen notes that studies have indicated a "close and apparent causal relationship between recommendations and dispositions."[58] However, Dawson cautions that the probation officer may write into the report the recommendation that he thinks will be well-received by the judge.[59] Another caution is provided by Goffman. In his work on *Asylums*, Goffman discusses *case-history construction*, a retrospective look at a person "designed" to demonstrate the validity of (negative) conclusions that have already been drawn. Although Goffman is specifically discussing the mental patient, his observation is relevant for criminal justice. Any criminal justice record or report tends to highlight information about a person that is usually considered "scandalous." In this way, decisions to apply severe sanctions can be justified as the report is constructed to show that the offender has shown asocial or antisocial tendencies throughout much of his life.[60] Schrink provides a breakdown of the steps or stages involved in preparing a professional report in criminal justice.[61]

The purpose of the report will serve to determine what information it should contain and how that information is to be organized, in particular, who will read the report and what kind of decisions will be based on it. The client has a lifetime of information which the writer could conceivably delve into. However, since time is of the essence, the writer must develop a "minimax" standard—the minimum data which will result in the maximum understanding.

Clients themselves are the best source of information. If the report writer can convince the client that frank answers are in the client's best interests, much valuable information can be obtained. Of course, the client's answers must be checked out with the same thoroughness as any other source of data. The better report writers have developed a vast pool of individuals or agencies whom they can contact for information concerning their clients. They carefully cultivate these resources and as a result can often obtain a great deal of information in a most efficient manner. By talking with veteran report writers and reviewing old reports, the neophyte can begin to develop a list of the more conventional resources, e.g., school, law enforcement, welfare. Identifying contact persons in each agency and working through them will increase the resource's confidence in the report writer and hopefully will result in more complete and candid sharing of information.

[58]John Hagan, "The Social and Legal Construction of Criminal Justice: A Study of the Presentencing Process," *Social Problems* 22 (June 1975): 623.
[59]Robert O. Dawson, *Sentencing* (Boston: Little, Brown, 1969), p. xi.
[60]Goffman, p. 145.
[61]Schrink, pp. 35–40.

Everything else being equal it is preferable to have a face-to-face, unstructured interview with each individual who has information concerning a case. Since time is limited, due to the usually heavy caseloads in most criminal justice settings, report writers must make some determination of the method they will use and the amount of time they will expend on each resource. As a rough rule of thumb, the more crucial or subtle the information the more time report writers will want to spend gathering it. They will want to carefully plan the type of questions they want to ask so that time is not wasted. Being unprepared can cost the writer future cooperation from the resource.

Because of the potential impact of the report on the client, any information important enough to be included should be subjected to a verification process. The more important the data will be in making a decision about the client, the more serious the need for verification. Verification may be as simple as contacting a school to see if the client did indeed complete a given grade level or contacting an employer to determine whether the client did have a satisfactory work record. Other types of information may be more difficult to verify, and the writer may need to be innovative. In the end, the writer may be unable to determine the accuracy of some information. The report writer then faces the decision of whether or not to include it in the report. If the writer includes such information he/she must carefully separate it from verified data and to include the caveat that it is unverified or that "it is alleged."

Most agencies have developed a standard format for their reports so the task of organizing the data is greatly simplified for the writer, although there are still important decisions to be made concerning whether a given piece of information is to be mentioned in several sections or in just one. Once the determination is made that the information in each section is complete and logically organized, the writer can begin to look for threads or patterns to identify and elucidate. The writer's own observations, however, should be carefully identified and separated from statements of fact. The writer should remember that the goal is to prepare an accurate statement of facts about some person so that others can make meaningful decisions about that person. This means that the writer must strive to remain objective. This is not always easy because the writer may unconsciously project his/her own values into the report.

Most client-oriented reports in criminal justice contain a section dealing with the writer's conclusions, evaluations, and/or recommendations. However, this is not always the case. The consumer (e.g., judge, parole board) may specifically direct that this section not be included as part of the report. In such instances the consumer prefers to draw his own conclusions. Or the consumer may direct that such a section accompany the report, but be embodied on a separate sheet. Under this arrangement the consumer may conveniently use the section or ignore it. The writer must be realistic enough to realize that this section may be the only one that anyone reads, so that it must be able to stand by itself. Specifically, a reader should be able to read this section and gain an appreciation of what the report as a whole is all about. Conclusions, evaluations, and/or recommendations made in this section should be drawn from the report and be based on specific facts. In this section no new material should be sprung upon the reader, and no groundless conclusions should be included. The reader should be able to follow each conclusion, evaluation, or recommendation back to some specific fact or facts in the body of the report.

A frequent complaint of consumers in this area is that recommendations are often broad, "pie-in-the-sky" statements which cannot be easily implemented. The writer will find decision makers following report recommendations much more closely if recommendations are very clear and specific. The writer should also be prepared to defend all recommendations and conclusions, not only to the consumer, but to the client. Having to defend their views to the client can be a difficult situation, one that many writers try to avoid.

Cunningham views the presentence phase as one of crisis.[62] She explains that a "crisis arises when the adaptive mechanisms generally drawn upon are not totally adequate for some severe stress." Certain points in the criminal justice process are more apt to produce a state of crisis than others: arrest, detention, and the presentence phase, among others. However, within this time of crisis much can be done for the client.

> It is almost axiomatic in corrections to say that more can be accomplished with a client during the presentence phase than in an extended period of probation.... [The defendant] is in limbo "waiting for the other shoe to drop." He may be coming down from the trauma of the guilty verdict while having to gear up for the threat of sentence.[63]

Cunningham describes what steps may be taken to help a client during the presentence phase:[64]

---

[62]Adapted from Gloria Cunningham, "Crisis Intervention in a Probation Setting," *Federal Probation* 37 (December 1973): 19–23. Reprinted by permission of Federal Probation.
[63]Ibid., p. 19.
[64]Ibid., pp. 19–23.

By the time of the first interview with the probation officer the client may have been in a crisis state for some time and may have developed some new mechanisms for dealing with these recurrent and similar threats. He may be sullen and defiant, super cool, totally confused and immobilized, or perhaps more typically, in a state of fluctuation between helplessness and control. The first task of the probation officer is to make some decisions and choices as to which of the coping mechanisms can be supported as constructive. This is determined partly on the basis of a quick assessment of the person and the broader implications of his crisis situation. For example, the guilt-ridden breast-beating, remorseful defendant may kindle joy in the hearts of defense counsels, but it is not the most desirable state for the client for an extended period of time. People in such a state are apt to do self-destructive things like confessing their guilt unnecessarily to their employers or mother-in-law. It may be more helpful to move a defendant beyond this point to more constructive behavior such as finding a new job or mending a sagging marital relationship.

Successful intervention by the probation officer at this point in time is limited by the extent to which he has knowledge of the probable sentence. Certain defendants will probably be placed on probation; others will probably be incarcerated. While the probable outcome may be stressed, it is helpful to many clients in crisis to discuss all possible dispositions and to do this in the light of the kinds of decisions and planning the client will have to make. What resources does the family have if the breadwinner is sent to prison? Do children have to be told if their father is on probation? Many clients bring up such questions anyway, but many others, especially first offenders, are either too unfamiliar with the reality or too immobilized to be able to ask such questions. Crisis theory suggests that these considerations which tend to be postponed until after sentencing may serve several purposes if discussed during the presentence phase. Their discussion lessens the sense of the unknown and reminds the client that whatever the disposition and in spite of limited autonomy he will have continuing rights, responsibilities and relationships. . . .

Many of the problems identified during the presentence phase cannot be even partially resolved during the period of a few days or weeks it takes to conduct the investigation. Some can, however, and in many other situations the probation officer can set in motion problem-solving efforts on the part of the defendant or can call into the picture enough supplemental resources so that the client can continue to work out his problems with only minimal intervention from a probation officer. An alternative in communication patterns between spouses brought about during a crisis period may have continuing impact on the resolution of both long-standing and emerging difficulties. Putting a destitute offender in touch with appropriate welfare resources may be the single most effective task an officer can do to reduce the likelihood of another law violation. In situations which require more extended activity on the part of client and worker it is suggested that an agreement to this effect be determined prior to the disposition. This agreement would include shared recognition of certain aspects of the client and his situation which need further attention and the open understanding that if he receives probation an attempt will be made to deal with these aspects in more depth. Further the amount of time to be devoted to this activity should be limited and specified in advance. For example, if the problem area is one involving relationships with other family members, four or five closely spaced joint or individual interviews can be projected for shortly after the onset of probation. If the issue is one of developing a community resource then a short period of intensive work with both client and resource is indicated. Setting the agreement in advance of the disposition takes advantage of the stronger motivation operating during the crisis state. Specifying and limiting in advance the amount of time the worker and client will have to invest in this activity takes into consideration the time limitations of the worker and the possible need for the client to withdraw from too intensive an involvement with the officer. Focusing on what is actually remediable will prevent both from indulging in grandiose goals of rebirth and rejuvenation and the inevitable disappointment this entails. Once outstanding difficulties have been dealt with in some way the client can be placed on a nonintensive reporting schedule with the understanding that intensive contacts can be resumed for short periods of time if other problems develop.

An additional task for the officer during this time is to come to terms with the client's emotional and/or physical withdrawal as effectively as he can. Probation officers are realists and by and large do not expect large doses of gratitude, respect, and admiration from their clients. It can be disconcerting however, when the defendant who has been so dependent and responsive prior to sentencing suddenly has difficulty remembering the officer's face and name, much less appointment times and monthly report forms, and all of this in spite of the fact that the officer was such a nice guy in recommending probation. We are accustomed conceptually and in practice to deal with the authority elements of our role. We have developed a general philosophy, techniques, and individual styles in the constructive blending of our responsibilities to the court, community and the offender. We interpret to the client that yes, under certain conditions, we can and do ask for revocation of supervision and incarceration. This is an overwhelming but straightforward reality. Reference to the crisis framework provides help in recognizing some of the more subtle effects of this apparent conflict in role responsibilities on the relationship between client and worker. What the officer should understand and maybe help his client to understand is what a truly pervasive, deeply rooted threat he, the officer, is to some clients. In addition to the objective reality of incarceration the officer may also precipitate once again the same frightening processes of personal disintegration, the "almost annihilation" the person has just struggled through with a tremendous expenditure of psychic energy. As with every other aspect of the crisis response, individuals will evidence this withdrawal in individual ways. It may be low level and temporary or intense and enduring. The potentially negative results of the withdrawal can probably be reduced by the extent to which the officer is able to give positive help and direction in crisis resolution prior to sentencing. The important insight for the officer is to be able to recognize it for what it is, a normal and permissible response within certain limits, and perhaps even a desirable step in the client's restored or improved functioning.

## In an Institutional Setting

### PRISON/TRAINING SCHOOL

The correctional setting of an institution presents criminal justice practitioners with their greatest challenges. In the adult institution the criminal justice practitioner is dealing with those offenders who have reached the end of the criminal justice sequence; for the most part, lesser offenders have been screened out before reaching this segment. In the juvenile institution the youngsters' immaturity, while it presents a real opportunity to effect change, makes them, unpredictable, often irresponsible, and sometimes quite dangerous.* In either the adult or

*Collins provides an insight with historical dimensions that has implications for social service workers in coercive settings:

> Throughout history, slaves, prisoners, and oppressed minorities have acquired the reputation of being dull, childish, irresponsible, and careless. Dominant classes have incorporated this into a self-justifying ideology. But the behavior results from the situation of being coerced without opportunity for rebellion or escape; being noncooperative is the only means left for retaining subjective dignity. and appearing stupid and irresponsible is the best cover to avoid being punished. Even in extreme cases of unequal resources, the fight for autonomy goes on, even if it must go underground. Given the fact that there is an element of coercion in any form of

juvenile institution the primary focus is on custody and security; this is particularly acute in a prison setting. The criminal justice practitioner must operate within the restrictions imposed by security considerations. While treatment is (purportedly) a primary focus in juvenile institutions, this is not the case in prison. "The mandate given to the prison by society is to isolate those of its members who have been defined as refractory and threatening to the social order."[65]

The theoretical basis for treatment is in dispute. Gibbons states that treatment workers use a crudely articulated behavior theory "which holds that most offenders are emotionally maladjusted and in need of intensive individual therapy."[66] However, Foren and Bailey state that intensive casework cannot be carried out in prison, and "it is also highly doubtful whether more than a relatively small proportion of the prison population needs and would be amenable to intensive casework."[67] Cressey maintains that there is a basic incompatability between individualized treatment and the need for organizational discipline and order" in a prison.[68] Foren and Bailey refer to the "anomalous position" of the caseworker in a prison setting:[69]

Casework in prison, though not essentially different from casework in other settings, must necessarily involve a more limited range of techniques. The majority of the clientele, because of personality factors, are unlikely to be susceptible to insight-promoting techniques. Even if they were, the closed environment may make it dangerous to apply them. The extent to which the

control in which someone can back up his orders by bringing undesirable consequences (including such milder forms of coercion as taking away rewards or the privileges of membership), we can see why the culture of order-taking classes is always built around some degree of implicit rebellion against authority.
Randall Collins, *Conflict Sociology: Toward an Explanatory Science.* (New York: Academic Press, 1975), p. 299.

[65]George H. Grosser, "External Setting and Internal Relations of the Prison." In *Prison Within Society*, ed. Lawrence Hazelrigg (Garden City, N.Y.: Doubleday, 1969), p. 9.
[66]Don C. Gibbons, "Some Notes on Treatment Theory in Corrections." In *Prisons Within Society*, p. 330.
[67]Robert Foren and Royston Bailey, *Authority in Social Casework* (Oxford: Pergamon Press, 1968), p. 176.
[68]Donald R. Cressey, "Limitation of Treatment in the Modern Prison." In *Theoretical Studies in Social Organization of the Prison*, ed. Richard Cloward et al. (New York: Social Science Research Council, reprinted by Kraus Reprint Co., Millwood, N.Y., 1975).
[69]Foren and Bailey, p. 177.

immediate environment can be modified is greatly reduced, though it must be recognised that relatively minor changes (such as a change of employment within the prison, or a change of cell) can become a matter of great importance to the prisoner.

Paradoxically, they note that:[70]

the prisoner who is resentful and hostile toward the regime may be more susceptible to casework help than the "model prisoner," and *may* be a potentially better citizen. The prisoner who is overly dissatisfied with his lot in prison may be willing to look with the social worker at his own part in the conflict.

Thus, if the criminal justice practitioner decides to use ego supportive techniques he/she is faced with a dilemma:[71]

Should he support the conforming aspects of the prisoner and perhaps thereby reduce in the long run that client's capacity for social rehabilitation outside, or should he support the "healthy" part of the personality which reacts adversely to an alien regime? The prison welfare officer may seek to avoid discussing the prisoner's here-and-now situation, partly because it is largely unalterable and partly because he does not wish to be seduced into taking sides in any conflict between the prisoner and the regime.

The inmate subculture[72]—a dynamic combining the institutional environment and the outside culture brought in by inmates—usually creates problems in juvenile and adult correctional institutions. Yet, it may be used for correctional treatment.[73] Ianni maintains that "prisons and the prison experience are the most important locus for establishing the social relationships that form the basis for partnerships in organized crime, both among blacks and among Puerto Ricans."[74] Ohlin

[70]Ibid.

[71]Ibid., p. 185.

[72]For a more extensive look at the inmate subculture see Donald Clemmer, *The Prison Community* (New York: Holt, Rinehart & Winston, 1958); John Irwin and Donald R. Cressey, "Thieves, Convicts and the Inmate Culture," *Social Problems* 10 (Fall 1962): 142–55; and Francis A. J. Ianni, *The Black Mafia* (New York: Simon and Schuster, 1974), pp. 157–98. See also: C. W. Thomas, "Prisonization and Its Consequences: An Examination of Socialization in a Coercive Setting," *Sociological Focus* 10 (January): 53–68; Rose Giallombardo, *The Social World of Imprisoned Girls* (New York: John Wiley, 1974).

[73]Don C. Gibbons, *Society, Crime, and Criminal Careers* (Englewood Cliffs, N.J.: Prentice-Hall, 1973), p. 476.

[74]Ianni, p. 158.

and Lawrence note that the inmate code or subculture may seriously impair the effectiveness of treatment methods.[75] They point out that "an inmate culture and an informally organized system of social relationships competes with the official system for the allegiance of inmates."[76] The authors note that the institutional treatment approach usually focuses on deviant behavior as a manifestation of internalized conflicts and conditions. They caution, however, that in contrast to this clinical orientation, there is a sociological dimension which views delinquency as a social disorder arising out of group life: "Nowhere does the influence of one's peers seem to exert such a profound control over a person's responses to social interactions as in the closed social systems of correctional institutions."[77] Continuing with their sociological perspective, the authors note the socially degrading aspect of being an inmate: the inmates, faced with this degradation of status, develop a common solution through intimate association with one another. They do this through the process of subculturalization, an alternative "opportunity to achieve compensatory status and privilege roles."[78] Conforming behavior to the inmate code and subculture places a prisoner at odds with treatment efforts.

Leonard Cottrell, in his forward to Polsky's *Cottage Six*, states:[79]

> Polsky demonstrates beyond cavil that is possible for at least a significant segment of the resident population of even a first-rate institution like Hollymeade[80] to create, maintain, and transmit a separate deviant subculture[81] that supports values and a social system that are counter to those of the institution itself and in substantial part negate even the most intensive and skillful individual therapeutic efforts.

Polsky highlights the cultural differences between the social service staff and the residents:[82]

---

[75]Lloyd E. Ohlin and William C. Lawrence, "Social Interaction Among Clients As A Treatment Problem," *Social Work* 4 (April 1959): 3.

[76]Ibid., p. 4.

[77]Ibid., p. 5.

[78]Ibid., p. 6.

[79]Howard W. Polsky, *Cottage Six: The Social System of Delinquent Boys in Residential Treatment* (New York: Wiley, 1962), pp. 6–7.

[80]Hollymeade is a pseudonym.

[81]A persistant collective behavior and related value system of a circumscribed group that violates conventional social norms.

[82]Polsky, *Cottage Six*, p. 156.

While the boys' orientation to the group favors authoritarianism, middle-class Jewish professionals stress individualism. Conflict between the caseworkers and administration often stems from the former's feelings that their integrity is being transgressed. Individualism is highly valued in social workers' families and is related to the parents' desires to have their children compete successfully with school peers.

The staff's extreme individualistic, achievement, and future-directed value orientations contribute to their assumption that the boys naturally will have similar orientations.

In a juvenile institution the social service staff has a central function; indeed, the institution is often administered by social service personnel. In a prison setting, social service is usually one (small) aspect of institutional life. Sanger Powers discusses the purpose of a prison social service unit:[83]

The purpose of treatment provided by the Social Service Unit within a prison setting is twofold. The first is to help the inmate to adjust to the institution in order that he may utilize the training and treatment facilities to the fullest extent. The second purpose is to assist him in making a satisfactory adjustment to life in a free community once release from the institution is accomplished by way of parole or discharge.

Areas of special interest to social services include reception and quarantine activities, records and identification, case records, inmate welfare, counseling and guidance, classification, mail and visiting, release planning, liaison with the parole board and parole staff, a close working relationship with the psychiatrist, psychologists, and chaplins.

Carpenter and Weber review intake and orientation procedures in a juvenile institutional setting.[84] The principal objectives of this process are:

1. to establish a working relationship with the youth;
2. to provide pertinent information about the institution to the youth;

[83]Sanger Powers, "The Social Services in a Correctional Setting." In *Correctional Classification and Treatment*, Leonard J. Hippchen, ed. (Cincinnati, Ohio: W. H. Anderson, 1975), pp. 150, 152.
[84]Kenneth S. Carpenter and George H. Weber, "Intake and Orientation Procedures in Institutions for Delinquent Youth," *Federal Probation* 30 (March 1966): 37–42.

3. to develop a diagnostic picture of the youth; and

4. to arrange a program based on the diagnosis.

Interwoven throughout is the "welcoming process:" "to help them relate positively to the other youth as well as to the staff, to adjust to the
institutional setting, and to get started on the 'right foot.'" The process
also serves as a backup screening mechanism: "If a youth has inappropriately been sent to the institution or if his needs can be met more
adequately in another setting, the intake and orientation procedures
will pick this up and the parent agency should be so informed."

The youth's new environment and the controls inherent in it are
anxiety-producing; The youngster may also be fearful and angry. The
authors point out that the youth may be unrealistically hopeful or
scheming to manipulate and exploit others—perhaps a mixture of the
two. The authors caution against undue delay between the youth's
arrival and the initial interview: "He has traveled a long route—at least
by experience. Undue delay at this point produces unhealthy tension
and negativism toward the setting." They continue:[85]

> Once comfortably seated in the office the worker must take time to
> welcome the youth in a manner that is appropriate to his mood. If
> he is trying to be cheerful, the intake worker should respond in
> kind. If he is discouraged, the worker should be supportive and
> friendly. He must be careful to respect his feelings and not make
> light of them. If he is silent, his silence should be inquired about
> sensitively. If he is sullen, a matter-of-fact approach may ease the
> tension and will not be inflamatory. The youth must sense from
> the worker's manner that he is welcome, that his situation is ap-
> preciated, and that adequate steps will be taken to help him with
> his problems.

The worker explains both the general operations and routine and
the specific rules of the instution, e.g., the cottage in which the youth
will live, when school starts, visits, release, etc. After the initial interview the worker introduces the youngster to the cottage staff and the
other youths encountered during the visit. The worker should schedule
a "tour" of the facility's shops, recreation areas, etc. The authors provide a caution with respect to the ongoing interview:[86]

> [The worker's] comments or questions might bias or have some
> unintentional effect on the youth; for example, a misunderstood

[85]Ibid., p. 38.
[86]Ibid., p. 40.

question might stimulate his defensiveness or induce him to present an overly favorable picture of himself.

The authors recommend the use of group orientation sessions:[87]

The experience of being part of a group of newly admitted youth meeting daily under the guidance of the intake worker, can help him in accepting his commitment and getting him started in the program. The worker can also make diagnostic observations of the youth and the way he gets along in a group.

## In a Probation/Parole Supervision Setting

While the social service worker is present in all of the segments of the criminal justice supervision, it is in probation and parole that he/she is the focal point of activity. Probation and parole supervision are part of what is referred to as community-based corrections. Charles Newman notes that "most correctional institutions make no claim to the provision of more than a custodial program for their inmates." It is in the community that treatment can be most effective, and Newman provides a three-stage treatment process for the criminal justice practitioner in a probation/parole setting.[88]

In the *investigation* stage we attempt to find out what is and was within him and outside him that made him the person with whom we are dealing. With skillful questioning, he will find himself looking at aspects of his life, so very necessary if he is to gain insight into the nature of his behavior. The *diagnosis* is the codification of all that has been learned about the individual, organized in such a way as to provide a means for the establishment of future treatment goals. As we learn more about the individual the diagnosis will be modified, and the treatment goals raised or lowered as indicated by the progress of the case.

The *supervision* process entails the elaboration of knowledge about the individual through the process of communication, so that the individual will gain a more realistic appraisal of his own behavior, thereby enhancing his own ability to function more acceptably in the community. The provision of certain material services may also be involved in the treatment process.

---

[87]Ibid., p. 41.
[88]Adapted from Charles L. Newman, "Concepts of Treatment in Probation and Parle Supervision," *Federal Probation* 25 (March 1961): 11–18. Reprinted by permission of *Federal Probation*.

In the *finding-out* process, the most important source to help the officer is the offender himself. He frequently is also a most difficult source. The offender may consider it to his interest and advantage to give a misleading picture. The extent to which a person reveals himself is in direct proportion to the degree of rapport which the worker has succeeded in developing. The investigation should give a comprehensive picture of the offender's own world, his personality, his relationship to others, and his immediate environment as seen in relation to himself. We should know something about his likes and dislikes, his hopes and desires, his values and disappointments, his ambitions and plans (or lack of them), his assets and qualities as well as shortcomings. We need to find out the type of relationship which has existed between the person and other significant people in his life: natural family, family by marriage, friends, neighbors, co-workers.

We have no hesitation about discouraging continued contact with previous associates. But what about family? Are these relationships always worth maintaining? With knowledge about those interrelationships, it may be most desirable to encourage the person to stay far away from his family as well as previous associates. Even though our culture strongly supports the notion of enduring marriage, we cannot assume, *a priori*, a positive family relationship exists solely because a man and a woman are living together in marriage.

An interview is a conversation with a purpose. In his role, the criminal justice practitioner is not interested in persons in the aggregate, but in the specific individual. The goal, through the interview process, is to be able to know the offender's personality in action. We are interested in his immediate environment, the way he reacts to frustrations and opportunities. We want to know his attitudes toward others and himself. From that point, we can assist him to gain a better self-understanding, thereby affecting his ability to function constructively in the community around him. It is important to recognize that both the worker and the offender bring prior life experiences into the interview situation. If the worker has been able to develop insight and self-awareness about his own behavior, there is a likelihood that he will be more tolerant and effective with the persons with whom he is working. This is particularly necessary in the implementation of authority.

The first contact is of extreme importance. In all probability the offender will be experiencing a certain amount of anxiety which, with skillful handling, can be mobilized from the very beginning to achieve the treatment goals. The person should be given the feeling that there is no need to hurry in exploring the many avenues which may develop in the initial interview. If the worker takes time to listen, the probability is that he will hear more than if he devotes the time to talking himself. At the beginning, the offender is making a number of observations about the officer, the office, and comparing his current impressions with his own preconceptions. At the same time, the worker should be making his own observations, such as the person's appearance, the way he enters the office, the way he conducts himself, how he sits down, how he talks, the tone of his speech, and other nonverbal communicative aspects. Whether we are capable of observing it or not, in many instances a *transference*[89] occurs from the individual to the officer from the very beginning. The mature worker will recognize that fact, and interact accordingly.

The content of the first interview, as with all subsequent contacts, will vary with the individual. Part of the time is spent in gathering factual information. However, unless there is reason to believe that information already on file is erroneous, generally there is no need to repeat the operation. Being asked the same questions over and over again can easily give the impression that it does not matter too much what you say since no one pays any attention to the answers. Accurate recording (even though it takes time) is of vital necessity if we hope to do a respectable job of treatment. By recording basic information as well as progress contacts, we are in a better position to see the progress which has been made in the case and alter treatment goals accordingly. Without such information, a shift in caseload requires the new worker to start out from the beginning, which we would agree is a great waste of time and effort.

After the initial interview, the officer is faced with the monumental task of making a fast appraisal, on the basis of a single interview, of the person's ability to reside in the community with only limited external controls. One of the better means of appraisal comes from an understanding of the degree of discomfort which the individual feels in relation to his social or emotional problem. Further, the officer will have to determine what part others may have in the problem, and the extent to which they are affected.

---

[89]The tendency of clients to identify a new situation or person with unconscious memories to which are attached significant emotional experiences of earlier life. "The feelings and attitudes surrounding the earlier situation are transferred to the new relationship, so that the worker can find himself the object of hostility, flattery or undue dependence." Foren and Bailey, p. 17. Herbert and Jarvis suggest that "the relationship between the social worker and the delinquent enables the latter to re-experience more successfully the emotions involved in his early family relationships," thus "a curative relationship for the delinquent is one in which he can deal afresh with his hating and loving feelings; one in which he can have an object for these feelings in a person who is neither destroyed nor overwhelmed by them and who shows concern, interest and consistency in spite of them." W. L. Herbert and F. V. Jarvis, *Dealing With Delinquents* (New York: Emerson Books, 1962), p. 46.

The timing of subsequent interviews must, in large measure, be determined by a variety of factors, including the type and immediacy of the problem, the size of caseload, and the need of the person for support and control. Unfortunately, too much of probation and parole supervision is little more than routine monthly reporting. Admittedly, in some cases, this minimal type of control may be quite adequate, but generally speaking where problems of adjustment to the home and community exist, it is questionable whether any value is derived from infrequent contact. In too many probation and parole offices, moreover, a person is seen only after he has demonstrated some emergent problem situation. To insure the protection of the community, as well as to assist the person in adjustment, probation and parole supervision *must* provide preventive as well as remedial treatment services.

### Surveillance Versus Counseling

Within the context of the need for sound correctional treatment programs, several elements emerge. First, we must recognize that the community continues to be concerned about the activities of the probationer and the parolee. Whether or not he is involved in further illegal activity, the law violator has demonstrated his capacity to disregard society's rules and regulations. By virtue of his prior activity, the community is justifiably concerned.

Secondly, we mut recognize that it is neither feasible nor desirable to maintain continuous surveillance of the offender's activities. At best, we can samplehis behavior at various moments and hope that we are able to detect certain indicators which suggest tht the person is more of a presumptive risk to himself and to the community. Greater protection than this to the community through surveillance is not possible in a democracy. . . .

It becomes obvious, then, that the correctional worker (whether in the institution or field services) should be in a position to recognize, understand, and deal effectively with subtle as well as obvious shifts in the behavior and personality of the offender. Not infrequently, these shifts can be indicative of problems which the individual is experiencing and for which he is unable to find a solution. [This does not] mean to suggest that to find a person in a particularly irritable mood during a field visit is cause for revocation. On the other hand, such irritability, persistently detected, may be a clue which directs our attention to the movement of the person into behavior which ultimately may get him into difficulty.

There are certain complexities that are endemic to probation/parole—items that are different from other areas of social service practice. The probation/parole officer is more than an authority figure—he possesses real power over his client's freedom. The sanction of imprisonment is always explicit or implicit in a probation/parole setting. The offender-client has been legally identified as a potential threat to the community and the criminal justice practitioner in a probation/parole setting is expected to exercise control over the offender, reducing the potential threat. However, the exercise of this control is limited since the worker's contact with his/her client is limited. Too many clients and too much paperwork are complaints common to probation/parole practice.

The probation/parole supervision process usually begins subsequent to conviction/adjudication or release/parole from a correctional institution. The client reports in person to the agency where he/she is assigned to the caseload of a probation/parole officer. He/she is provided with a copy of the rules of probation/parole,[90] which are universally applied to all offenders within the particular jurisdiction. Many times, the specific rule may not have any particular relationship to the offender and his prior conduct. The imposition of rules and conditions can have a therapeutic value. However, to do so, the rules must have a relationship to the prior behavior pattern of the individual upon whom they are imposed. Limit-setting, an important aspect of probation/parole supervision, involves specifying what behavior the officer will or will not accept from the offender. The degree of rule-enforcement, the actual imposition of sanctions such as imprisonment, varies from officer to officer and agency to agency. However, every criminal justice practitioner recognizes that probation/parole clientele may commit crimes which can receive a great deal of media coverage, always an embarrassment to an agency. Somewhere between the two variables of sanctions and recidivism is a (mythical) line-formula which maximizes deterrence while maintaining rule flexibility (in statistical terms, a "probation/parole line of regression"). Every agency and every practitioner strives to approximate this line.

Often both client and community expect more from a criminal justice practitioner than is reasonable or realistic. The probation/parole client usually has an extensive history of failure—at home, at school, at work. The ability of the criminal justice practitioner to provide help or exercise control is obviously limited by community hostility, fear or contempt for offenders, and a lack of adequate rehabilitative resources, e.g., financial assistance, education and training. It is these structural realities that cause the criminal justice practitioner, who may be well-versed in theory or who might otherwise be motivated to seek better

[90]A sample copy appears in Appendix E.

theoretical groundings for practice, to abandon abstractions on the altar of pressing realities. In a paper on probation counseling, Arcaya refers to the "multiple realities."

Arcaya points to the differential levels of understanding involved in the probation officer-client relationship:[91]

1. the shared level, generally objective, legal, or formal, and
2. the subjective attitudinal, or informal meanings held by each.

While he refers to these differences as the "multiple realities" which are inherent in probation counseling, they are also inherent in parole. Arcaya states:[92]

> In probation work we find a situation where two individuals are joined by legal force in a counseling and (supposedly) trusting relationship. From the beginning, the probation officer is confronted with a problem which not only entails communicating meaningfully with an unknown individual (a meeting of two realities, difficult enough under voluntary conditions), but one which, if he is at all flexible, constrains him to pay heed to two different perspectives, simultaneously: his obligations as a court-appointed supervisor of probationers, and the idiosyncratic needs of the probationer as client in a counseling relationship. Inherent in the job of probation officer is this tension of perspectives. It localizes itself between the officer and the court (how closely to abide by its formal rules of supervision), the officer and the client (how many breaks to give an offender), and between the officer and himself (what kind of officer to be).
>
> When a probationer enters a probation office for the first time part of his awareness is occupied by a nagging feeling of apprehension. Viewed from the eyes of the probationer, the office represents a power that can, and does, limit his freedom. It is an institution to which he must submit involuntarily [as a "client," euphemistically stated]. In the background of this submission is an implicit assumption made by our legal system that a probationer is in need of supervision, rehabilitation, or guidance. Thus, even before the first contact is ever made between officer and client, the client is already lead to believe that he is considered less than a responsible human being. It is not surprising, therefore, that the probationer encounters his supervising officer with a mixture of fear, wariness, and defiance. Generally, in the

[91]Jose Arcaya, "The Multiple Realities Inherent in Probation Counseling," *Federal Probation* 37 (December 1973): 58. Reprinted by permission of *Federal Probation*.

[92]Ibid., pp. 58–59.

beginning of his introduction to the probation system, the probationer's attitude is to obey the formal rules of probation and maintain a respectful, if distant, relationship with whoever might be assigned to work with him. During this initial contact period the probationer's "sniff out" evaluates his officer, determining to what extent he may be trusted.

At the other pole of this meeting is the officer himself who has little to say with regard to who is assigned to his caseload. He, too, meets a stranger for the first time. Like the probationer's experience, fear and apprehension accompany the initial meeting. The officer is fearful because he knows nothing of the individual's capacity to cooperate, follow the rules, or give a hard time. He is apprehensive because he knows there might come a day when he will have to reprimand, admonish, or even incarcerate his new client. Maybe, from past experience, he feels he has failed to really help many of his probationers. Perhaps the memories of these failures haunt him now. Yet, in spite of these discouragements, he maintains an optimistic hope that the relationship will be worthwhile for the probationer. He desires the probationer's betterment through his experience on probation. With these feelings in mind, the officer chooses one of two broad counseling approaches toward his new ward.

### Roles[93]

First, he may choose to put out of his awareness the ambiguity of his position—that he is both counselor of the individual and the representative of a legal situation. Instead of integrating the two responsibilities, he may dichotomize the functions and choose to act on one more than the other.

The *authority-figure* role is inevitably presented by an officer hoping to cover his own fear of the interpersonal counseling experience. He conveys an image characterized by a determination to show the client "who's boss." He sees probation work to involve the legal surveillance of his cases. To this end, his major occupation centers around keeping his paperwork in order, taking appropriate legal action when a clear violation of rules has occurred, and providing the person on probation with clear and strong reminders of the latter's probation responsibilities.

The *nice-guy* officer is as inflexible and thoughtless as the authority figure. This individual chooses the other extreme of the spectrum by giving the probationer power over *him*. He has little consideration for the rights of society as a whole or, for that

[93]No individual officer completely fits either of the "pure" approaches that are described.

matter, the basic welfare of his client. He is an example of someone who believes that any rule broken is unimportant. By his silence, he subtly fosters and condones antisocial behavior on the part of the probationer. This officer is "bent" on being like, proving that he is "humanistic," that he is, in short, a "nice guy."

The alternative stance is what is here termed a "dwelling" presence. This attitude openly accepts the ambiguity of feelings and responsibilities attached to probation work and uses this ambiguity to bring the client an awareness of the officer's own humanity. Here the officer attempts to share with the person on probation the personal tensions he experiences in counseling within the legal system and discloses his difficulties in accomplishing this feat. The client is not made to feel that he confronts an unerring, larger-than-life, authority who has all the answers or a permissive, easily deceived fool. The officer has no interest in either having power over the probationer or having the probationer having power over him. Rather, in the dwelling stance the officer creates a relationship that encourages both to relate as equals. A respect for the inherent worth of both individuals is presumed in spite of the fact that one is a convicted criminal and the other a court-appointed supervisor. This stance acknowledges that there are no privileged positions in authentic human communication: The lasting benefits of a counseling relationship derive from the mutual trust and lack of power conflicts.

To accomplish this rapport the client and officer must develop a common ground of communication as a result of the experience with each other. This means building a *shared world* of meanings which occurs principally from a willingness to not only talk, but also listen. To truly listen implies to dwell in what the other says. It is not the absence of talk which characterizes listening, but the effort to interpret the other's words from his perspective. Communication proceeds only to the extent the speaker feels that someone is trying to understand him. In the most fundamental sense, listening communicates more than talking. The problem of multiple realities is no more than the challenge of really understanding what the other says.

In a dwelling stance with the probationer, the officer tries to make sense of what his client has to say from the reality of the client's own "words." To meaningfully "be" with the other necessitates entering into his "world," trying, as much as possible to leave one's own world apart. Let us examine two dimensions of responsiveness: listening and speaking.

*Active listening* means that the officer actively attempts to put aside preconceptions of what the client is saying. He tries, instead, to silently remain with the language which the probationer uses as much as possible, allowing him to describe what he means in his own words. The officer does not try to define the reality and experience of the client for him. He accords the individual enough respect to assume that he will relate his story better than the officer could. Nevertheless, it will occur that, as the officer listens with this end in mind, many uncertainties about what is actually said will arise. When this happens, the officer may ask the probationer to clarify what he means. This request, however, must be phrased also in the "language" of the client if the question is to be meaningful to him.

Through this and numerous other clarifications of the probationer's language and behavior, the officer slowly builds up an image of the style and perspective of the probationer. As a result of this type of inquiry, he actively listens to what the other says by having him serve as his own source of "reference." Meanings of words and body gestures are understood not through some independent "dictionary" definition but in terms of the inner "logic" of the client. Thus, the probationer is, for the listening officer, a self-defining being. Success in understanding someone as he understands himself comes only slowly and laboriously....It could be that the client is surprised or threatened that the officer [is] so close to his emotional world. Chances are that no breakthrough in communication would be accomplished through one inquiry. This does not matter. What is of greater importance is that the client see that the officer cares enough to consult with *him* about what *he* means without prejudging his experience. Of greater benefit than any discovered "facts" is the feeling conveyed to the probationer that someone is attempting to hear him. Listening requires patience.

*Responsive talking* means, according to this stance, to really *respond*. One talks as a consequence of having understood the client as he himself allows one to understand him. This means that the officer works together with the client through dialogue to contextualize and situate the latter's world. Any suggestions, recommendations, or, even orders originate from the mutual dialogue. A set of probation goals is not the outgrowth of unverified and unshared prejudices of what *should* be best for the client. The client always serves as his own best advisor of action. While certainly this does not mean that the officer must capitulate his responsibilities to the courts and not abide by the guidelines of probation, it does mean that any rules enforced or any unpopular decisions made by him must, at the very least, be documented to the probationer in terms of the latter's concrete behavior.

Fink et al. provide some cautions about the supervision process for the criminal justice practitioner:[94]

[94]Arthur E. Fink, C. Wilson Anderson, and Merrill B. Conover, *The Field of Social Work* (New York: Holt, Rinehart & Winston, 1968), p. 315.

[A not] uncommon practice of untrained probation officers is to direct the lives of their probationers. What seems to give sanction to such a practice is the obvious fact that the individual by his very act of transgressing the law has shown his inability to manage his own life, and hence what is more natural than to tell him what to do, to make the decisions for him that will oblige him to conform? Furthermore, the very injunction of the court to report any serious violation of probation seems to make it all the more imperative to keep the offender good. Despite the plausibility of this position, there is a fundamental contradiction inherent in it. The one unmistakable conclusion about the offender is that he needs help in accepting responsibility for his behavior. For someone else to direct his life means that the worker has robbed the client of the decision for his own life. This might be very well if probation officers supervised the offenders throughout their lifetime, but the real fact is that all probationers finish with probation at some time either successfully and by discharge or by failure and commitment. Someday the individual will need to make his own decisions, and the surest way to prepare him for that day is to help him while he is under supervision. Another aspect of this question pertains to what is happening to the individual when another person makes his decisions for him. Instead of the probationer carrying the responsibility for his decisions, he can always shift it over on the probation officer who made them. Thus the very opposite of the probation objective is accomplished; instead of helping the individual to do more for himself the probation officer makes it possible for him to do less.

In the community setting of probation/parole supervision, the criminal justice practitioner comes face-to-face with the real problem of *labeling*. The stigma that attaches to probationers and parolees is quite intense. This stigma coupled with minority (racial or ethnic) status often makes offenders "doubly handicapped." If we consider that most probation/parole clients are not equipped, educationally or vocationally, for skilled or satisfying work, we have an additional dimension to the dilemma. All this adds up to frustration—perhaps rage. In a report prepared by the American Bar Association, Hunt et al. conclude:[95]

The existence of arbitrary restrictions on an offender's job opportunities suggests a basic ambivalence by society towards the rehabilitation of the offender. We expect our corrections system to

---

[95]James W. Hunt, James E. Bowers, and Neal Miller, *Laws, Licences and the Offender's Right to Work* (Washington, D.C.: American Bar Association, Commission on Correctional Facilities and Services and Criminal Law Section, 1974), p. 17.

correct, but we hinder that process by allowing the former offender to be subjected to continued restrictions that deny him fair consideration for a job or license even after he has supposedly "paid his debt to society."

Armore and Wolfe, in a booklet for employers, point out the problems of the offender seeking employment, that the ex-offender is often under a threat of serving "a life sentence on the installment plan:"[96]

(a) The average ex-offender feels that his or her time spent behind bars has been a degrading experience, to say the least;

(b) The average ex-offender seeking to start up again is woefully aware that prison life has for the most part, not provided meaningful vocational rehabilitation;

(c) Though, in the main, ex-offenders want to find an honest means of making a living, they suffer from the feeling of desperation that comes from seeing no light at the end of the tunnel;

(d) Ex-offenders are painfully aware that revelation of their past lives creates fear in many employers, who perpetuate a dehumanized image of them without examining their past crimes and their current needs on a one-to-one basis.

In a pamphlet geared to businessmen, the National Alliance for Businessmen states:[97]

> ... A few will have admitted to a prospective employer that they had just come from prison ... only to see the smile of a personnel officer turn to stone. One ex-offender describes how quickly he was considered "a Humphrey Bogart-like character with a contagious disease." Another tells of sensing immediate fear from his interviewer, although the man applying for work had served time for a "white collar" infraction of the tax laws. Few are articulate enough to make the case that although murderers and rapists are probably the most frequent source of fear to the public, **less than one percent of all criminals are incarcerated for these crimes.**
> A few will have tried to hide their prison records. Their stories usually end with disclosure and dismissal.
> In all, their reactions will point up one key fact: that poor

---

[96]John R. Armore and Joseph D. Wolfe, Introduction to *Dictionary of Desperation* (Washington, D.C.: Communications Department of the National Alliance of Businessmen, 1976), p. 7.

[97]A xerox copy from the National Alliance for Businessmen was sent to the author.

civic response teaches ex-offenders that crime pays—only because nothing else does!

Pati, an authority on training and educating offenders, provides some observations based on his efforts to assist offenders by convincing employers to hire ex-offenders:[98]

> It took a long time to persuade managers to tell me their opinions on hiring ex-convicts. In fact, most company personnel that I approached did not want to talk at all. They were very uncomfortable with my curiosity and often questioned my identity. Some personnel managers thought I was snooping around to find possible violations of EEO compliance activities; one even thought I was a communist. In general, though, after reassurance, the majority agreed to discuss their programs. Practically all requested that I keep their company's name confidential.
>
> "We don't want any more trouble." [Vice president]
>
> "If we give our name, all the ex-cons will be out here looking for jobs. We can't hire everybody." (Personnel director)
>
> "What do you think the people in this neighborhood are going to think? We can't afford to scare the local community." (President)
>
> "Before we give our name, we want to see what others are doing." (Plant superintendent)

In an interview with two representatives of the National Alliance of Businessmen, Mario Bruschi and Harold Edelson, several problems were enumerated with respect to offender employment:[99]

1. Employers ask: "Why should I risk employing an ex-offender when there are so many nonoffenders available for employment; and
2. there is fear of creating "employee problems" as the result of other workers being resistant to working with an ex-offender.

The two officials pointed to particular types of offenders who are "almost impossible" for them to place: drug addicts and sex offenders. They also noted a particular organizational problem encountered in the area of offender employment: metropolitan areas have been saturated with tax-supported, but private, programs to help offenders. These agencies are highly competitive, and their efforts are fragmented with the result being that employers are continually barraged by job de-

---

[98]Gopal C. Pati, "Business Can Make Ex-Convicts Productive," *Harvard Business Review*, May–June 1974, p. 72.
[99]Personal Interview by Writer.

velopers. The National Alliance of Businessmen is attempting to provide the needed coordination with mixed results.

Compounding the problem of stigma is the lack of some of the very basic "skills" needed for securing employment; e.g., being on time for interviews and dressing properly. While these items are basic to most middle-class persons, they are often absent in offenders. Job interviews can be quite traumatic to the offender, who often lacks skills and an extensive employment history, is fearful cf the impact of revealing his record, and is unsophisticated in some of the basic aspects of presenting a good impression during a job interview. (See checklist with interview instructions for offenders in Appendix C.)

## In a Victim-Oriented Setting

Knudten et al. state that "most elements of the criminal justice system are directed to conviction of the offender and the maintenance of regularized system operation." Thus, the victim of crime "is treated as an intervening actor and not a person in need within the system."[100] The victim of the crime "is victimized as a result of the crime event and as a result of their entrance into the criminal justice system." *Secondary victimization* often results in the loss of income and/or time as a result of court appearances and the trauma of additional victim-offender courtroom confrontations.[101]

In recent years, concern for the victim as a "victim," as opposed to being merely a complainant or witness, has increased. Services heretofore not available (or limited to offenders) have become a reality for some victims of crime. Victim services can generally be classified according to their basic programmatic thrust, although any one program may offer a combination.

The *victim-witness advocate* program usually operates out of a prosecutor's office. The primary concern is to avoid losing cases because of the failure of witnesses to cooperate in prosecution. There are more than a hundred such programs in operation throughout the United States.[102] Caplan notes that "information from the victim and witnesses—not detective work—is the critical factor in solving most

---

[100]Richard D. Knudten, Anthony C. Meade, Mary S. Knudten, and William G. Doerner, *Victims and Witnesses: Their Experiences With Crime and Criminal Justice System* (Washington, D.C.: United States Government Printing Office, 1977), p. 12.
[101]Ibid., p. 4.
[102]Ordway P. Burden, "Reaching Out to Assist Victims of Crime and Criminal Justice," *Law Enforcement News*, November 15, 1977, p. 5.

serious crimes," and witness cooperation is often a crucial factor in successful prosecution.[103]

*Victim compensation programs* are increasing on state and federal levels, although compensation laws usually have ceilings and other limiting clauses. In New York, for example, there is a $20,000 ceiling for loss of earnings, and full payment for medical expenses. The New York law, however, requires a showing of serious financial hardship.

*Victim restoration programs* stress restoring the victim's previous state of functioning, and where that is not possible, providing services to maximize some form of restoration. These programs seek to deal with the residual effects of the trauma of victimization. In certain appropriate instances reconciliation between victim and perpetrator is effected through a mediation role. These programs often find that the mere offer of help has a salutory effect on the client-victim. Goeke and Stretch note that even when the services offered were limited, there appeared to be a positive effect on the victim as a result of reaching out and offering even limited aid.[104] They also report a heightened concern for safety as a result of victimization and they point to the need to link victim assistance to community group involvement in order to reduce feelings of helplessness and isolation. They provide an important methodological suggestion for the criminal justice practitioner by noting that a basis for treating the offender is dealing with his/her attitude toward the victim.

Restorative programs usually provide:

1. receptive and empathetic communication;
2. interaction with other victims;
3. information on criminal justice operations, in particular the role of the victim in his involvement with the prosecution of the case; and
4. a variety of counseling, social casework and group services, and psychological and psychiatric consultations and treatment, depending on the level of agency resources.

Persons interested in victim-oriented research and practices are advised to subscribe to:

---

[103]Gerald M. Caplan, in the Forward to Frank J. Cannavale, Jr., and William D. Falcon, *Improving Witness Cooperation* (Washington, D.C.: United States Government Printing Office, 1976), p. vii.

[104]John C. Goeke and John J. Stretch, remarks delivered in conjunction with their paper. "The Design and Evaluation of Services to Victims of Crime," presented at the Annual Meeting of the American Society of Criminology, Atlanta, November 18, 1977.

Victimology
Visage Press
3409 Wisconsin Avenue, N.W.
Washington, D.C. 20016

Those interested in joining a national victim advocate organization should write to:

NOVA
c/o Department of Criminal Justice
University of Southern Mississippi
Southern Station, Box 5127
Hattiesburg, Miss. 39410

The greatest amount of programmatic response in the area of victimization has been for victims of sexual offenses, the result of the increasing influence and activity of women's groups. In discussing the "rape crisis center." Brodyaga et al. note: "Centers are often spinoffs of a consciousness-raising group, a women's center, or a militant women's organization."[105] These centers tend to be staffed by both professionals and volunteers, the latter, as well as the victim-clients, are usually middle-class whites. The authors report that the paucity of minority women involved with the centers is a major problem.[106] An exemplary program assisting victims of rape is described by Bryant and Cirel.[107] This report also contains some excellent pointers for the social service worker dealing with the victims of rape or sexual assault. (These pointers appear in Appendix I of this book.)

> [Polk County Rape/Sexual Assault Center] provides social services to rape and sexual assault victims in three main ways: (1) by lessening the victim's trauma during the immediate post-crisis period; (2) by easing the victim's return to normal life; and (3) by supporting the victim and her family through all criminal justice proceedings. Since many of Polk County's social service professional agencies and community organizations have representatives on the Center's Board of Directors, coordination with social service agencies has progressed well. During the first operational year R/SACC received 42 referrals from 19 agencies and referred 20 victims to other agencies. All center services are free to clients and confidentiality is assured.

[105]Lisa Brodyaga, Margaret Gates, Susan Singer, and Richardson White, *Rape and Its Victims: A Report for Citizens, Health Facilities and Criminal Justice Agencies.* (Washington, D.C.: United States Government Printing Office, 1975), p. 123.
[106]Ibid., p. 126.
[107]Gerald Bryant and Paul Cirel, *Polk County Rape/Sexual Assault Care Center, Des Moines, Iowa* (Washington, D.C.: United States Government Printing Office, 1977).

# 5

# Practice Based on Theory

## Practice Based on Sociological Theory

In 1961 Empey and Rabow noted: "Despite the importance of sociological contributions to the understanding of delinquent behavior, relatively few of these contributions have been systematically utilized for purposes of rehabilitation."[1] They conjectured the reason for this: sociological tradition views sociology as primarily a research discipline and not a treatment one. In 1955 Cressey observed:[2] "Sociological theories and hypotheses have had a great influence on development of general correctional policies, such as probation and parole, but they have been used only intermittently and haphazardly in reforming individual criminals. Since sociology is essentially a research discipline, sociologist-criminologists have devoted most of their time and energy to understanding and explaining crime, leaving to psychiatrists and others the problem of reforming criminals." It is in the context of these observations that a recent development in sociology—clinical sociology—is of some import.[3]

[1]LaMar T. Empey and Jerome Rabow, "The Provo Experiment in Delinquent Rehabilitation," *American Sociological Review* 26 (October 1961): 679.

[2]Donald R. Cressey, "Changing Criminals: The Application of the Theory of Differential Association," *American Journal of Sociology* 61 (September 1955): 116.

[3]John F. Glass, "Clinical Sociology: A New Profession," paper presented at the Annual Meeting of the American Sociological Association, Chicago, 1977. See also Marshall Edelson, *Sociotherapy and Psychotherapy.* (Berkeley: University of California Press, 1970) and by the same author, *The Practice of Sociotherapy* (New Haven: Yale University Press, 1970).

*The Provo Experiment.* A noted experiment in applying sociological theory towards the rehabilitation process was reported by Empey and Rabow in a paper based on their work with juveniles in Provo, Utah.[4] The Provo Experiment was based on the following observations:

1. The greater part of delinquent behavior is not that of individuals engaging in highly secretive deviations, but is a group phenomenon—a shared deviation which is the product of differentiated group experience in a particular subculture; and

2. Because most delinquents tend to be concentrated in slums, or to be the children of lower-class parents, their lives are characterized by learning situations which limit their access to success goals. Success is thus translated into deviancy by the presence of a delinquent system which supplies status and recognition.

The authors note that the home and/or parents "may have been instrumental at some early phase in the genesis of a boy's delinquency," but it is his current identification with a delinquent reference group that is, in the form of an intervening mechanism, the immediate cause of his delinquency." Treatment can, thus, focus on either his "early phase," using transference and introspective therapy, or it can focus on the nature of his membership in the delinquent system and "direct treatment to him as part of that system." Provo opts for the latter method.

The Provo program deals with upwards of twenty boys, habitual offenders, fifteen to seventeen years of age, who spend between four to seven months at the school. "Norms dictate that no one in the group can be released until everyone is honest and until every boy helps to solve problems."[5] Failures are sent to the Utah State Industrial School. The basic approach is *Guided Group Interaction,* which "grants to the peer group a great deal of power, including helping to decide when each body is ready to be released." The authorities "do not go out of their way to engage in regular social amenities, to put the boys at ease, or to establish one-to-one relationships." There is no individual counseling, testing, gathering of case histories or clinical diagnosing. The school is located in the community and the boys live at home spending only a part of each day at the center.

There is a deliberate lack of formal structure and boys are seldom told why they are in trouble or why the authorities are doing what they are doing:[6]

[4]Empey and Rabow, pp. 680–96.
[5]Ibid., p. 687.
[6]Ibid., p. 686.

The absence of formal structure helps to do more than avoid artificial criteria for release. It has the positive effect of making boys more amenable to treatment. In the absence of formal structure they are uneasy and they are not quite sure of themselves.

This fluid situation sets the stage for treatment:

1. It produces anxiety and turns boys toward the group as a method of resolving their anxiety.
2. It leaves boys free to define situations for themselves.
3. It binds neither authorities nor the peer group to prescribed courses of action. Each is free to do whatever is needed to suit the needs of particular boys, groups or situations.

The only "conventional" aspect of the program, that which is similar to other treatment programs in institutional settings, is the daily group discussions.

*The Synanon Program.* Volkman and Cressey report on the *Synanon* drug rehabilitation program, citing it as an example of the successful application of the theory of differential association.[7] The Synanon program emphasizes alienating the addict from his previous group values which support deviance, while assisting him in assimilating a new orientation which is conducive to nondeviant behavior. The authors illustrate the antideviance nature of the Synanon subculture:[8]

> First, there is a strong taboo against what is called "street talk." Discussion of how it feels to take a fix, who one's connection was, where one took his shot, the crimes committed, or who one associated with is severely censured.
> Second, a member must never in any circumstances, identify with the "code of the street," which says that a criminal is supposed to keep quiet about the criminal activities of his peers.

Cressey and Volkman note that the addict, "who as a criminal, learned to hate stool pigeons and finks with a passion must now turn even his closest friend over to the authorities, the older members of Synanon, if the friend shows any signs of nonconformity." The authors report: Cohesion is maximized by a "family" analogy and by the fact that all but some "third-stage members live and work together. The daily program has been deliberately designed to throw members into continuous

---

[7]Rita Volkman and Donald R. Cressey, "Differential Association and the Rehabilitation of Drug Addicts," *American Journal of Sociology* 69 (September 1963): 129–42.

[8]Ibid., pp. 133–34.

mutual activity." Status is gained according to one's attitude toward crime and the use of drugs:[9]

> The Synanon experience is organized into a career of roles that represent stages of graded competence, at whose end are roles that might later be used in the broader community.

Regular group sessions (without any trained therapists) emphasize the enforcement of anticriminal and antidrug norms.

Cressey argues: "If the behavior of an individual is an intrinsic part of groups to which he belongs, attempts to change the behavior must be directed at groups."[10] He points out that the group should be used to develop new attitudes and values: "if criminals are to be changed, either they must become members of anticriminal groups, or their present procriminal group relations must be changed."[11] The target for change is the group: "When an entire group is the target of change, as in a prison or among delinquent gangs, strong pressure for change can be achieved by convincing the members of the need for a change, thus making the group itself the source of pressure for change."[12]

### UTILIZING GROUP METHODS

Konopka states that group work "is one of the methods used predominantly in the context of the face-to-face group and which uses the group as a medium of action."[13] She points out that, of the various specialities in social work, group work did not completely accept psychoanalysis "partly because it entered the social work family at a time when psychoanalytic thinking had begun to change and partly because the underlying concepts of group work were derived from such early sociologists as Simmel and Weber."[14]

There are five basic reasons for utilizing group methods in criminal justice:

1. *Group methods reduce tension.* The criminal justice practitioner is an authority figure, and the offender may find the casework interview a rather trying, if not traumatic, experience. The tension that

[9]Ibid., p. 136.
[10]Donald R. Cressey, "Changing Criminals: The Application of the Theory of Differential Association," *American Journal of Sociology* 61 (September 1955): 116–20.
[11]Ibid., p. 118.
[12]Ibid., p. 119.
[13]Gisela Konopka, Social Group Work: A Helping Process (Englewood Cliffs, N.J.: Prentice-Hall, 1972), p. xi.
[14]Ibid., p. 13.

exists, especially early in the relationship, may hinder the ability of the criminal justice practitioner to help his/her client. In a group, however, the offender is part of the majority: There are several offenders but only one criminal justice practitioner. The authority of the criminal justice practitioner and its effect on the client is dispersed among the group members. The offender is free, or at least freer, in the group where he/she can participate actively or passively.

2. *Group methods reduce class-racial ethnic differences.* It is the exceptional case where the criminal justice practitioner and the offender can identify with each other on the basis of class, race, and/or ethnicity. Often, even when race and ethnicity are the same for criminal justice practitioner and client, class differences are present. That these factors can inhibit the creation of a sound helping relationship has been discussed extensively in professional and popular literature. In the group, these differences tend to be less important, since, in the hands of a skilled worker, the group utilizes interaction between members to provide the medium of help.

3. *Group methods reduce feelings of isolation.* When the offender enters the group situation, he/she recognizes that other persons encounter similar problems; the group members are persons with similar backgrounds and experiences who share like aspirations and/or feelings of alienation. The group provides comfort to each member as he/she realizes that such a situation is not unique, it is not an isolated one. The group allows offenders to "let their hair down" without the fear of losing status.

4. *Offenders aid each other.* The group is effective because in this setting the client is the helping person—not some "honky," "gringo," and/or agent of the establishment. The criminal justice practitioner must facilitate the helping process, but he/she does not find solutions to problems; it is the client, who must live in the *real* world, and find solutions that are relevant. The skilled worker is able to keep the "work" of dealing with problems flowing in the group.

5. *Group methods provide a "safe" milieu.* In the group setting, offenders can relate to each other in a way that is different from their previous peer experiences. The need to be "tough," or "conning," for example, is not a pressing consideration in the group. The group, if under the aegis of a skilled worker, provides a nonthreatening milieu where feelings can be expressed, where new roles can be tried, and where otherwise relatively helpless persons become helpers. The feelings of mutual aid that can be generated in a group setting lead to a cohesiveness that allows the group to be a medium of help.

In a chapter of his book which discusses "social deviance," Heraud states that traditional social casework approaches have little chance of success for persons experiencing anomie in the form of normlessness, and persons who respond to anomie by retreatism: "casework based on clarification and strengthening of goals.... will have little chance of success in cases of severe retreatism."[15] He advises the worker to distinguish between "marginal" and "hard-core" situations of normlessness. In the latter case, the deviant family has retreated from accepted norms and can *justify their own deviant standards.* Heraud suggests that casework can be successful in the "marginal" cases.[16] The difficulty, according to the author, is that traditional methods of social service cannot deal with what is essentially a problem of social structure.[17] Instead, he suggests that the worker stress the broker or advocate role: "social work can help to grapple with such [structural] problems by intervention at levels which are intermediate between the individual and society—the school, the neighborhood, and the community."[18]

### ADVOCACY

Our earlier review of sociological theory and the criminal justice sequence provides a basis for discussing the role of the criminal justice practitioner as an advocate:[19]

> *Basis 1*-The "justice system" is often unfair, at least insofar as it accentuates the misbehavior of specifically disadvantaged groups as compared to more advantaged groups;
>
> *Basis 2*-Much of what eventually happens to an offender is determined by such idiosyncrasies of the criminal justice system as caseload size, the personality of the agents of control, e.g., the policeman, the prosecutor, the judge, and the circumstances of the victim—class, race, etc.
>
> *Basis 3*-The goal of social work is to prevent or at least to alleviate the socially and psychologically damaging effects of social injustice.

Shireman notes that a basic task of social work is to produce change in the way social institutions confront their clients. He states

[15]Brian J. Heraud, *Sociology and Social Work: Perspectives and Problems.* (Oxford: Pergamon Press, 1970), pp. 166–67.

[16]Ibid., p. 167.

[17]Ibid., p. 168.

[18]Ibid., p. 169.

[19]Walter A. Friedlander, Introduction to *Concepts and Methods of Social Work* (Englewood Cliffs: Prentice-Hall, Inc., 1976).

that an emphasis on advocacy "represents a healthy refocusing on social functioning in the broader sense," as opposed to a focus mainly on treating intrapsychic disorders. He maintains that a major challenge of social work in criminal justice is to deal with the system, not just the offender.[20] Friedlander states that the social worker, as a community organizer, "encourages the leaders of the community to provide the necessary social services and facilities to procure opportunities for learning and to realize physical health, cultural growth, and pleasure for those individuals and groups for whom present conditions have not secured these means."[21] Like Shireman, Friedlander notes a two-fold (*dualistic*) aim of social work, focusing not only on the individual, his family and groups of persons, but "also concerned with the improvement of general *social conditions* by raising health and economic standards, advocating better housing and working conditions, and supporting constructive social legislation."[22]

In Chapter Three we reviewed specific junctures within the decision-making process of the criminal justice system. Gottfredson states that "criminal justice may be portrayed schematically quite well, depicting the interrelated nature of its parts, by a flow diagram showing the series of points at which decisions may be triggered by a report of a crime."[23] Figure 5-1 is a schematic diagram based on Gottfredson's recommendation.

Using the *decision-making points* shown in Figure 5-1, we will focus on the formal in addition to the informal or unofficial aspects of the criminal justice system to see how the practitioner can maximize his/her role as an advocate. For our purposes, the advocate role will be limited to the practitioner's "normal" responsibilities in the criminal justice system. This will involve collecting information, evaluating offender needs, providing recommendations designed to meet these needs, and engaging in appropriate activities designed to facilitate client help. How is this put into operation?

The criminal justice practitioner can offer an alternative to further processing. The practitioner may, for example, indicate to the police that more appropriate means of disposing of a particular case are available as an alternative to arrest and continued processing. If the social service worker is available, the service may be offered even prior to an

---

[20]Charles Shireman, "The Justice System and the Practice of Social Work," *Social Work* 19 (September 1974): 563.

[21]Friedlander, pp. 5–6.

[22]Ibid., p. 7.

[23]Don M. Gottfredson et al., eds. *Decision-Making in the Criminal Justice System: Reviews and Essays* (Rockville, Md.: National Institute of Mental Health, 1975), p. vi.

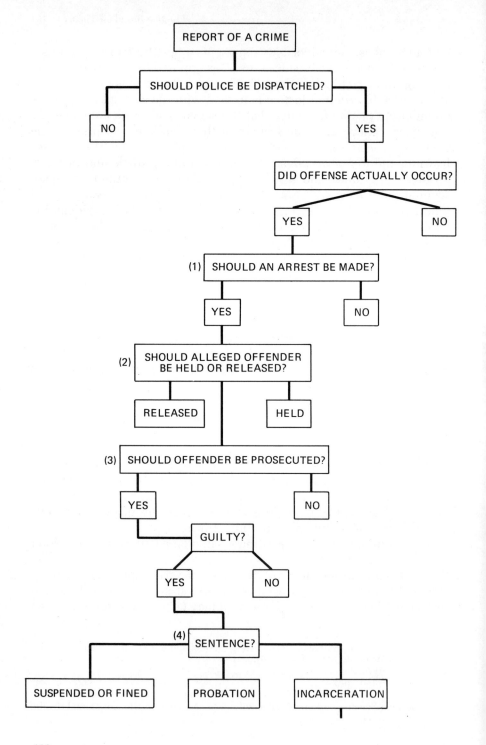

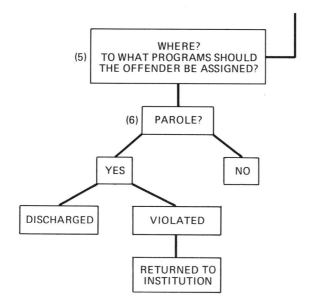

**Figure 5-1.** Decisions Triggered by a Report of a Crime

arrest—point (1) on our diagram. Timely intervention is crucial in the criminal justice system since once the wheels begin to turn they are difficult to stop or reverse.

In the schematic, point (2) relates to the police decision to issue a summons or arrest, detain and hold for arraignment. As in point (1), timely intervention is crucial. The third key point—point (3)—is prosecution or its equivalent in juvenile court. The criminal justice practitioner can provide psychosocial and agency resource information which can be useful in convincing the prosecution to drop or defer prosecution. The sentencing process—point (4)—is an obvious area in which the criminal justice practitioner functions as an advocate. The practitioner may be a probation officer or employee of a private voluntary or legal aid agency. In the juvenile court the criminal justice practitioner, usually a probation officer, must offer treatment alternatives to the court. A particular difficulty in this regard is the reluctance of many private treatment programs to accept "serious" delinquents into a program, even when the probation officer believes the program is the most appropriate one for a particular youngster. The practitioner acting as an advocate may mobilize the influence of the court to secure a proper private agency placement. Thus, as we see in point (5), the criminal justice practitioner may play an important role in determining where an offender is sent if incarceration is indicated. Within point (5) is the classification process, in which the criminal justice practitioner is an active participant but not usually an advocate. At point (6), parole, the criminal justice practitioner finds himself playing in a crucial role, for the information that he provides the paroling authorities may decide the question of parole release. Private or public agency personnel may operate as advocates at this stage by offering services to inmates that will increase their chances of receiving favorable parole consideration—employment or training, for example.

As an advocate, the criminal justice practitioner helps to individualize and personalize cases. He/she helps to convert a rather dehumanizing situation into one which focuses on the person as a human being, not merely a case or docket number. Another aspect of the criminal justice practitioner as an advocate concerns dealing with noncriminal justice agencies, private employers, and persons. The practitioner may help to secure services from such public agencies as the welfare department, hospitals, and schools (including colleges). The criminal justice practitioner must be aware of the possibility that public or private agencies or employers may discriminate against offenders because of their offender status or race, etc. Often the client will not be aware of such practices, or he/she may perceive them when they are not grounded in fact. When discrimination is apparent the criminal justice practitioner may intercede directly on behalf of the client or draw upon private or public agencies having jurisdiction or interest in preventing discriminatory practices.

Della'Apa et al. note that correctional client populations, probationers and parolees, tend to be composed of "low-status losers from a highly stratified and complex society."[24] The authors state: "The punishment administered by assignments to corrections is not too different from the punishment they routinely receive on the streets from an indifferent society."[25] They present a plan for helping offenders which they state "represents a radical departure from contemporary practices." Their *Community Resources Management Team* (CRMT) approach is based on the need for an improved delivery services model, as opposed to the medical model approach. Therefore, practitioners must assume the role of an advocate in order to secure services needed by the offender that are available in the community service network, or they must "assume a community organization and resource development role for needed services that do not exist." In the CRMT model, the criminal justice practitioner acts as an advocate-broker, which the authors maintain is a complete reversal of traditional roles. They state

[24]Frank Della'Apa, Tom Adams, James D. Jorgensen, and Herbert R. Sigurdson, "Advocacy, Brokerage, Community: The ABC's of Probation and Parole," *Federal Probation* 40 (December 1976): 37–44.
[25]Ibid., p. 37.

that the CRMT model "transforms the way workers assess their clients. The client is now a person whose future depends not only on how well he adjusts and adapts to the environment, but additionally, on how well he is linked to social institutions."[26] Thus, "a new balance is struck between the traditional role of counseling and controlling the client and community development."[27]

*The Adolescent Diversion Program.* The Adolescent Diversion Project of the University of Illinois at Champaign embarked on a program involving child advocacy. The following is a view of the theory and practice underlying this aspect of the program.[28] Advocates are undergraduate student volunteers supervised by professionals.

### Child Advocacy

The underlying rationale for the child advocacy approach is that youth have the *right* to community resources. The needs of the youth are met by adapting the community resources to the individual youth rather than by specifying which resources are needed by all youth and making them generally available. The intervention focuses on individual rights and the assessment of individual needs.

The advocate's role can be broadly construed, as " ... his client's supporter, his advisor, his champion, and, if need be, his representative in his dealings with the court, the police, the social agency, and other organizations that affect his well being ... "[29] Or the conception can be a narrower one in which advocates primarily supply their clients with information about their environment and youths eventually become their own self-advocates.

In either case, the advocate serves the essential function of opening up opportunities to "legitimate means" of attaining desirable goals—education, the acquisition of skills leading to a decent job, a certain minimum of material and psychological well-being. In child advocacy theory, delinquent behavior is less a function of individual personality than a product of available social and community resources. The thrust of the child advocacy approach, then, is to secure the rights of the child with respect to generally available community resources and to open access to opportunities which otherwise may have been beyond the reach

[26]Ibid., p. 41.
[27]Ibid.
[28]Richard Ku and Carol Holliday Blew, *A University's Approach to Delinquency: The Adolescent Diversion Project* (Washington, D.C.: United States Government Printing Office, 1977). References in the original deleted.
[29]National Association of Social Workers, report of the AD HOC committee on Advocacy, 1969, p. 17.

of the child. . . . the child advocacy approach assesses the youth in terms of unmet needs that result because personal or community resources are unavailable or unexplored, rather than because interpersonal problems exist. Mutual identification of resources for change (*individuals* who have power over the delivery of personal and community resources) provides the basis for advocacy intervention.

The range of strategies available to the student employing the child advocacy approach may begin with simply convincing a community agency to provide resources to meet a specific need of the referred youth. A more radical strategy would employ media exposure or pressure on political figures or persons with substantial community influence to convince existing agencies to deliver resources to the youth. Provision of information to a critical individual about an unmet need of the youth, without direct involvement in that intervention, represents a somewhat passive strategy. Obviously, the choice of a strategy is highly dependent on the degree to which the advocacy-based intervention acts *for* the youth, rather than instructing that youth to take such actions himself.

Taking educational resources as an example of the range of advocacy strategies, in a case involving unmet educational needs a number of targets for change are possible. At one end of the continuum, the student could "plead his case" to the individual teacher(s) involved with the youth in question. A middle-ground strategy would involve attempting to change educational resources by consulting a school principal. At the top end of the continuum, the student could take the case to the local board of education or superintendent of schools. Individual strategies for cases are selected jointly by the student, the youth, and the supervisors on the basis of previous knowledge about the persons involved, about the prospects of success with a particular approach, and about previous attempts relevant to the specific case. In sum, the child advocacy model for ADP involved the following activities on the part of the student intervention agent:

1. During the first two weeks of contact, the student attempted to get to know the individual youth and began to determine *with* the youth the problem areas and targets for change.
2. The student became involved in manipulating resources for the youth, applying a variety of advocacy strategies.
3. Sometime around the third month of intervention the student instructed and encouraged the youth to initiate his or her own advocacy actions.
4. During the last month of the intervention, the student prepared the youth further for his or her own advocacy role and

for the termination of formal intervention by the student. The student assumed a passive role, limited to consulting the youth while the youth carried out his or her own advocacy efforts.

In the following two case studies, the conceptions and techniques of the child advocacy intervention approach are illustrated.

---

### CHILD ADVOCACY CASE

Mike was a sixteen-year-old who at the time of his referral was facing charges for attempted murder and aggravated assault. This was Mike's first offense in the local community since moving here from a large urban area five weeks earlier. Mike lived with his mother who was employed as a surgical aide in a local hospital. Before coming to the local community, Mike had been deeply involved in gang activity. He had been on probation in his previous community. After intake and pre-assessment, Mike was assigned to a student volunteer.

By the student's report, Mike was very quiet during that first meeting. The student said that "He called me 'Sir,' and I freaked out." After a rather uncommunicative hour, the volunteer asked Mike what he would like to do, and he indicated an interest in shooting pool. As a result, they went to the University Union and talked and played pool. Their next two weeks together involved mostly recreational activities. They attended a University basketball game, had dinner at the student's house, and shot pool. Before the first two weeks were up, the project was informed that the prosecuting attorney's office intended to file a petition on the attempted murder charges even though the police had agreed to divert Mike to the project. Mike received a five-day notice to appear in court for a preliminary hearing. He called the student and asked him what he should do. The student suggested that they go to the preliminary hearing together, and that the first step should be to request an attorney.

Mike, his mother, and the volunteer attended the preliminary hearing and, at the volunteer's suggestion, Mike remained silent except to request an attorney. A continuance was granted for two weeks to allow for a court-appointed attorney to be involved in the case.

Two days after the initial court hearing, Mike went to the student's house and initiated a discussion of what they should do next. According to the student, this was the first time that he had any indication that Mike was interested in actively participating in the project. A lengthy discussion followed in which the student explained the whole notion of advocacy and that they would have to "have their case together" if they were to convince the court that severe action was unnecessary. He explained that it would be important that they be able to convince the judge that the project provided a positive alternative to probation or placement away from home.

During the next two weeks, the student and Mike talked on the phone three times per week and continued their recreational activities. They discussed various community programs and activities which would interest Mike. Mike expressed a particular need to do this since he was new to the community. Because the shooting incident in question involved some of the "prominent" kids in his neighborhood, he was pretty much a loner socially.

Together they identified the following needs and community programs:

1. *Department of Vocational Rehabilitation.* Mike was considerably behind in school and was interested in part time employment. He was behind to the point that he was unable to read and continuing to attend regular ninth grade classes was of little potential benefit.

2. *Junior varsity basketball team.* Mike was a good basketball player but had not gone out for the basketball team because he was not aware of when and where practice and tryouts occurred.

3. *Recreational activities.* Mike felt that he needed additional activities to meet other youth in the community.

Mike and the student discussed the need for developing a strategy to gain access to the desired programs. They spent an afternoon going over a catalogue of programs in the local community and determining who was going to take responsibility for making the necessary contacts. The student agreed to set up a meeting with Mike and his school counselor so they could get more information concerning the vocational program available through the school. Mike agreed to approach the basketball coach, explain his situation, and request permission to try out. They agreed to go together to look into several recreational programs available through the Boy's Club and the park district.

Mike's scheduled court hearing was postponed for a month due to the absence of the presiding judge. Mike's attorney indicated that they would request a further continuance, to give them time to demonstrate that formal court supervision was not necessary for Mike.

Mike was successful in gaining permission to try out for the basketball team and started playing regularly. Gaining access to the vocational resources proved more difficult. A number of pre-assessment screenings were necessary for Mike to enroll in the school district's vocational rehabilitation program. The meeting with the school counselor culminated in an appointment for physical and psychological testing. The actual testing was delayed on two occasions, however. Finally, the student confronted the school counselor and vocational rehabilitation coordinator for an explanation of the delays. They indicated that Mike had been missing school on several occasions, and they weren't sure he was a "good risk." The student next went to the district director of the program and demanded that Mike be admitted to the vocational and work study program, threatening intervention by Mike's attorney. Within two weeks Mike was enrolled in half-day vocational classes and participating in work/study employment the other half day.

When the formal court hearing was finally held (three months after referral), the student and Mike's attorney were successful in convincing the judge that formal intervention by the court would be counterproductive. An informal review was scheduled in 60 days, but Mike was not formally adjudicated. At this point, the student began reviewing the principles of advocacy with Mike. Unfortunately, however, two weeks prior to his termination, Mike was arrested for theft (shoplifting) and was formally placed on probation at his review hearing.

## Practice Based on Psychoanalytic Theory

Frazier provides a review of his work with inmates at the Deuel Institution of the California Youth Authority. In his paper he focuses on the use of casework with young drug addicts. These youngsters are usually fearful of forming relationships, especially one in which the addict knows that the purpose is to give up "his one satisfying experience in life," drug usage.[30] The absence of this satisfaction in the institution may motivate the addict toward a new approach to interpersonal relationships as a way of handling his conflicts and anxieties which can no longer be anesthetized with drugs: "As he increased the dosage of heroin during the past months or years to keep going, so he now has a supply of the caseworker's understanding, acceptance, warmth, and trust that he can use in increasing amounts as his capacity for an interpersonal relationship increases."[31]

According to psychoanalytic theory, drug abuse is symptomatic of neurosis which manifests itself during adolescence. Freud states: "From the time of puberty onward the human individual must devote himself to the great task of *freeing himself from the parents;* and only after this detachment is accomplished can he cease to be a child and so become a member of the social community."[32] Freud points out that in neurotics this detachment is not accomplished.[33] Frazier focuses on the addict's distorted pathological relationship with his/her parents which was characterized by becoming overdependent or being rejected. This experience can effect the present relationship with the worker, who, by the mechanism of transference, is a parental figure. The worker builds on this transference, providing a healthy and constructive relationship through which the addict can go on to learn that "he is accepted with his shortcomings as well as his strengths," with the goal being greater understanding of himself and his ability to handle problems with his parents on a more real basis: "becoming more independent of them in the manner he has learned to be more independent of the worker."[34]

[30]Thomas L. Frazier, "Treating Young Drug Users: A Casework Approach," © 1962, National Association of Social Workers, Inc. Reprinted from *Social Work,* Vol. 7, No. 3 (July 1962), pp. 94–101.

[31]Ibid., p. 95.

[32]Sigmund Freud, *A General Introduction to Psychoanalysis* (New York: Washington Square Press, 1961), pp. 345–46.

[33]Ibid., p. 346.

[34]Frazier, p. 95.

Frazier notes that the addict's identification with his father (or father figure) is "at best shakey and laden with hostility."[35] The addict, despite anger expressed towards the father, often identifies with him and his failures. This identification serves as a basis for help, as the worker enables the addict to deal with these feelings without resorting to drugs or other acting-out behavior. "The ability to check impulses, to control feelings, to endure some pain, to feel a little more adequate as a man will figure largely in the inmate's ability to get along on parole."[36] Having recognized more clearly the positive factors in his identification with his father (through a transference relationship with the caseworker), he can now use this insight as a base to delve into similar feelings he has toward his mother. For instance, he may begin to point out how the mother sometimes drove the father out of the house. He may even side with the father against the mother, and if this happens at all on a feeling level, he may eventually try to express some feelings of hostility toward his mother. The author notes that while anger toward the father is often permissible, expressing anger towards a mother figure is wrought with psychological difficulty. "In the final stages of treatment the caseworker is compared with the father before he is compared with the mother. At first the addict may recognize his father's weaknesses and say he would like to have a father who has the qualities of the caseworker. When he recognizes that no one can be just like the caseworker he can then separate his father's 'good points' from his 'bad' ones. Finally, through the caseworker's acceptance he will accept his father and thus himself."[37]

Frazier notes that the addict's relationship with his mother usually includes a long history of emotional deprivation:[38]

> Frequently, a tense, dominant, autistic, unhappy mother forced the child into becoming an adjunct to herself rather than allowing him to develop as an independent person. The feeling of hostility toward the mother and the inability to form any close satisfactory relationships date back to these earliest years. The addict's conflicts reflect this oral deprivation in an infantile helplessness, and the drug helps him regress to a "happy" infancy that was never really happy. The effects of the drug handle his hostility and reduce the tensions which are symptoms of these life-long conflicts. The hostility toward the mother generally remains unconscious, but it is expressed through the drug which not only "destroys" the user but also symbolically destroys the mother whom he has incorporated through identification.

[35]Ibid., p. 97.
[36]Ibid., 97.
[37]Ibid., p. 98.
[38]Ibid.

Through the casework relationship, the addict is encouraged to explore his ambivalent love/hate feelings toward his mother and to recognize how the use of drugs was an attempt to reconcile these anxiety-producing feelings.

Frazier provides an interesting explanation as to why the "recovery" rate for aggressive offenders is greater than that of drug addicts:[39]

> The armed robber, for instance, is aware of his hostility toward his victim or the world; he generally has little difficulty discussing it and therefore, hopefully, little difficulty in handling it in the treatment process; the young drug user who robs is seldom aware of any anger toward the victim or toward his parents who originally generated his hostility. The drug has handled the hostility, and his main interest in criminal activity is to obtain more drugs. The actual crime (burglary, theft, and—infrequently—armed robbery) is far removed from the original seat of hostility whereas the use of the drug is one step closer to it.

Fenichel presents some of the psychoanalytic dynamics involved in drug addiction:[40]

1. There is a combination of "the need to get something that is not merely sexual satisfaction but also security and assurance of self-assertion. . ."
2. Euphoric drugs are protections "against painful mental states, for example, against depression, and are indeed often very effective."

He concludes that "addicts are persons who have a disposition to react to the effects of alcohol, morphine, or other drugs in such a way that they try to use these effects to satisfy the archaic oral longings which is sexual longing, a need for security, and a need for the maintenance of self-esteem simultaneously."[41] This pathology has its origins in infantile sexuality, both oral and Oedipal.

St. Pierre reviews some of the attributes of drug addicts[42] treated in a hospital setting:[43]

---

[39]Ibid., p. 100.

[40]Otto Fenichel, *The Psychoanalytic Theory of Neuroses* (New York: W. W. Norton, 1945), pp. 376–77.

[41]Ibid., p. 376.

[42]Those persons addicted to opiates, i.e., heroin, or opiate-like substances such as methadone and barbituates.

[43]C. André St. Pierre, "Motivating the Drug Addict in Treatment," © 1971, National Association of Social Workers, Inc. Reprinted from *Social Work*, Vol. 16, No. 1 (January 1971), pp. 80–88.

1. Drug usage usually begins during adolescence out of curiosity, thrill-seeking, and peer influences;
2. The "high" approximates the orgasm, and serves as a substitute for sexual involvement—drugs suppress the sexual drive;
3. Drugs provide relief from psychic tension, reducing anxiety;
4. The hospital may serve as a refuse from street hustling and it provides an opportunity to reduce the quantity of drugs needed to sustain a "good high." Since addicting drugs produce a tolerance, the person seeking a "high" must constantly increase his/her dosage. When this is no longer financially or physically possible, the addict may seek hospital care as the most painless method of withdrawing from the drug. Obviously, motivation is not to give up drug usage, but merely to bring it back to a point of pleasure.

St. Pierre provides additional insight into unconscious motivations.[44]

[The addict patients] were not fully aware of their great lack of incentive. They overworked the ego defense mechanisms of denial and projection, which obviously interfered with this awareness. Denial was used in two ways. The addict rejected the reality of his physical and personal deterioration and indulged himself in the wish-fulfilling fantasy of the "beautiful feeling of heroin," thereby shutting out the "madness of it all." Projection was found to be especially useful in avoiding the uncomfortable reality of responsibility for continuing the addiction. For example, when methadone was denied, addicts often said: "You're forcing me to go back on the street and use drugs." To this the counselor was tempted to say: "Why is this a crisis? What have you been doing for the past two years?" Another projection frequently heard was the addict's blaming his relapse on another person: "A friend stopped by and gave me some."

St. Pierre states that The addict usually has little insight into the motivations for his drug use. St. Pierre states:[45]

Actually patients never gave the matter much thought before it was brought up in therapy. They really had to be helped to see that they were taking drugs to meet certain needs, emotional as well as physical. Simply asking the patient: "What do drugs do for

[44]Ibid., p. 84.
[45]Ibid., pp. 85–86.

you?" often established what drugs really meant to him. It is most important that the patient verbalize these needs in order to return the crucial focus to his own words.

Invaribly all patients brought out directly and indirectly two major reasons for drug use: (1) they thoroughly enjoyed the satiating euphoria of the high and (2) the drug brought considerable relief from psychic pain, tension, and anxiety. Patients verbalized quite easily that drugs relaxed them. Surprisingly, however, patients soft-pedal the importance of the high to them. Only later as therapy progresses does the overwhelming importance of the high and its primacy in the patient's relapse emerge.

The clinical observation is that the standard psychodynamic formulations for explaining relapse become secondary to new drives generated in the personality after the patient has tasted the effect of drugs. The pleasure principle now appears to take hold. What is now being dealt with is a hungry man who has a new appetite, an appetite for the feeling he knows drugs will give him. The chief motive for relapse was observed repeatedly to be the attempt to recapture the first high—such is the impact it has made on the addict's mind and feelings. Bringing this to his awareness eventually elicits a concession by the patient that this is the case. This proved to be extremely important in giving the patient an understanding of why he was using drugs.

The self-destructive impulse appeared for most patients to be a component part of addiction. Additional guilt brought on by addiction compounded the situation. In this regard patients reported taking larger and larger dosages in order to achieve the desired oblivion. Also, the need to expiate showed itself as the addict flirted dangerously with death by overdose. The clinical picture viewed here is that of the addict standing motionless, arms hanging limp, observing himself plunging headlong downhill to self-destruction and doing nothing about it. He apparently splits himself off from his feelings, using the ego defense mechanism of isolation, and thereby does not see himself as a participant in this tragedy. When challenged by the counselor with: "You see what's happening; why don't you do something about it?" the addict usually replies with a naive rationalization: "I don't know how." Were the patient able to be more honest his reply would be: "I won't struggle," which is the crux of the motivation problem.

The reality of the situation appeared to be that in heroin addiction, as with all other forms of addiction, one is unable to stick to a system. The addict finds himself psychologically helpless to set any limits on his use of drugs. He becomes "greedy," as some patients put it. Furthermore, changes are going on in his body; a tolerance develops. The body demands more and more of the drug to achieve the desired feeling, and eventually high dosages are needed simply to prevent withdrawal sickness. There is no status quo—and this fact has to be reinforced continually.

Fenichel notes that addicts represent the most clear-cut type of *impulse neurotics*: "They betray a characteristic *irresistability*, which is different from that of a normal instinctual drive, and which is caused by the condensation of instinctual urge and defensive strivings."[46] St. Pierre notes the impulsive nature of the addict:[47]

> In this phase the patient has to be helped to develop an appreciation of the power feelings have over his behavior. Typically (which is likely the condition of the majority of the general population), the addict is unaware of the world of feelings. He goes through life without understanding why he feels the way he does. With regard to his addiction, rational thinking and behavior are submerged under waves of impulses.

In order to deal with this impulsiveness, St. Pierre suggests that the addict must be helped to distinguish between "knowing and feeling":[48]

> [The addict] may know that drugs are destructive; however, his feelings may not respond according to his best interests. His impulses might continue to demand gratification despite the injurious consequences. The patient is told that his *knowing* could be considered an expression of the intellectual portion of his personality, whereas his *feelings* are the expression of the instinctual forces.

To do this the practitioner must help the patient become aware of his adult, mature and rational self, as opposed to the demanding, childish, and narcissistic aspect of his nature and "its associated uncontrolled impulses." St. Pierre states:[49]

> When the patient has mastered the stages of knowing why he uses drugs, developing an intellectual conviction that this is self-destructive, and achieving some insight into his feelings, his ego is seen to be in a much stronger position to contain and attempt mastery of his craving for drugs. What was observed clinically was an excruciating turmoil in and struggle on the part of

---

[46]Fenichel, p. 367.
[47]St. Pierre, p. 86.
[48]Ibid., p. 86.
[49]Ibid., p. 87.

the patient. Some patients compared it to taming a wild animal in themselves, a predicament that can readily be appreciated.

Using an approach based on the psychoanalytic theory of growth and development, Geiger discusses counseling in a probation setting:[50]

> This person on probation has arrived there because of his emotions which are affected by threats to the ego and he has reacted to these according to the manner in which his emotions have developed and the balance he has achieved in his reactions. The id or the primitive impulses are counteracted by the superego which is largely in the subconscious zone and is a composite representation of the parents. It takes the place of the actual parents in the management of the id or primitive impulses and is the critical faculty of the unconscious. The probation officer acts similarly on the conscious level. The ego, the result of the stimuli from the outer world and from within, represents what is commonly known as reason, logic, sanity. The id is the driving power and the ego is the operator of the vehicle. The ego is the achieved balance between the instinctive energy of the id and the superego. The ego evolved by the influences of the world on the more primal structure, the id, the superego, largely in the unconscious zone but contacting both the id and the ego and being the critical faculty must all be able to balance to some degree if personality organization occurs.

Geiger notes that emotional blocks require discharge, and that antisocial behavior can provide an outlet for repressed emotions. In the healthy, mature individual, emotional reactions that are potentially harmful are suppressed or sublimated in a socially acceptable manner. This is part of adult adjustment to reality. With the offender, this is problematic. Therefore, she advises a review of emotional reactions before, during, and after the offense to help the offender:[51]

> Learn to endure the pain that strikes deeply into the emotions, to postpone or give up satisfactions, that is, immediate desires, and to direct primitive instinctual urges into socially acceptable outlets. It is to be remembered that sometimes those with less cultural background, because of their differences, have less ability to suppress the instinctual drives and must be dealt with in ways suited to their understanding. Only under restrictions, and

[50]Sara G. Geiger, "Counseling Techniques in Probation," *Federal Probation* 18 (March 1954), p. 28. Reprinted by permission of *Federal Probation*.
[51]Ibid., p. 29.

sometimes painful ones, does the probationer learn to curb impulse and accept the demands of society with or without conflict.

Geiger stresses the importance of the relationship between the worker and the offender; in order to be helped, the offender must enter into a good object-relationship with the worker. The offender "becomes convinced that the therapist is a good object when he works through positive and negative transferences and 'discovers' that the analyst loves him in a mature, adult sense, freeing him for more satisfactory relationships in his outer world." The difficulty of establishing this kind of relationship within the authoritarian setting of criminal justice is stressed, especially since previous contacts with criminal justice personnel may have been essentially negative:[52]

> Handicaps from early contacts with law-enforcing agents enter the picture, but the officer is a counselor and a therapist during the period of probation, despite the fact that the police role is also thrust upon him. There is no more difficult situation in which to establish and maintain rapport than that in which each is ordered to be friendly one to the other.

Geiger stresses the need to plan for treatment, which is often problematic given the usual high caseloads and deficient information that characterizes criminal justice practice:[53]

> In order to achieve a counseling plan one needs to know what the diagnosis is. Work of high quality cannot be achieved with a large case load. A diagnosis and a knowledge of the dynamics of the behavior make it possible to allocate time for counseling. Should there have been a presentence investigation, one has knowledge from which to proceed. Should there have been no presentence investigation, the officer must find his way alone and arrive at his own conclusion, or diagnosis, relative to the man with whom he works.

After determining the problem from the tentative diagnosis, the worker "will define the immediate problems of the individual and how they have or have not extended into his family, social, and work situation." Geiger expresses concern that the worker may become discouraged when working with offenders who are often difficult clients:[54]

[52]Ibid., p. 30.
[53]Ibid.
[54]Ibid.

So that the officer does not become discouraged, it must be remembered that habits of any kind are learned; they are adaptive acts and they become automatic. Among probationers habits of any kind, especially thinking and acting, are very difficult to unlearn. The forming of new habits is a major task. Corrective emotional experiences are essential and they are painful. Once a man sees the challenge in and the fun of changing behavior that is harmful to him and understandingly comes in contact with his own conflicts, which he has made himself, usually unconsciously, he is practically certain to recover. He will see what his behavior has done to himself and to others and how in the future he can modify his reactions, although the set period of probation may hinder progress.

She advises discussing with the offender:[55]

his strong points, and his assets as he needs to believe in himself and to know that you do not see him as a failure. A few regard probation as a disgrace, but they are the ones who have been unable to face the fact that they did wrong, that they were caught, that according to law they must be punished. There has been a severe blow to the ego. Some time elapses before these men grow to the point where they can accept their reality situations. Some are never able to face them. Sometimes it takes over a year before the emotional and the intellectual, that is the ego, the superego, and the id, can arrive at an approximate level and function comparatively harmoniously together. Usually these men expect the probation officer to be a threat. This he must not be with this particular group and preferably with none, though at times it cannot be avoided.

According to psychoanalytic theory, ambivalence (love/hate) toward the father is a normal manifestation in all male children. "The hostility toward the father should drop out with the relinquishing of the rivalry between them and there follows an intensification of the primary identification with the father."[56] When this ambivalence progresses into adolescence and adulthood it is often manifested in hostility toward authority-figures and authority in general. The antagonism toward the father and the power that he represents is transferred to other societal representations of authority, such as teachers or policemen. Handler states: "Learning to deal with authority is often a neces-

[55]Ibid.

[56]William Healy, Augusta F. Bronner and Anna Mae Bowers, *The Structure and Meaning of Psychoanalysis* (New York: Knopf, 1930), p. 134.

sary first step in rehabilitation and one that some people can learn best in a setting where escape is literally impossible and where learning can proceed slowly and can bring valued rewards, i.e., privileges and amenities."[57] Hardman strikes a similar theme: "Since one of the basic components of delinquency is a history of negative experiences with authority figures, one of the most beneficial services I can render to a delinquent is a new and constructive relationship with authority."[58]

Bromberg and Rodgers state that "the influence of authority on the development of the delinquent's personality and on his mis-behavior is particularly pertinent for the reason that authority is the most vital and challenging factor in his every social relationship."[59] The authors discuss the dynamics of delinquent behavior and author-ity:[60]

> Limited antagonism to authority is a normal reaction in all indi-viduals and is a derivative of the infantile emotional life of each person. In our culture, it is manifested in society through accept-able forms, such as expressed resentment over taxes, dislike of rationing, ridicule of government officials, humorous or pointed references to the law, minor infractions of ordinances, and so on. Within these limits, most individuals adjust to the dictates of authority. This is accomplished through a recognition of reality demands and a perception of their need to conform. The occa-sional open verbal expression of resentment to law and regu-lations permits the average citizen to adjust to authority comfort-ably. Normal individuals, though retaining some antagonism to authority during much of their early life, only occasionally resort to criminal expression. The point at which antisocial behavior is least probable is reached at maturity, when the concept is firmly imbedded that acquiesence to the demands of authority results in communal benefits.

In contrast to the "normal" reaction to authority, is that of the delin-quent:[61]

> The immature and psychopathic offender regards his inac-cessibility to authority as a virtue, a triumph of his individuality.

[57]Ellen Handler, "Social Work and Corrections," *Criminology* 13 (August 1975): 249.

[58]Dale G. Hardman, "Constructive Use of Authority," *Crime and Delin-quency* 6 (July 1960): 250.

[59]Walter Bromberg and Terry C. Rodgers, "Authority in the Treatment of Delinquents," *American Journal of Orthopsychiatry* 16 (1946): 672–85.

[60]Ibid., p. 674.

[61]Ibid.

His social values are reversed and mature standards of submission to authority are derided as those of weakness. This special viewpoint makes for unusual difficulties in the task of providing insight and modifying behavior patterns.

In an application of psychoanalytic theory that complements Walter Miller's observation on *autonomy* and the lower-class delinquent, Bromberg and Rodgers state:[62]

> . . . the psychological basis of the ever-present antagonism toward authority in immaturity lies in the denial of a basic unconscious dependence on the very authority-figure against which the rebelliousness is directed. Contrary to common opinion, the particular individual who most vigorously express their rebelliousness are those with the strongest unconscious dependency feelings.

Based on their findings, Bromberg and Rodgers recommend that practitioners avoid "a completely passive attitude" because "the delinquent does not recognize that any figure in his environment is truly passive toward him;" thus, such an attitude on the part of the criminal justice practitioner will merely confuse the client.

As we have noted, it is basic to social service practice in criminal justice that the offender must learn to deal with authority. Most offenders have a long history of difficulty with authority figures, starting with parents and school officials, and ending with personnel in criminal justice. Geiger states that the worker cannot expect that a man who has been negativistic or hostile toward authority all of his life will suddenly accept limitations and adjust. She cautions:[63]

> Verbally he may seem to be adjusting on a satisfactory level but basically he has no intention other than living through the period of probation. He does as he pleases, when he thinks he cannot be found out. His total rejection is frustration and he feels strongly. So, his attempts at adjustment may be consistently superficial. The officer may need to interpret by asking if this or that was intended as it seems, or if the response is inadequate, or if it was intended this way or that, giving the positive and more healthful interpretation. Some attempts at adjustment may be direct and these can be welcomed heartily, met sincerely, and evaluated. Again, the attempt may be inadequate, which requires tactful stimulation and at times a mild shock, or the attempt may be ade-

---

[62]Ibid.

[63]Sara G. Geiger, "Counseling Techniques in Probation," *Federal Probation* 18 (March 1954), p. 31 (This was fully given in fn 50).

quate and appreciated as such by the officer. It can be expected
that there will be repetition of satisfactory probation experiences
except in the deviate personality who follows the same law but is
of a masochistic type, needing and achieving punishment by repetition of the behavior which necessitates his supervision.

Studt stresses the legal relationship, with all its implications for
control, between the criminal justice practitioner and the offender.[64]
Society has created agencies to administer restricted status assignments, probationers/parolees, for example, and the criminal justice
practitioner has the responsibility for supervision during the period of
restricted status. Studt refers to the power to "limit," as well as the
practitioner's authority to help the offender learn to act differently toward other authorities in the community: "It can be said, for instance,
that his job is to reinterpret the authority of the community to the
client."[65]

In psychoanalytic theory *resistance* is a central concept. According to the theory powerful unconscious forces oppose any change in
mental condition. In psychoanalytic treatment the therapist strives to
aid the client to overcome these forces thus allowing unconscious mental processes into consciousness. Freud notes that overcoming resistance is the essential work of psychoanalysis.[66] In psychoanalytic treatment the techniques that are used to overcome resistance include
dream analysis and free association. In criminal justice practice, although the level of inquiry and treatment is not the unconscious, resistance is a central problem for the criminal justice practitioner. The
client may feel quite content with his mode of thinking and acting; it is
only getting caught and punished that is problematic. Ankersmit notes
that resistance is a crucial problem found in the involuntary probation
setting:[67]

> Resistance must be dealt with freely and openly before any
> genuine contract can be made. The probationer should be allowed
> to ventilate his hostile feelings toward probation, police, parents,
> and authority in general. This is not to be interpreted as allowing
> the probationer to make excuses for his behavior, but at this early
> stage, non-judgmental listening is essential. It greatly strengthens

[64]Elliot Studt, "Casework in the Correctional Field," *Federal Probation* 18
(September 1954): 18–26.
    [65]Ibid., p. 24.
    [66]Freud, *Introduction to Psychoanalysis*, p. 302.
    [67]Edith Ankersmit, "Setting the Contract in Probation," *Federal Probation*
40 (June 1976): 28–32. Reprinted by permission of *Federal Probation*.

a relationship if the client believes that the probation officer is really hearing his feelings. Disillusionment, frustration, hopelessness, anger may emerge. At this stage the probation officer listens and reflects back the feelings.

Ankersmit points out that resistance will continue in various degrees throughout the period of probation supervision. "It can crop up in many forms, such as failed appointments or in not following through on plans made. The temptation for the probation officer is to either deny or overlook the resistance or to berate the probationer. Instead he should clearly point out the resistance and listen for feelings: 'You failed your last two appointments. Does that have anything to do with how you feel about coming here?' "[68] In a probation (or parole) setting resistance has a distinct bottom line: "Of course if the resistance is expressed in the form of a serious violation of probation, the probation officer will have to take the matter to court. Unlike a counselor in a voluntary agency, the probation officer does have a great deal of power, but this may reach exaggerated proportions in the offender's mind." Thus, she recommends: "explore the client's fantasy about this power. A somewhat paranoid client may think the probation officer can see into every corner of his life. Women may think they can be penalized for their sexual activities, or for poor housekeeping."[69] Resistance is positively correlated to the degree of power the probationer thinks the probation officer has:[70]

> The more areas of his life he thinks the officer can control, the more secretive he will be. An admission of limited power paradoxically gives the probation officer more power to be effective. He is no longer the omnipotent parent figure to be resisted at all costs. His frankness helps establish a more trusting relationship, and he serves as a model to the probationer in terms of honesty.

Ankersmit recommends the use of a "contract" for overcoming resistance. Setting the contract is a social work concept used quite often in work with groups. Schwartz states that the contract is a convergence of two sets of tasks, the client's and the agency's. The contract "provides the frame of reference for the work that follows and for understanding when work is in process, when it is being evaded and when it

[68]Ibid., p. 29.
[69]Ibid., p. 29.
[70]Ibid.

is finished."[71] Ankersmit explains the concept as "simply a means of reaching agreement with the client as to what goals he will work toward achieving."[72] She states that the concept gives clarity and direction to the work of the probation officer. Since often the rules and regulations of probation (and parole) are not clearly defined, she recommends that the officer formulate a *verbal* contract establishing individual probationer's particular goals and responsibilities. The contract may be reduced to written form if the officer believes that the offender needs more structure because of immaturity or confusion. Ankersmit provides an example of contract setting:[73]

> When the probationer participates in setting the contract, a key question is, "Is there an area in your life you want to work on?" Of course, there are some probationers who will never share their goals with a probation officer. But it is possible with many offenders to uncover the motivation for working on constructive goals. The crucial factors in tapping a probationer's motivation are working through resistance and clarification of power, as described above. A probationer can be so angry at first at being forced to see a probation officer that he will deny he has any problems. Allowing him to express this anger, which is a part of dealing with resistance, is an essential first step. Often just letting the probationer know that he has a choice to accept counseling or not frees him to accept it. For example, I often say, "You're on probation, so you have to see me, but it's your choice as to whether or not you want to use our time to talk about what's bothering you."

Ankersmit indicates three possibilities with respect to setting the contract:[74]

(1) *The "Barebones" Legal Contract.*—No counseling contract can be made because the probationer does not want counseling. His attitude is clear: "I have to be on probation. I don't like it, and there's nothing I want from you." If regular reporting is one of the legal conditions of probation, the client must still report. But it is explicit that this reporting is routine and

---

[71]William Schwartz, "Address Delivered to the Annual Workshop for Field Instructors and Faculty," Columbia University School of Social Work, April 21, 1966, p. 2.
[72]Edith Ankersmit, "Setting the Contract in Probation," *Federal Probation* 40 (June 1976): 28–32. Reprinted by permission of *Federal Probation*.
[73]Ibid., p. 30.
[74]Ibid., pp. 31–32.

that no casework is offered. The client should be made aware that he must, as must all probationers, take the consequences of his behavior should he run afoul of the law.

(2) *The Counseling Contract.*—The probationer may want job counseling, or marital counseling, or personal counseling, e.g., to learn how to channel his anger in a less harmful way. The simple desire to stop breaking the law because of the unpleasant consequences is a very acceptable contract, and often the only one that can be set with a sociopathic personality. With such an offender it is futile to moralize or preach. A hard-nosed approach about the discomforts of being incarcerated is best. Asking the probationer to talk in great detail about his personal experiences in jail or prison reminds him vividly of the unpleasant consequences of law-breaking.

This contract to stay out of trouble needs to be refined in terms of what specific behavior leads to getting into trouble and what alternatives there are to such behavior. One useful technique is to ask for a step-by-step account of the circumstances leading up to an offense.

(3) *The Supportive Relationship.*—No verbal contract is set because the probationer is not capable of it, nor is he receptive to counseling in a goal-oriented sense. Nevertheless, he relies heavily on a supportive relationship. This applies particularly to probationers who fit the schizophrenic or borderline diagnosis. For these probationers the probation officer, if he has the time, can become a very important person.

The work here is mainly in helping the probationer deal with his day-to-day crises. Often these probationers should receive psychiatric help, but refuse it. The probation officer may be the only stable person in their lives. As the mental hospitals close down, more and more of these probationers find their way into probation officers' caseloads. A relationship contract of this sort cannot be explicit. To make the contract explicit might frighten the probationer or injure his pride.

For the probation officer, available time is a critical factor in committing himself to this type of contract, since it is by far the most time-consuming and emotionally exhausting type. The officer must also feel empathy for the particular probationer. The schizophrenic or borderline personality needs, most of all, the experience of a genuine person-to-person relationship.

## Practice Based on Behavior Theory

A noted application of the principles of behavior modification is reported by Cohen and Filipiczak in their book on the National Training School (NTS) in Washington, D.C.[75] A token economy was initiated whereby inmates (NTS is a training school for delinquents) would receive points that could be converted into such items as:

renting a private room for sleeping

special clothing

special food items

room furnishings

plane transportation to home on furloughs

use of lounge

various miscellaneous items

The program used purchasing power as the extrinsic reinforcer to initiate academic behaviors: "Some young men are willing to wait for their delayed reinforcement, good report cards, diplomas, and so on, but our delinquent student inmates wanted to know, 'Man, what's the payoff *now*?' "

The authors describe how the point system provided immediate reinforcement:[76]

> The points they received for correct answers to programed or semiprogramed educational problems, tests, and other academic performances could at any time be converted into material or social reinforcers. They could rent and decorate a private room, order clothes and other materials from a mail order catalog, or buy entrance into a recreational lounge, for example. They chose their own rewards and did not have to convert their points into any specified reinforcer; points could also be saved. By recording the points rather than distributing them in money or token form, we avoided the transference of negotiable points from one student to another. Points could not be acquired in any way unrelated to the learning specified by the staff.
>
> The academic program was voluntary and individualized. The student-inmate did not have to do academic work. He worked at his own pace on individualized curricula based on the results of his pretesting. The only way he could earn sufficient points was to

[75]Harold L. Cohen and James Filipczak, *A New Learning Environment* (San Francisco: Jossey-Bass, 1971).
[76]Ibid., p. 9.

study and complete the educational material recommended to him. The variety of tests he took upon entering the project determined his standing in various school subjects (he might score at a high school level in mathematics and a third grade level in reading). After consultation with an advisor, he was assigned programs which allowed him to start work at the appropriate level for each subject. A grading system was developed which gave the student immediate access to his own progress and the adequacy of his understanding. A grade of at least 90 per cent or better was required on all programed instruction. After he had completed a unit of study and had achieved 90 per cent correct responses, the student was given an exam through which he could earn additional points.

The program also provided for secondary reinforcement:[77]

> For example, when a student especially well on an exam (earned a grade of 100 per cent) the staff brought the accomplishment to the attention of the other students and commended him genially— "Gosh, that was great," or "Man, that's cool." Such a reward was recognition for a task performed. However, only a task that required some competent behavior or a large effort won such recognition. The student knew the difference between a task that required lots of competent behavior and one that was "Mickey Mouse."

The program also empowered correction officers to award points for exemplary student behavior:[78]

> This opportunity was a distinct change in the officer's role. In conventional institutions, he used aversive control over social behavior. In the NTS program the officer's relationship to the student was enhanced by his ability to award points, and several officers experienced great pleasure—and relief—at being able to assume a positive rather than a threatening role.

The result of the program was a significant improvement in the academic achievement of the inmates. However, while the youngsters stayed out of trouble longer after release than a similar NTS group "the total recidivist rate may be near the norm. The program evidently delayed the delinquent's return to incarceration, but his behavior would require additional maintenance in the real world for the program ex-

[77]Ibid., p. 12.
[78]Ibid.

perience to remain effective after the first year in preventing recidivism."[79]

The *Adolescent Diversion Project* of the University of Illinois at Champaign uses behavioral contracting as one method of treatment. Youngsters are referred to this program by the police as an alternative to juvenile court petitioning. The program utilizes undergraduate student volunteers to provide direct service. Delinquent behavior is seen as the result of reinforcement of antisocial behavior and lack of approval and support for positive behavior. The behavioral contracts for this project were developed as follows:[80]

> Students were urged to direct the statements of the agreements in *positive*, rather than negative, terms (i.e., what should be *done*, not what should be *stopped*) and to make them highly specific and focused only on the most important changes for the individuals involved. For example, a contract might contain the terms of an agreement between the youth and parents for the youth's curfew hours to be liberalized if he or she came home on time for some specified time period. The students filled the role of facilitator, performance monitor, and mediator in any disagreements that arose over the performance specified in the contract. The behavioral contracting method stressed "the inherent principle of reciprocity." Each negotiated contract involved a direct exchange of responsibilities and privileges between the agreeing parties. One individual's responsibilities are the other person's privileges, and vice versa. The student was charged with insuring that this proper balance was maintained.
>
> Contract renegotiation represented another important concern in successfully implementing the behavioral contracting approach. Since the time of contract renegotiation is of critical importance, several general guidelines were set forth for students:

> Renegotiation should not be considered until at least four weeks following implementation of the initial agreement.
>
> The same procedures should be followed in renegotiation as established in the initial contract agreement.
>
> All parties, including the supervisory group, should have input to the renegotiation process.
>
> Renegotiation should be based on information gained from execution of the initial contract.

[79]Ibid., p. 134.

[80]Richard Ku and Carol Holliday Blew, *A University's Approach to Delinquency: The Adolescent Diversion Project* (Washington, D.C.: United States Government Printing Office, 1977).

The desire to renegotiate a contract may reflect a lack of commitment on the part of either or both parties (in which case contract renegotiation would be an easy out) or may imply that appropriate reinforcers were not identified and employed. If the terms of a contract are unrealistic in terms of either party's obligations and rewards, it is important that this be detected at an early stage. If renegotiation involved augmenting contractual agreements, students were cautioned to maintain an equitable balance of responsibilities and privileges.

In sum, the behavioral contracting model involved the following activities on the part of the student intervention agent:

During the first two weeks of contact the student attempted to build rapport with the youth and began to assess areas of interpersonal conflict. Attention was focused on the home and school and on selection of behaviors to be modified and critical persons to be involved.

The following week the student involved the youth and those persons with whom he or she had a "dysfunctional relationship" in a process of specifying the behaviors or attitudes each would like changed.

Sometime near the fourth week, the student "negotiated" the written agreement between the parties. The contract specified what each person would change in the relationship and what each could expect.

Throughout the intervention, the student functioned as a mediator, assisted in the renegotiation of the contract, as necessary, and helped the parties achieve satisfactory results from the process.

Approximately four weeks prior to termination, the student attempted to instruct the youth and other persons involved in the contract in how to maintain an ongoing process of behavioral contracting. After instruction and sufficient practice, student involvement was terminated.

The following case study highlights the principles, activities, and anticipated outcomes of the behavioral contracting method of intervention.

---

### BEHAVIORAL CONTRACTING CASE

Joe was a sixteen-year-old who had come to the attention of the juvenile division for possession of marijuana and violation of the municipal curfew laws. Prior to the referral to the Adolescent Diversion Project, Joe had had five contacts with the police, including possession of controlled substances, truancy from school, and curfew violation. Joe lived in a middle-class area of Urbana-Champaign and both of his parents were employed. His father worked as a maintenance department supervisor and his mother was a salesperson in a local store. During intake and pre-assessment Joe had expressed a sports interest and was assigned to a male student volunteer who had a similar interest.

After being assigned to Joe, the student called Joe at home and set up a time for them to get together. Joe invited the student to his house for the following evening. At that initial meeting, the student explained the project briefly to Joe and his parents. He and Joe were then left alone by Joe's parents. Conversation was initially difficult, and the student had to carry the conversation for the first hour by talking about such day-to-day things as what he was taking at the University, what life in Chicago (student's home town) had been like, and the student's intramural football team. Although Joe had been rather quiet initially, particularly in the presence of his parents, he gradually began to discuss his own situation. Joe indicated that he was in high school but was pretty turned off to the whole school situation. He said that he skipped whenever he got the chance. He talked of his interests in sports, particularly the Babe Ruth baseball team he pitched for and the Sunday afternoon football group he hung around with. In discussing his home situation, Joe said that he didn't really mind it at home, but that "I spend as much time as possible away from home, with the guys or my girlfriend." The initial contact ended with Joe and the student making plans for the upcoming weekend, either to go to a football game or to play football together. Two days later, Joe called the student and invited him to play football on Sunday with Joe and his friends. In the words of the student, "As he put it, it's tackle and it's rough—somehow I have the feeling this was my first test. . . The game was pretty tough, but it was good. . ."

During the remainder of the initial two weeks Joe and the student went to a movie, played football again, had dinner together and talked on the phone several times. During this time the student had some difficulty getting in touch with Joe but each time they talked, the student stated that "he's genuinely glad to hear from me."

Following the initial "get acquainted" period, the student began to work on assessing Joe's situation more specifically in order to initiate a contract between Joe and his parents. The student proceeded by setting up two somewhat more formal sessions with Joe and his parents. These sessions were held at Joe's home. The student began by explaining the idea of behavioral contracts, and what was required by both parties. This initial "contracting session" resulted in a consensus on the general areas of change desired by both Joe and his parents. Joe's parents thought Joe should show more responsibility around the house, keep better hours, and improve his appearance. Joe wanted to get his parents off his back and get a component stereo set. At the conclusion of this session, the student asked both Joe and his parents to specify these changes in greater detail prior to the next meeting.

At the next meeting the parents specified some agreements they would like to exact from Joe. They felt he should: (1) inform his parents where he was after school and return home before 5:00 p.m.; (2) make his bed and clean his room daily; (3) put out the garbage on Wednesday and Fridays; (4) set the table for dinner each night; (5) mow the lawn or shovel the snow as needed; (6) cut his hair; (7) improve his grades in school. Joe specified for the contract that he (1) be allowed to earn at least $5.00 per week toward the stereo he wanted; (2) be allowed to go out four week nights and two weekend nights; (3) be allowed to choose his friends without interference or harassment from his parents.

On the basis of this information, the student drew up a tentative agreement between Joe and his parents. During the two week period required to initiate the contract the student also spent about two hours each week talking with Joe's parents about their several concerns. At the beginning of the sixth week the following contract was implemented.

---

*Joe agrees to:*

1. Call home by 4:00 p.m. each afternoon and tell his parents his whereabouts and return home by 5:00 p.m.
2. Return home by 12:00 midnight on weekend nights.
3. Make his bed daily and clean his room daily (spread neat; clothes hung up).
4. Set table for dinner daily.

*Joe's parents agree to:*

1. Allow Joe to go out from 7:30 to 9:30 Monday through Thursday evenings and ask about his companions without negative comment.
2. Allow Joe to go out the subsequent weekend night.
3. Check his room each day and pay him $.75 when cleaned.
4. Deposit $.75 per day in a savings account for Joe.

*Bonus*

If Joe performs at 80% or above #1 through #4 above, his parents will deposit an additional $3.00 in his account for each consecutive seven day period.

*Sanction*

If Joe falls below 60% in #1 and #2 above in any consecutive seven day period, he will cut two inches off his hair.

---

At this time the student also set up daily checklists on each of the terms of the contract to be jointly used by Joe and his parents to record each other's performance.

Following the implementation of the initial contract, the student began meeting with Joe and his parents on a weekly basis to go over the checklists on the contract specifications. In addition, the student and Joe spent three to five hours per week in various recreational activities. These included sports events, a party at the student's house, and riding around in the student's car.

Joe's performance on the contract was consistently 90% or above. However, two weeks after it began, Joe received grades for the term. Although the student's earlier visit with Joe's teachers had indicated that they were "completely satisfied with Joe's performance," he received an F, two D's, one B, one C and two incompletes. This report card created considerable controversy between Joe and his parents. The student held an extra meeting with Joe and his parents in which he suggested that school performance be included in the contract.

The result was the combination of the household responsibilities (bed making, table setting) into a single responsibility with payment on a weekly rather than daily basis. Daily checksheets were established with Joe's teachers and he was able to earn additional savings towards his stereo. During the same time period, Joe had located a part-time job doing maintenance work and the use of his earnings had become a heated domestic issue. A further addition was made to the contract whereby Joe agreed to save $15/week in return for the use of his parent's family room for his friends on one weekend night.

Within two weeks, Joe was consistently performing at a 100% level on all contract items and both he and his parents reported to the volunteer that they were more satisfied with the situation. In addition, Joe had been in no further difficulty with the police, and his next report card contained one A, one B, and three C's.

During the seventeenth and eighteenth weeks, the student held two final sessions with Joe and his parents. These sessions focused on a general discussion of the contracting approach and its use on an ongoing basis. They role-played negotiations of several situations that had become troublesome in the past and the student coached them in specifying what each party wanted, stating requests in terms of positives, negotiating reciprocal agreements, and monitoring the contract. The student explained that his involvement with them had come to an end since they had made some real gains and that they should use the procedures in the future when difficulties arose. The student reported that they parted on a very friendly basis and that he had heard from Joe spontaneously several times before leaving the University.

---

Milan et al. report on the use of a token economy at the Draper Correctional Center in Alabama.[81] They examined "the feasibility of systematically deploying the technology of applied behavior analysis to aid in the understanding and solution of the problems confronting those charged with care and rehabilitation of the institutionalized felon."[82] The authors describe the project:[83]

Participants of the cellblock economy were fifty-six inmates incarcerated at Draper Correctional Center, Elmore, Alabama, a maximum security state institution whose all-male population consists primarily of younger offenders serving sentences for their

[81]Michael A. Milan, Larry F. Wood, Robert L. Williams, Jerry Rogers, Lee R. Hampton, and John M. McKee, *Applied Behavior Analysis and the Imprisoned Adult Felon, Project 1: The Cellblock Token Economy* (Montgomery, Alabama: Rehabilitation Research Foundation, 1974).
[82]Ibid., p. 14.
[83]Ibid., p. 17.

first or second felony conviction. The only general constraint governing consideration for participation in this project was that inmates be eligible for either parole or unconditional release within ninety days of the project's termination date.

Participation was voluntary. (The term "voluntary" should be used with caution in criminal justice where coercion, when it is not overt, is often subtle, particularly in a prison setting.)

Tokens consisted of points acqui ed and expended through a simulated checkbook banking system. Each inmate received checkbooks, and as they completed the reinforced target behaviors or academic assignments, a staff member computed the number of points earned and these were credited to the inmate's account. Points, through the medium of checks, could be used to purchase various forms of recreation—TV, lounge, poolroom, and to purchase canteen items or other special items from a Sear's or Penney catalog.

Target behaviors involved routine maintenance—housekeeping tasks—and academic achievement. The results of the program, in comparison with the "aversive control procedures usually used by correctional staff, indicated that high levels of performance generated by token reinforcement demonstrate that the token economy is indeed a viable alternative to such aversive control procedures."[84]

Following termination of the program, experimental performance deteriorated. The authors state:[85]

> It should not be surprising that performance deteriorated following the termination of the token economy at the end of the project, . . . for the power and importance of the contingent relationship between performance and token reinforcement has been previously demonstrated by the deteriorations in performance when the tokens were either awarded on a noncontingent basis or not awarded at all.

There is a paucity of material on the use of behavior modification with offenders in a community, noninstitutional setting. One paper, which appeared in the literature over a decade ago, considers the use of behavior therapy with juvenile delinquents on probation and residing with their parents. The technique used was operant conditioning; the positive reinforcers were such items as praise, attention, privileges, money, food, TV, use of the car, etc. Negative reinforcers consisted of withdrawal of rewards, ridicule, etc. The medium through which the conditioning was operationalized was the youngster's parents. Because

[84]Ibid., p. 55.
[85]Ibid.

the youngsters were residing at home under their parent's care, the reinforcements could be controlled. The authors provide some case examples:[86]

---

**CASE 1**

Claire is a bright, moderately attractive 16-year-old who was referred to the project for truancy, poor grades, and incorrigibility at home. The parents were divorced 6 years ago and the mother now supports the two of them as a maid. The father is out of state, as is Claire's older married sister.

When the referral came from a local high school, it stated that Claire was going to be expelled for truancy. The staff persuaded them to hold up expulsion for several days, which they were willing to do.

The mother was eager for help, although she lacked the physical or emotional resources to assist very much. Clair had been staying home from school for days and was now threatening to run away. Her mother had withdrawn all money, the use of the telephone, and dating privileges. These were all very powerful reinforcers to Claire but, unfortunately, her mother had not provided any clear way for Claire to earn them back.

Obviously, the most pressing problem was Claire's truancy and it was imperative that an intervention plan be prepared immediately to prevent suspension from school. Also, Claire's attending school would be very reinforcing to mother who was, at this time, somewhat dubious that a "noncounseling" approach would be successful. By winning her confidence it would be possible to begin shaping her to regard Claire in a more positive perspective, which would be necessary before a more amicable relationship could be worked out between them.

An intervention plan was agreed upon by mother, Claire, and a staff member. Telephone privileges and weekend dates were contingent on attending school all day. The school attendance officer would dispense a note to Claire at the end of each day if she had attended all of her classes. On presenting the note to mother, Claire earned telephone usage (receiving and calling out) for that day. If she received four out of five notes during the week she earned one weekend date night, and five out of five notes earned two weekend date nights. Phone usage on the weekend was not included in this plan.

Much to mother's astonishment Claire accepted the plan. Mother herself felt the plan "childish" and was apprehensive about Claire complying with it. Staff emphasized the necessity and benefit of praising Claire whenever she brought a note home. This would be difficult for mother, who was inconsistent, ineffectual, and emotional in all her relations with Claire. However, she was given support through several brief phone calls every week.

Despite frequent family upsets Claire attended school regularly from the first day of intervention. The plan was altered (in technical

---

[86]Gaylord L. Thorne, Roland G. Tharp, and Ralph J Wetzel, "Behavior Modification Techniques: New Tools for Probation Officers," *Federal Probation* 31 (June 1967): 21–27.

terms the schedule was "thinned") after a month so that Claire would receive only two notes a week. A note on Wednesdays would mean she attended all her classes on Monday, Tuesday, and Wednesday. This was backed up by the privilege of one weekend night out. A second note on Friday meant full attendance on Thursday and Friday, which was backed up by a second weekend night out. The telephone privileges were taken off contingency. About 7 weeks later the notes were stopped entirely.

The results were quite impressive. During the first 46 days of school (baseline period) Claire missed 30 days of school (65.2 percent absent). While working with the project for less than 3 months she was illegally absent twice (6.6 percent). She was *never* illegally absent again following termination, which covers the entire second semester of school. Grades were beyond redemption during the first semester mainly because of absences, thus causing her to fail two subjects. This dropped to one failure during the second semester.

According to her counselor at school, Claire continued to experience a poor relationship with her mother but did begin expressing positive attitudes and interests in her classes. Thus, the project was successful in preventing this girl from being expelled from school and probably running away. This was accomplished with a very modest expenditure of staff time.

## CASE 2

Mark is a 7th grade boy referred by the local juvenile court for (1) incorrigibility—refusing to do chores, disobedient, defiant; (2) destructiveness—toys and family property were often impulsively destroyed; (3) stealing—both at school and at home; and (4) poor peer relations—he has few friends and frequently fights with his siblings. He lives with his natural parents and two younger sisters.

The case is particularly interesting because of the great difficulty the staff had in gaining parental cooperation. The mother and father seemed to be people who derived little from experience. The father handled all discipline problems with a combination of extended lectures and punishment. His whippings were commonly followed by some destructive act by Mark, but the father still would not reduce his corporal punishment. The mother was also prone to lecture Mark, as well as being quite vague and inconsistent in her expectations of him. The destructive acts around home were serious enough to require immediate attention. Money, praise (especially from father), and a new bicycle were found to be highly reinforcing to Mark. His allowance had been placed entirely contingent on report card grades at school, which meant long periods of nonreinforcement.

The parents were persuaded to reinstate the allowance contingent on daily nondestructive behavior at home. If he did destroy or damage something, he would lose money for that day, plus having to pay for repairs. In addition, Mark could earn points each day for the successful completion of chores at home, points that would accumulate toward the purchase of a bicycle in about 6 months. Regular assignments were encouraged from school so that Mark could be rewarded for studying at least 30 minutes after school. When father would arrive home from work he praised Mark for studying. Should he study each day of the week father would "bonus" him with an extra allowance or special weekend outings together. Father was to ignore Mark on any day that he did not study. The parents kept daily records on these behaviors. The records were collected every other week.

At the end of 7 weeks Mark had not committed a single destructive act, there had been no reports of stealing, he rarely missed completing a day of his chores, and he was studying at least one-half hour 6 nights a week. The parents were pleased but informed the project that Mark did not need to be praised and rewarded for appropriate acts—this was just "bribery." It was so alien to the nature of these parents to use rewards to shape behavior that they were seriously considering dropping the plan despite its considerable success. Fortunately, report cards came out at this time and Mark showed improvement in both academic and behavior grades. Therefore, it was possible to persuade them to continue.

A disaster did occur several weeks later, though. Mark broke his eyeglasses. This prevented any studying for a week, but worse still it precipitated an infuriated reaction in his father because of the expense. Mark was castigated and the bicycle point-chart was indefinitely suspended.

Some 6 weeks passed before any consistent plan of action was reinstated. School work, intermittently reinforced with father's praise, was maintained at its prior high level. Two minor acts of destructiveness occurred at home (he broke some bathroom tile and a toy) and he exhibited some defiant behaviors toward his mother. Completion of chores began dropping again, and probably was most responsible for the parents in accepting the suggestion to make a chart for the chores and reward completion of them. The "back-up" (reward) would be interaction with father plus his praise. Earning money and the bicycle were still not allowed by the parents.

About five weeks were spent in keeping a daily chart on Mark's completion of chores. He would place a star on the chart and then the parents would praise him. The frequency of chore completion soon rose to 100 percent and this so pleased the father he decided to reinstate the bicycle point-chart. Completion of chores and obedient behaviors would then earn points, and when an arbitrary total was accumulated he would get a new bicycle. Mark got the new bicycle in 34 days. In this period he had 170 individual behaviors that could earn points, and he was reinforced on 168 of them.

The parents are fully persuaded as to the importance of making rewards contingent, and the efficacy of shaping behavior with positive reinforcement. No daily charts are now kept on Mark. A 6-week followup shows no return to previous misbehaviors. Originally, he had earned two D's and an F in eight subjects on the midterm report card. His final report card had no mark below a C.

## CASE 3

Blaine is a 14-year-old boy whose limited ability (IQ in low 80's) had contributed to a number of adjustment problems at home and at school. His father referred him to the project because he had been setting fires in and around his home, and frequently messing up the home. The school complained of his antagonism toward peers and general incorrigibility. The father had tried occasional spankings, lectures, and restriction of TV (the most effective). The school had tried paddling, scolding, restriction of playground privileges, plus the principal inviting him to the gym to put on the boxing gloves!

The mother had died 2 years previously in an airplane crash. Blaine and his 12-year-old brother were cared for during the day by a neighbor, while the father worked as a policeman. The neighbor lady was capable of setting limits on Blaine, but was not a source of much reinforcement. The father was quite reinforcing and capable of using his reinforcers on contingency.

The most urgent matter of business was to stop the playing with matches. Several minor fires had been started by Blaine, and his father realistically feared a serious one. A daily chart was kept by the father and the babysitter. A star was put up each day that Blaine refrained from playing with matches. This was backed up daily by praise from his father and access to evening TV. A week of success also gained him 25 cents. If on any day he was caught playing with matches, he did not get his star, he lost his TV privileges, and his quarter on the weekend. A second chart was simultaneously begun for the completion of chores (the details are unimportant here). No intervention was begun at school.

In the 2 weeks prior to intervention, Blaine had been caught playing with matches four times. Blaine continued on the chart system for nearly 6 months. He had 161 opportunities for reinforcement (no playing with matches) and he missed only one of them. Equally interesting, though, were the side effects that occurred after he was put on a positive schedule of reinforcement. Both Blaine and his brother began doing their chores regularly, thus receiving attention, praise, and money. The school reported a steady improvement in Blaine's attitude and behavior. No misbehavior incident was reported on him at school from the time following intervention. Recent followup showed no changes—the school was full of praise for his behavior and playing with matches had not recurred.

## CASE 4

The final case is particularly instructive because it demonstrates some of the strengths and limitations of behavior modification techniques. Loren is a 16-year-old boy who lives with his stepfather, mother, and two younger brothers. He was referred for (1) assaultive behavior—threatening to shoot his stepfather and trying to fist fight with both parents; (2) defiance of nearly all parental requests (coming home early at night, completing his household chores, mowing the lawn, not taking the car without permission); and (3) habitual truancy. Police had been called for several of these incidents, and referral was made from the local juvenile court.

Assessment of the family revealed that Loren was on an entirely aversive reinforcement schedule. He was denied allowance, restricted to the house, restricted from the car, continually threatened with the police, and verbally abused. None of these was effective. Money, use of the car, and nights-out were considered positively reinforcing, but the parents were so angry with Loren they provided no clear way for him to earn these. An interview with Loren confirmed the latter.

Loren's parents were where many are at the point of referral—desperate. They had been meeting each infraction with punishment until a point of no return was reached. The thought of rewarding Loren for approximations of "good" behavior had not occurred to them and the suggestion was met with great skepticism. However, since they had exhausted their own repertoire of controls, the project staff member was able to persuade them to at least give his suggestions a try.

Two points in the family assessment were quite important. First, Loren apparently had never been given a clear idea of his parents' expectations. For example, instructions such as, "Be in at a decent hour," made for much uncertainty. Second, it became obvious that his stepfather wanted the boy out of the home and was trying to accomplish this through unrealistic and vacilating demands.

The intervention plan consisted of a carefully devised schedule—more nearly a contract—which would allow Loren to earn money for completion of chores and being obedient (e.g., on a weekend night he must be in by midnight). Failures brought not only a loss of money but also carried a fine in the form of 15-minute blocks of restricted time from use of the family car. For the first time he knew exactly how to earn money and time away from home, and exactly what the consequences would be for not conforming. The parents were not to hedge on the contingencies, and biweekly phone calls from our staff plus a posted copy of the "contract" were used to prevent this.

Rapid changes subsequently occurred in Loren's behavior. In the first 35 days, he was rewarded an average of 81 percent of the time in each of four areas of responsibility (range 75 to 89 percent). Prior to intervention he met these obligations rarely (0 to 10 percent).

At this point a second contract was drawn up because Loren's stepfather was continuing to nag him despite tremendous improvement and because Loren's car insurance had expired and his stepfather refused to renew it. The new contract was negotiated in the presence of both parents. Loren, and a project staff member. It allowed for points to be earned for chores and responsibilities which could be applied to the car insurance premium (stepfather agreed finally to this). Loren could earn a maximum of 50 points a week, and needed 250 for the premium. The first week he earned 22 points and then the full 50 on each week thereafter.

Loren began driving the car again, but only by meeting specific contingencies agreed to by his parents, himself, and staff. In addition, he re-entered high school, achieved satisfactorily, was not truant, and had applied for an after-school job. The case was maintained at this level of success for 24 days, requiring only one phone call to the parents and two brief home visits. Loren's stepfather and mother expressed satisfaction over the changes and felt that he was doing so well that the "contract" should be abandoned. Our staff member vigorously tried to discourage this, feeling that such a drastic change was premature. However, the parents persevered and abruptly ceased abiding by the agreements and contingencies.

Events following the parents' return to preintervention conditions illustrate an unfortunate collapse of environmental controls. Loren was truant for the succeeding 7 school days, and was arrested 11 days later for burglary. His parents refused to visit him during his 2 days at a detention home. In addition, they told the probation officer that Loren was "hopelessly" bad despite all the good things they had done for him. The court placed Loren on probation and reluctantly allowed him to return to his home. The project had recommended foster placement but none was available. His adjustment remains exceedingly tenuous at home, but the parents have refused further help.

Loren's case demonstrates the validity of behavior modification techniques—behavior can be changed by altering environmental consequences, while simultaneously exhibiting its limitations, and uncooperative parents can defeat productive change. Probation officers adopting operant techniques will thus have to accept a shortcoming common to all known forms of helping children, namely, bad parents yield bad results.

---

Stumphauzer presents a paper on the use of behavior therapy with a twelve-year-old girl involved in stealing.[87] The girl had been referred to the author's clinic (Child/Adolescent Clinic, Los Angeles) by school officials because of repeated incidences of theft: "According to reports from school and parents, the girl had suffered from 'uncontrollable stealing' almost daily for five years (taking small objects at home, at school, and most recently in stores)." She was seen by the therapist on an outpatient basis for a total of fifteen sessions over a period of five months; first on a weekly and later once every four weeks. The sessions included the girl and family. The early sessions involved a behavioral analysis and stealing was measured on a chart daily by the girl's mother. The author presents the behavior therapy utilized in this case:[88]

> Self-control techniques were based on an analysis of the exact circumstances under which theft occured and what the patient said to herself. She expressed interest in stopping but said, "I can't control myself." We role-played seeing the usual kind of things she would steal (e.g., money in a classmate's purse on the playground) and then alternate interesting things and activities she could shift her attention to which were to be followed by self-reinforcement (e.g., "I'm proud of myself.").

Beginning with the fourth session the patient was encouraged also to measure her own stealing on Daily Behavior Graphs in addition to the measures from parents and her teacher.

[87]Jerome S. Stumphauzer, "Eliminating Stealing by Self-Reinforcement of Alternative Behavior and Family Contracting," *Journal of Behavior Therapy and Experimental Psychiatry* 7 (1967): 265–68.
[88]Ibid.

Eventually the girl composed self-evaluative daily measures:

(1.) I'm trustworthy, I keep my hands to myself . . .
(2.) I watch to make sure everything is in its place at home . . .
(3.) At the store I look for what I'm supposed to and not things that will get my interest.

Reinforcement from the family included praise and an allowance for each day of not stealing, and a special activitiy, such as a trip, for a whole week of not stealing. The author reports remarkable progress and an eighteen month follow-up revealed no further stealing.

## Concluding Remarks

This book is, at best, a starting point for theoretically based social service in criminal justice. As theories are tested and refined, or as new theories are formulated, they must be made relevant for practice. Unless practice is based on theory, the worker will begin each case anew, without the benefit of accumulated knowledge and experience. The worker who uses practical methods based on theory is best able to serve his clients and the criminal justice agency.

Keeping abreast of the vast array of literature relevant to criminal justice practice is no easy task. There are few periodicals which are geared to criminal justice practice; for the most part, periodicals must be reviewed for material relevant to practice. In order to help the reader, the following list of periodicals has been annotated with *** indicating the most relevant to criminal justice practice.

\*\*\*

CRIME AND DELINQUENCY
411 Hackensack Avenue
Hackensack, New Jersey

FEDERAL PROBATION
Supreme Court Building
Washington, D.C. 20544

OFFENDER REHABILITATION
The Haworth Press
149 Fifth Avenue
New York, New York

\*\*

BEHAVIOR MODIFICATION
Sage Publications
275 South Beverly Drive
Beverly Hills, California 90212

CRIMINAL JUSTICE REVIEW
Georgia State University
University Plaza
Atlanta, Georgia 30303

CRIMINOLOGY
Sage Publications
P.O. Box 776
Beverly Hills, California 90213

JOURNAL OF CRIMINAL
JUSTICE
Maxwell House, Fairview Park
Elmsford, New York 10523

JOURNAL OF CRIMINAL LAW
AND CRIMINOLOGY
Northwestern University School
of Law
357 E. Chicago Avenue
Chicago, Illinois 60611

JUVENILE JUSTICE
P.O. Box 8978
Reno, Nevada 89507

SOCIAL CASEWORK
44 East 23rd Street
New York, N.Y. 10010

SOCIAL SERVICE REVIEW
University of Chicago Press
Chicago, Illinois 60628

SOCIAL WORK
2 Park Avenue
New York, N.Y. 10016

\*

AMERICAN JOURNAL OF
SOCIOLOGY
1130 East 59 Street
Chicago, Illinois 60637

AMERICAN SOCIOLOGICAL
REVIEW
1722 N Street, N.W.
Washington, D.C. 10036

SOCIAL PROBLEMS
114 Rockwell Hall
State University College
1300 Elmwood Avenue
Buffalo New York 14222

# Appendices

A

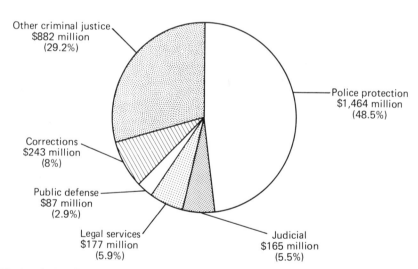

$3,019 million

Other criminal justice
$882 million
(29.2%)

Police protection
$1,464 million
(48.5%)

Corrections
$243 million
(8%)

Public defense
$87 million
(2.9%)

Legal services
$177 million
(5.9%)

Judicial
$165 million
(5.5%)

**Figure A-1.** Federal government criminal justice system total expenditure, fiscal year 1975

*The eight diagrams that are presented here show the level of spending for various segments of the criminal justice sequence. Of greater importance is the percentage of distribution of criminal justice expenditures.

Source: *U.S. Department of Justice, Law Enforcement Assistance Administration and U.S. Bureau of the Census,* Expenditure and Employment Data for the Criminal Justice System: 1975 (*Washington, D.C.: United States Government Printing Office,1977*).

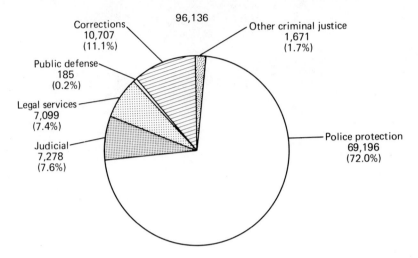

**Figure A-2.** Federal Government criminal justice system full-time equivalent employment, October 1975

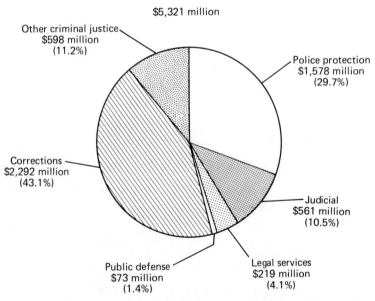

**Figure A-3.** State government criminal justice system total expenditure, fiscal year 1975

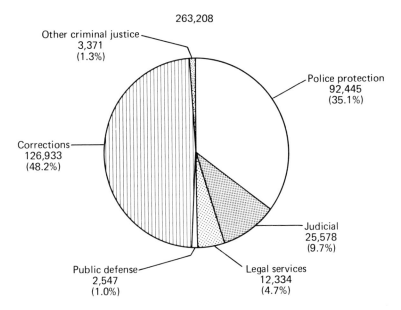

263,208

Other criminal justice
3,371
(1.3%)

Police protection
92,445
(35.1%)

Corrections
126,933
(48.2%)

Judicial
25,578
(9.7%)

Public defense
2,547
(1.0%)

Legal services
12,334
(4.7%)

**Figure A-4.** State government criminal justice system full-time equivalent employment, October 1975

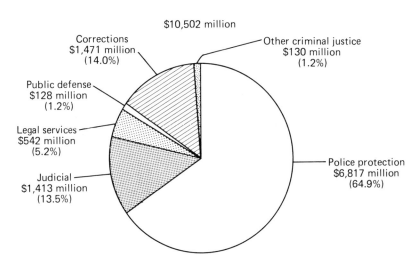

$10,502 million

Corrections
$1,471 million
(14.0%)

Other criminal justice
$130 million
(1.2%)

Public defense
$128 million
(1.2%)

Legal services
$542 million
(5.2%)

Judicial
$1,413 million
(13.5%)

Police protection
$6,817 million
(64.9%)

**Figure A-5.** Local government criminal justice system total expenditure, fiscal year 1975
*Because of rounding, detail does not add to total of $10,502 million.*

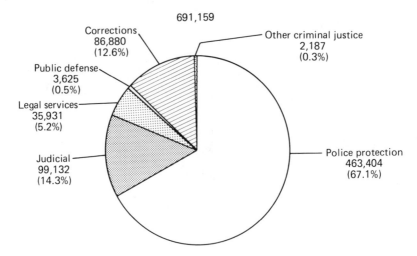

**Figure A-6.** Local government criminal justice system full-time equivalent employment, October 1975

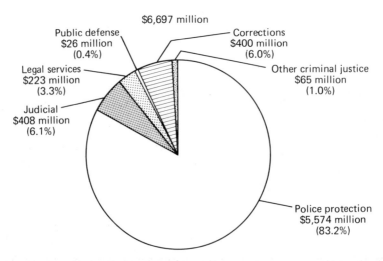

**Figure A-7.** Municipal government criminal justice system total expenditure, Fiscal year 1975
*Because of rounding, detail does not add to total of $6,697 million.*

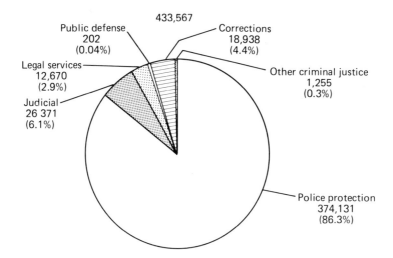

**Figure A-8.** Municipal government criminal justice system full-time equivalent employment, October 1975

**Table 1.** Percent Distribution of Expenditure for the Criminal Justice System, by Level of Government, Fiscal Year 1976

| Activity[1] | Amount | | | | Percent distribution | | |
|---|---|---|---|---|---|---|---|
| | All governments[1] | Federal Government[2] | State governments | Local governments[1] | Federal Government[2] | State governments | Local governments[2] |
| Total criminal justice system[3] | 19,681,409 | 3,322,073 | 5,986,650 | 12,068,308 | (X) | (X) | (X) |
| Direct expenditure | 19,681,409 | 2,450,229 | 5,204,226 | 12,026,954 | 12.5 | 26.4 | 61.1 |
| Intergovernmental expenditure | (³) | 871,844 | 782,424 | 133,855 | (X) | (X) | (X) |
| Police protection[3] | 11,028,244 | 1,615,714 | 1,789,471 | 7,723,588 | (X) | (X) | (X) |
| Direct expenditure | 11,028,244 | 1,611,640 | 1,696,460 | 7,720,144 | 14.6 | 15.4 | 70.0 |
| Intergovernmental expenditure | (³) | 4,074 | 93,011 | 59,390 | (X) | (X) | (X) |
| Judicial[3] | 2,428,472 | 219,445 | 663,068 | 1,633,645 | (X) | (X) | (X) |
| Direct expenditure | 2,428,472 | 219,445 | 585,151 | 1,623,876 | 9.0 | 24.1 | 66.9 |
| Intergovernmental expenditure | (³) | — | 77,917 | 18,123 | (X) | (X) | (X) |
| Legal services and prosecution[3] | 1,047,929 | 149,402 | 253,591 | 653,502 | (X) | (X) | (X) |
| Direct expenditure | 1,047,929 | 149,402 | 247,723 | 650,804 | 14.3 | 23.6 | 62.1 |
| Intergovernmental expenditure | (³) | — | 5,868 | 3,142 | (X) | (X) | (X) |
| Public defense[3] | 331,102 | 103,718 | 78,622 | 157,364 | (X) | (X) | (X) |
| Direct expenditure | 331,102 | 103,718 | 70,139 | 157,245 | 31.3 | 21.2 | 47.5 |
| Intergovernmental expenditure | (³) | — | 8,483 | 1,279 | (X) | (X) | (X) |

| | | | | | | | |
|---|---|---|---|---|---|---|---|
| Corrections[3] | 4,385,512 | 285,973 | 2,589,609 | 1,678,879 | (X) | (X) | (X) |
| Direct expenditure | 4,385,512 | 256,352 | 2,474,783 | 1,654,377 | 5.9 | 56.4 | 37.7 |
| Intergovernmental expenditure | (3) | 29,621 | 114,826 | 49,547 | (X) | (X) | (X) |
| Other criminal justice[3] | 460,150 | 947,821 | 612,289 | 221,329 | (X) | (X) | (X) |
| Direct expenditure | 460,150 | 109,672 | 129,970 | 220,508 | 23.8 | 28.3 | 47.9 |
| Intergovernmental expenditure | (3) | 838,149 | 482,319 | 2,374 | (X) | (X) | (X) |

— Represents zero or rounds to zero.

X Not applicable.

[1]Local governments data are estimates subject to sampling variation; see text for data limitations.

[2]Federal Government data is for the fiscal period beginning July 1, 1975 and ending June 30, 1976. Data for the transition quarter from July 1, 1976 to September 30, 1976 are displayed separately.

[3]The total line for each sector, and for the total Criminal Justice System, excludes duplicative intergovernmental expenditure amounts. This was done to avoid the artificial inflation which would result if an intergovernmental expenditure amount for one government is tabulated and then counted again when the recipient government(s) ultimately expend(s) that amount. The intergovernmental expenditure lines are not totaled for the same reason.

237

**Table 2.** Percent Distribution of Employment and Payrolls for the Criminal Justice System, by Level of Government, October 1976

| Activity | All governments[1] | Federal Government | State governments | Local governments[1] | Percent distribution | | |
| --- | --- | --- | --- | --- | --- | --- | --- |
| | | | | | Federal Government | State governments | Local governments[1] |
| **Total criminal justice system:** | | | | | | | |
| Total employees ... | 1,148,262 | 100,771 | 283,049 | 764,442 | 8.8 | 24.6 | 66.6 |
| Full-time employees ...... | 1,049,750 | 99,016 | 267,685 | 683,049 | 9.4 | 25.5 | 65.1 |
| Full-time equivalent employees ...... | 1,079,892 | 99,553 | 272,488 | 707,851 | 9.2 | 25.2 | 65.5 |
| October payroll .... | 1,277,120 | 159,726 | 311,636 | 805,719 | 12.5 | 24.4 | 63.1 |
| **Police protection:** | | | | | | | |
| Total employees ... | 670,724 | 72,301 | 97,887 | 500,536 | 10.8 | 14.6 | 74.6 |
| Full-time employees ...... | 617,132 | 71,207 | 89,175 | 456,750 | 11.5 | 14.4 | 74.0 |
| Full-time equivalent employees ...... | 628,347 | 71,421 | 90,884 | 466,042 | 11.4 | 14.5 | 74.1 |
| October payroll .... | 772,867 | 113,497 | 105,620 | 553,750 | 14.7 | 13.7 | 71.6 |
| **Judicial:** | | | | | | | |
| Total employees ... | 151,074 | 7,578 | 28,535 | 114,998 | 5.0 | 18.9 | 76.1 |
| Full-time employees ...... | 127,736 | 7,473 | 25,629 | 94,667 | 5.9 | 20.1 | 74.1 |
| Full-time equivalent employees ...... | 137,451 | 7,531 | 27,516 | 102,442 | 5.5 | 20.0 | 74.5 |
| October payroll .... | 154,466 | 13,733 | 42,786 | 97,948 | 8.9 | 27.7 | 63.4 |
| **Legal services and prosecution:** | | | | | | | |

| | | | | | | | |
|---|---|---|---|---|---|---|---|
| **Total employees** ... | 64,860 | 7,008 | 13,665 | 43,304 | 10.8 | 21.1 | 68.1 |
| **Full-time employees** ........ | 54,473 | 6,821 | 12,984 | 34,668 | 12.5 | 23.8 | 63.6 |
| **Full-time equivalent employees** ...... | 59,306 | 6,928 | 13,227 | 39,153 | 11.7 | 22.3 | 66.0 |
| **October payroll** .... | 77,140 | 12,427 | 17,623 | 47,050 | 16.1 | 22.8 | 61.0 |
| **Public defense:** | | | | | | | |
| Total employees ... | 7,623 | 219 | 2,912 | 4,492 | 2.9 | 38.2 | 58.9 |
| Full-time employees ...... | 6,735 | 219 | 2,809 | 3,707 | 3.3 | 41.7 | 55.0 |
| Full-time equivalent employees ...... | 7,255 | 219 | 2,843 | 4,193 | 3.0 | 39.2 | 57.8 |
| October payroll .... | 9,821 | 407 | 3,624 | 5,790 | 4.1 | 36.9 | 59.0 |
| **Corrections:** | | | | | | | |
| Total employees ... | 246,376 | 11,869 | 136,400 | 98,107 | 4.8 | 55.4 | 39.8 |
| Full-time employees ...... | 235,625 | 11,634 | 133,520 | 90,471 | 4.9 | 56.7 | 38.4 |
| Full-time equivalent employees ...... | 239,293 | 11,717 | 134,420 | 93,156 | 4.9 | 56.2 | 38.9 |
| October payroll .... | 252,890 | 16,938 | 137,928 | 98,024 | 6.7 | 54.5 | 38.8 |
| **Other criminal justice:** | | | | | | | |
| Total employees ... | 8,451 | 1,796 | 3,650 | 3,005 | 21.3 | 43.2 | 35.6 |
| Full-time employees ...... | 8,049 | 1,662 | 3,568 | 2,819 | 20.6 | 44.3 | 35.0 |
| Full-time equivalent employees ...... | 8,240 | 1,737 | 3,598 | 2,905 | 21.1 | 43.7 | 35.2 |
| October payroll .... | 9,935 | 2,724 | 4,054 | 3,157 | 27.4 | 40.8 | 31.8 |

[1]Local governments data are estimates subject to sampling variation; see text.

# B

## Confidentiality

Friedlander provides the essence of the social work principle of confidentiality:[1]

> If the client is to participate fully in the resolution of his problem situation, accepting the caseworker as a trustworthy and competent person, communicating with a minimum of social defenses a picture of his current role, and helping to individualize his situation, he often must be assured both directly and indirectly of the social agency's policy regarding the confidential nature of interview content. What the client tells the caseworker is never discussed outside the confines of the professional relationships that are aimed at helping the client. In practice, this means that the content of case records is never discussed in public or social circles—on a bus or a train or at a party. It also means, for example, that what a wife tells a caseworker is never subsequently communicated to her husband by the caseworker without the express permission of the client. Moreover, letters requesting information about the client from other professional or social agency

[1]Walter Friedlander, *Concepts and Methods of Social Work* (Englewood Cliffs, N.J.: Prentice-Hall, 1976), p. 69.

sources are never prepared without the permission of the client. In entering into a client-caseworker relationship, the client is generally expected to remain protected, within the limits of the law, from harm to himself deriving from what he divulges to a caseworker.

For the criminal justice practitioner, however, especially if he is employed by a law enforcement agency, the principle of confidentiality creates a professional dilemma. The practitioner has a duty to uphold the law and protect the public. Thus, he/she cannot fail to act on information which conflicts with either duty. The criminal justice practitioner should explain to the client that confidentiality will be compromised in favor of community protection if a conflict should arise. Although the practitioner will guard information from being used unofficially, the client must be told that official use includes review by supervisory staff and in certain instances by other social and law enforcement personnel.

The criminal justice practitioner must also be aware of statutory limitations on his ability to provide client information to other persons, even agency personnel who would seem to have a legitimate need and reason to have certain offender information. For example, in 1975, the federal government created new regulations for the protection of the confidentiality of alcohol and drug abuse records. Weissman notes that the scope of these regulations is rather comprehensive,[2] and they may be confusing to the criminal justice practitioner. It is incumbent upon the criminal justice practitioner to understand restrictions on confidentiality, those imposed by agency regulations, and those of a statutory nature.

Foren and Bailey state that in a prison setting "confidentiality is eroded to some extent by the requirements of custodial security within the prison, though strictly speaking, confidentiality is an ethical obligation of the agency and not the individual worker."[3] This latter statement provides little comfort to the criminal justice practitioner in a prison setting. The information received and recorded by the social service worker is often available to nontreatment personnel, e.g., security personnel. Indeed, because of the fact that inmates are used extensively in clerical and maintenance positions, inmates may also have access to the information. In New York, an inmate successfully sued

[2]James C. Weissman, "The Criminal Justice Practitioner's Guide to the New Federal Alcohol and Drug Abuse Confidentiality Regulations," *Federal Probation* 40 (June 1976): 11.

[3]Robert Foren and Royston Bailey, *Authority in Social Casework* (Oxford, Eng.: Pergamon Press, 1968), p. 190.

correctional officials who left his record unattended after a parole hearing, thereby permitting several inmates to see the folder and subject him to ridicule. Criminal justice practitioners should be very cautious about putting certain information in a record, and they should certainly be honest and open with their clients concerning their inability to insure confidentiality in certain settings.

Most criminal justice clients are "wise" enough to recognize that what is said in an interview is not confidential from others in criminal justice who have a legitimate need to have the information. They are usually aware of the fact that a criminal justice practitioner often has reports from other practitioners. However, the information compiled by the criminal justice practitioner is certainly withheld from the general public. The offender may not be aware of the extent of confidentiality to which he/she is entitled, and this should be explained by the practitioner.

While many of the principles of social service are put to a severe test in criminal justice settings, basic honesty should not be one. Both the worker and the client should be aware of the limitations of the setting with respect to confidentiality. There is a growing concern over the detrimental use of information processed by the criminal justice system. Laws preventing discriminatory practices against exoffenders are being passed. Severe restrictions are also being placed on information about arrests that do not result in convictions. In New York, for example, a law passed in 1976 (Criminal Procedure Law 160.50) makes confidential most of the records and papers concerning the arrest and prosecution of persons ultimately acquitted. The law requires that courts, with some exceptions,[4] order the sealing of all records of arrest and prosecutions and order the return of all fingerprints and other identifying data when a criminal action has been terminated in favor of the accused.

---

[4]Under the statute in New York, the sealing order must provide that access to all records be available to the accused or his/her agent, to a firearms licensing officer to whom the subject has applied for a license, and, with the permission of a superior court, to a law enforcement agency "where the interests of justice are found to so require."

# C

## Checklist for Offender Employment*

### A. GREET RECEPTIONIST

1. Give your name and reason for visit. Example—"Good morning, my name is John Smith and I have a 10:00 a.m. employment interview with Mr. Jones."
2. Be punctual. Example—For a 10:00 a.m. interview, try being there by 9:30 or 9:45 a.m.
3. Be prepared to fill out an application. Example—(Refer to #2)—By arriving at 9:30 a.m. or 9:45 a.m., you can fill out an application and go in at 10:00 a.m. to see Mr. Jones.
4. Have a copy of your social security number, names of past jobs with addresses and dates, names of references with addresses, etc., written on a card to aid you in filling out the application.

*Source: From Phyllis Groom McCreary and John M. McCreary. Job Training and Placement for Offenders and Ex-Offenders (Washington, D.C.: United States Government Printing Office, 1975), pp. 79–80.

5. Be prepared to take a test for the job you are applying for if required. Example—Electronic, clerical or industrial machines, etc.
6. Have a list of questions you wish to ask prepared. Example:
   a. How old is the company?
   b. How many employees are with the company?
   c. What is the potential for promotion and growth?
   d. What are the duties that the job entails?
   e. What is the starting salary?
   f. What is the top salary potential?
   g. What are the working hours?
   h. Is there paid overtime?
   i. What benefits are offered by the company.
   j. Does the company offer tuition for night school?
   k. Does the company promote from within?

### B. PROCEDURE FOR THE INTERVIEW

1. Walk slowly and quietly, stand right, hold your head up.
2. Greet the interviewer.
   a. Shake hands firmly if interviewer offers his hand.
   b. Look interviewer in the eye and say, "How do you do Mr. Jones."
   c. Stand until the interviewer asks you to be seated.
   d. Wait for the interviewer to start the interview and lead it.
   e. You may smoke if the interviewer states so.
   f. Be prepared to answer questions. Examples:
      Why do you want to work for this company?
      Where do you see yourself in five years?
      Are you planning to further your education?
      What do you know about this company?
      Do you have any particular skills or interests that you feel qualifies you for a position with this company?
      What makes you feel you are qualified for this particular job?
      Do you have any plans for marriage in the immediate future?
3. Now is when you present your questions.

## C. ATTITUDES AND BEHAVIOR DURING THE INTERVIEW

1. Sit up straight, feet on floor, hands in lap.
2. Sit quietly (do not keep moving around or fidget).
3. Use your best manners.
   a. Be attentive and polite.
   b. Speak slowly and clearly.
   c. Look interviewer in the eye (do not wear sunglasses).
   d. Use correct English, avoid slang.
   e. Emphasize your good points.
4. Speak of yourself in a positive manner.
5. Talk about what you can do.
6. Do not apologize for your shortcomings.
7. Do not talk to an excess about your personal problems.

## D. WHAT AN INTERVIEWER SEES IMMEDIATELY DURING AN INTERVIEW

1. Hygiene
   a. Bathe just before an interview.
   b. Clean and clip nails if necessary.
   c. Brush teeth.
   d. Use a good deodorant.
   e. Wear an outfit that is clean and conservative regardless of the fashion trend or style.

## E. INTERVIEWER CLOSES THE INTERVIEW

1. Do not linger when he indicates it is time to stop.
2. Be sure to thank the interviewer as you leave.

## F. STAYING ON THE JOB

1. With the great shortage of available jobs, employers can afford to be highly selective in choosing an employee.
2. Accepting positions in related fields so when positions are re-opened, you will have first choice at these positions.

# D

## Courts In The United States*

1. *Appellate courts* include courts of last resort and intermediate appellate courts. These are courts having jurisdiction of appeal and review, with original jurisdiction conferred only in special cases.

    a. *Court of last resort* is the court of final appeal within the judicial structure of each State. It is called the "Court of Appeals" in the District of Columbia, Maryland, and New York; the "Supreme Court of Appeals" in West Virginia; the "Supreme Judicial Court" in Maine and Massachusetts. In Texas and Oklahoma two courts of last resort are authorized—the "Court of Criminal Appeals" for criminal cases and a "Supreme Court" for civil cases. In every other State the court of last resort is titled the "Supreme Court."

    b. *Intermediate appellate courts* are those that are limited in their appellate jurisdiction by State law or at the discretion of the court of last resort. In 16 of the 25 States with a court of this type operating in fiscal year 1974–75 the name "court of appeals" is used. These States are:

*Source: U.S. Department of Justice Law Enforcement Assistance Administration

| Arizona | Kentucky | New Mexico |
|---|---|---|
| California | Indiana | North Carolina |
| Colorado | Louisiana | Ohio |
| Florida | Michigan | Oklahoma |
| Georgia | Missouri | Oregon |
| | | Washington |

In Illinois the title is "Appellate Court"; in Maryland, "Court of Special Appeals"; in Massachusetts, "Appeals Court"; in New Jersey, "Appellate Division of the Superior Court"; in New York[1], "Appellate Division of the Supreme Court"; and in Texas, "Court of Civil Appeals." In Alabama the civil and criminal cases are heard on appeal by separate courts—a "Court of Civil Appeals" and a "Court of Criminal Appeals." In Tennessee the "Court of Appeals" hears only civil appeals; a separate "Court of Criminal Appeals" reviews criminal cases before review by the court of last resort. In Pennsylvania the "Commonwealth Court" reviews all cases brought by or against the State government or its agencies; the "Superior Court" reviews all other appeals except those within the exclusive jurisdiction of the court of last resort.

2. *Courts of general jurisdiction* are trial courts having unlimited original jurisdiction in civil and/or criminal cases, the names of which vary considerably. The list below shows the title of the courts of general jurisdiction in each State. Several States are listed more than once because local situations led to the development of separate courts, either to hear cases involving different types of pleadings or to hear cases in particular local jurisdictions.

In many States, statutes either require or permit local governments to supplement the salary of State-paid judges of general jurisdiction courts. These judges were counted as part-time employees at both the State and local levels when actually receiving a check from both governments.

### Circuit courts

| Alabama | Kentucky | South Carolina |
|---|---|---|
| Arkansas | Maryland | South Dakota |
| Florida | Michigan[2] | Tennessee[2] |
| Hawaii | Mississippi | Virginia |
| Illinois | missouri | West Virginia[2] |
| Indiana | Oregon | Wisconsin |

[1]There are also three appellate terms of the Supreme Court that have jurisdiction in specific cases that would otherwise be heard by the appellate division.

[2]In these States, the above-named courts are supplemented in some counties and cities by general jurisdiction courts with varying names.

### District courts

| | | |
|---|---|---|
| Colorado | Minnesota | North Dakota |
| Idaho | Montana | Oklahoma |
| Iowa | Nebraska | Texas |
| Kansas | Nevada | Utah |
| Louisiana | New Mexico | Wyoming |

### Superior courts

| | | |
|---|---|---|
| Alaska | District of | New Hampshire |
| Arizona | Columbia | New Jersey |
| California | Georgia | North Carolina |
| Connecticut | Indiana² | Rhode Island |
| Delaware | Maine | Washington |
| | Massachusetts | |

### Chancery courts

| | |
|---|---|
| Arkansas | Mississippi |
| Delaware | Tennessee |

### County courts

| | |
|---|---|
| New Jersey | Vermont |
| New York | |
| Wisconsin | |

### Common pleas courts

Missouri
Ohio
Pennsylvania

### Supreme court

New York

3. *Courts of limited jurisdiction* are courts whose legal jurisdiction covers only a particular class of cases or cases where the amount in controversy is below a prescribed sum or is subject to specific exceptions. Included under this category are probate courts, juvenile courts and other courts of limited jurisdiction.

Probate courts are also called orphans courts, surrogate's courts, or courts of ordinary. The subject jurisdiction varies from place to place, but generally includes estate settlement; probate and contest of wills; adoption; commitment of the insane; administration of the affairs of orphans, mental defectives and incompetents; guardianship of minors; apprenticeship; receivership; change of name proceedings; and the administration of trusts.

Juvenile courts are those that deal primarily with delinquent and neglected children regardless of the name of the court. In various places such courts are called juvenile courts, family courts, juvenile and domestic relations courts, domestic relations courts, or other similar names. The jurisdiction of these courts can include crimes committed by persons under legal age; juvenile status offenses; offenses against children; probation of minor delinquents; adoption, custody, or disposition of minor and mentally incompetent children; child neglect or abandonment; child and wife support; and paternity.

Other courts includes various other State and local courts with limited jurisdiction such as justices of the peace, district magistrates, justice courts, county courts of limited jurisdiction, municipal courts, city courts, etc. Also included are specialized courts such as tax courts, courts of claims, and courts having jurisdiction over more than one type of case (e.g., a court that handles both juvenile and probate cases).

# E

STATE OF NEW YORK
DEPARTMENT OF CORRECTIONAL SERVICES

## GENERAL RULES GOVERNING PAROLE

When an inmate of a correctional institution is approved for parole or conditional release, he or she must agree to the following conditions of parole which are made a part of the release agreement:
In consideration of being granted release, I promise, with full knowledge that failure to keep such promise may result in the revocation of my release, that I will faithfully keep all the conditions specified on this sheet and all other conditions and instructions given to me by the Board of Parole or any of its representatives.

1. I will proceed directly to the place to which I have been released (spending funds only for necessities), and within twenty-four hours, I will make my arrival report to the designated office of the Department of Correctional Services.

2. I will not leave the State of New York, or any other State to which I may be released or transferred, or any area as defined

by the Parole Officer in writing, without the written or documented permission of my Parole Officer.

3. (a) I will fully comply with the instructions of my Parole Officer. (b) I will make office and/or written reports as I am directed. (c) I will reply promptly to any communication from a Member of the Board of Parole, a Parole Officer, or other authorized representative of the Board of Parole. (d) I am aware that making false reports may be considered a violation of the condition of my release.

4. (a) I will permit my Parole Officer to visit me at my residence or place of employment. (b) I will discuss with my Parole Officer any proposed changes in my residence, and I will not change my residence without prior approval of my Parole Officer. (c) I understand that I am legally in the custody of the Board of Parole and that my person, residence, or any property under my control may be searched by my Parole Officer or by any other representative of the Board of Parole at its direction. (d) If so directed, I will observe a curfew.

5. I will avoid the excessive use of alcoholic beverages. If so directed by the Parole Board or my Parole Officer, I will abstain completely from the use of alcoholic beverages.

6. (a) I will make every effort to secure and maintain gainful employment. (b) If, for any reason, I lose my employment, I will report this to my Parole Officer immediately and I will cooperate fully in finding new employment. (c) I will not voluntarily quit my employment without prior approval of my Parole Officer.

7. (a) I will lead a law-abiding life and conduct myself as a good citizen. (b) I will not be in the company of or fraternize with any person having a criminal record. If there are unavoidable circumstances (such as work, school, family or group therapy and the life), I will discuss these with my Parole Officer and seek his written permission. (c) I will support my dependents, if any, and assume toward them my legal and moral obligations. (d) I promise my behavior will not be a menace to the safety or well-being of myself, other individuals, or to society. (e) I will advise my Parole Officer at any time that I am questioned or arrested by members of any law enforcement agency.

8. I will consult with my Parole Officer before applying for a license to marry.

9. I will not carry from the Facility from which I am released, or

cause to be delivered or sent to any Correctional Facility, any written or verbal message or any object or property of any kind without proper permission.

10. (a) Upon my release, I will advise my Parole Officer as to the status of any driver's license I possess. (b) I will seek and obtain permission of my Parole Officer before applying for or renewing a driver's license. (c) I will request and obtain permission of my Parole Officer before owning or purchasing any motor vehicle.

11. I will not own, possess, or purchase firearms or weapons of any kind.

12. I will not use, possess, or purchase any illegal drugs or use or possess those that have been unlawfully obtained.

13. Should the occasion arise, I will waive extradition and will not resist being returned by the Board of Parole to the State of New York.

14. Special Conditions: (May be imposed by the Board of Parole).

# F

Supreme Court
of the
State of New York

*Presentence Report*
Re: Smith, John
    b. 1/3/59

### PREVIOUS COURT HISTORY

1. *Juvenile*
None
2. *Adult*

July 1, 1974    Youthful Offender    Criminal Court    Cond. Disch.
On May 16, 1974, at the corner of 101st Street and Eighth Avenue, Manhattan, the defendant with four others, forcibly took a wallet containing $8 from the person of Valerie Gronich.
The defendent was conditionally discharged relevant to the above offense because on June 7, 1974, he had voluntarily entered the program of the New York State Division for Youth. A representative of this agency refused to divulge without Court Order any details relevant to the defendant's adjustment at the program and date of discharge.

June 19, 1976    Obstructing        Criminal Court       Not Found
                 Governmental Admin. and
                 Resisting Arrest
No record of this arrest can be found in the files of the Criminal Court.

**PENDING CHARGES**

None

## I. Present Offense

### ABSTRACT OF COMPLAINT AND INDICTMENT

In the County of New York, on May 23, 1976, John and William Smith, armed with a knife, forcibly took some currency from Harold Jones.
COMPLAINANT: Harold Jones, 38 West 108th Street, Manhattan
The account which follows is based upon information obtained from the Court papers, the records of the District Attorney's Office, and the Arresting Officer, Detective Johnson, now attached to the 1st Precinct. On May 23, 1976, at about 8:00 P.M., Jones was going to visit a friend who lived at 132 West 108th Street, Manhattan. In the hallway of the abovementioned building, he encountered the two defendants, who produced a knife and dragged him to the basement. There, they took $38 in U.S. currency from Jones' possession and fled.
Jones knew the defendents from the neighborhood and reported this matter to the Police. Detective Johnson, who was then attached to the 5th Detective Division, after investigation, located the defendants in their home on May 28, 1976, and placed them both under arrest.
Both William and John Smith have each pleaded guilty to Robbery in the 3rd Degree and are similarly awaiting sentencing by Your Honor on January 11, 1977.

## II. Mitigating and Aggravating Circumstances

According to Detective Johnson, at the time of arrest neither defendant made a statement, and he considers them equally culpable.
The knife used in the robbery and the money were never recovered.
Jones, who apparently has moved from the abovementioned address was not available for interview by this Department, and therefore his attitude could not be determined. According to Detective Johnson, the complaining witness was not injured during the course of the robbery and suffered a total loss of $38.
William Smith reiterated his admissions of guilt and stated that he committed the robbery because he needed money for drugs.

John Smith, despite his admissions of guilt in open Court before Your Honor, stated he pleaded guilty because his counsel advised him to, and he desires that his plea of guilty remain.

## III. Family Setting

According to his mother, there was parental conflict during the defendant's formative years resulting in the separation and divorce of the parents. Thereafter, his mother re-married, and seemingly, according to her, the defendant made a good adjustment in the home and had a favorable relationship with his stepfather. She claims that he did not present any outstanding problems during his formative years.

John Smith is the third of five children born to Michael Smith and Susan nee Henderson, both aged 38, who were married in 1950. His father, a native of this City, deserted the family. His mother remarried, Kenneth Parker, now aged 42, and resides with him at 132 West 108th Street, Manhattan.

When interviewed, Susan Smith was extremely defensive of her son. She asserted that she did not believe he was involved in this offense, and she could not understand why he pleaded guilty.

The defendant's older brother, William, aged 20, is his co-defendant. There is another older brother, Louis, aged 21, a sister, Judith, aged 15, and a sister, Barbara, aged 14. The defendant also has a half-sibling, Jon Parker, aged 10.

Except when he was in a camp at the Division for Youth, the defendant has resided with his mother all his life in a seven room apartment for which she pays a rental of $126, at 132 West 108th Street, Manhattan.

## IV. Education

John Smith attended the public schools of this City, attending Public Schools 61, 93, and the John Brown High School, all in Manhattan, being discharged from the latter school in February of 1970, while still in the third term. His attendance was poor, and it was noted that he was failing all subjects because of absenteeism.

Smith now claims that he is attending Hamilton High School nights in order to get his high school diploma.

## V. Employment Record

Smith, who was arrested on May 28, 1976, was paroled on that date, and has since been at liberty.

At the time of his arrest, he was unemployed, and maintained by his mother and stepfather.

He had a brief period of employment for two months in October and November 1976 as a delivery boy, at a salary of $100 weekly, for Golden's Supermarket in Manhattan.

Smith appears to be vocationally unskilled, and does not have any long range employment goals.

## VI. Physical and Mental Health

This defendant was not referred to the Psychiatric Clinic of this Court because, at the time of interview, the need for such an examination was not indicated. He appears to be of average intelligence and states he is in generally good health.

## VII. Appearance, Character and Conduct

John Smith is a youth of average height and proportions, who, as an interview subject, appeared to be friendly, but somewhat subdued in manner.

Basically, he appears to be an individual of average intellectual and emotional attainments, who was reared in a somewhat disorganized home, but who apparently did not present any symptoms of maladjustment until late adolescence.

He appears to have had some problems which brought him to the attention of the Division for Youth, and according to his mother after being involved in their program, the defendant made a good adjustment and maintained satisfactory relationships in his home.

Basically, he appears to be a somewhat weak-willed and easily-led youth, who acts impulsively on occasion.

He has denied any involvement in the instant offense, but seemingly he was motivated by a desire to go along with the plans of his older brother.

## VIII. Recommendation

It is respectfully recommended that the defendant be sentenced to incarceration.

Taking the defendant's total life picture into consideration and the serious nature of the instant offense, probation does not appear appropriate. We recommend a reformatory sentence.

Respectfully Submitted,

Anthony Ariola
Probation Officer

Reviewed by:

Robert Kaplan
Senior Probation Officer

APPROVED:

Nelson Elwirth
Chief Probation Officer

# G

Sample of a presentence memoranda prepared by the New York City Legal Aid Society, Pre-trial Diversion and Presentence Program.

### I. INTRODUCTION

The Pre-Sentence Service Group is a social service program within Legal Aid designed to provide short-term counseling and referral for appropriate clients between the client's conviction and date of sentencing. J_____ W_____ was referred to us on August 14, 1975. Through our work with Mr. W_____ and with people who know him, we have examined the events of his life, his personality, and the interrelationship of these factors to his crime.

It is hoped that our evaluation, by providing more in-depth information that was previously available, will help the Court in making a decision concerning the defendant's future.

### II. BACKGROUND HISTORY

J_____ W_____ was born on February 2, 1928, in Newark, New Jersey. He was raised by both of his parents (deceased). His mother was a dancer and as a result the family traveled quite often. Mr. W_____ was close with both of his parents and suffered a great deal when they passed away. His mother died in 1971 and his father died two years later.

Mr. W_____ is the second oldest of nine children born of this marriage. From our observation and conversations with Mr. W_____'s family and friends, we have concluded that the client has a very good relationship with his family. His sisters, E_____ and L_____, informed us that Mr. W_____ is very helpful and that they can count on him. E_____ also told us that her brother enjoys working. "He'll work doing anything to make an honest dollar, rather than go out and hustle off anyone else."

Mr. W_____ attended P.S. 24, 89, Junior High School 40 and 139 in New York City, where he completed the seventh grade. He left so that he could work as his parents were having financial difficulties and could no longer support him. As soon as he left school (in 1944), he began working at a grocery store called Sunbeam on Madison Avenue as a delivery boy. In 1946, he went to work for the New Haven docks for six years. In 1952, Mr. W_____ was employed by Seamen Company, operating machines. From 1970–1972, Mr. W_____ was working at Jaymee Dyeing and finishing Corporation where he was "laid off due to a slow down in production." Attached is a letter from the plant manager, Clyde Kanner. The following year Mr. W_____ worked as a dishwasher in New Jersey. During the same time he held a job (part-time) as an elevator operator. In 1973, our client went to work for Marcher Molding Corporation at 909 Essex Street. He worked there for two years but was laid off because business was slow. Attached is a letter from Robert Bruce Gomez, his employer. As one can see from his long history of employment, Mr. W_____ enjoys his independence and is self-supporting. He is presently receiving public assistance because jobs are scarce and hard to come by. Mr. _____ has expressed his desire to work but has been unable up to this point to find employment.

We referred Mr. W_____ to the Office of Vocational Rehabilitation for possible employment. This agency offers training in various fields, thorough medical examinations, referral for employment and counseling. Mr. W_____ applied for their services and is waiting to be called.

Mr. W_____ was married in 1950 to B_____ J_____. A daughter, D_____ W_____ was born from this relationship. She is now a grown woman, and has two children of her own, B_____ and C_____. Although J_____ W_____ and his wife are separated, our client keeps in contact with his daughter and his grandchildren. Mr. W_____ was also living common-law for a few years with M_____ B_____. They separated in 1968. Two children were born from this union, J_____ Jr., fourteen years old and V_____ W_____, twelve years old. Mr. W_____ visits his children quite often and whenever possible, takes them out for the week-end.

Included at the end of this memorandum are letters from Paragon Progressive Federal Credit Union, where Mr. W_____ has been a member since September, 1967, and from the Church Mr. W_____ attends.

Ignoring a long list of juvenile and/or "Y.O." involvements, this defendant's adult criminal record begins with a 1948 sentence of Probation (the crime was burglary). Before completing Probation, he was convicted of another burglary and was sentenced to one year. That was in May, 1949. Mr. W_____ was then twenty-one years old. In early 1950, he was again arrested and convicted of assault on which he was sentenced to a jail term of six years. After serving four of the six years, he was released in March, 1954. Mr. W_____ was again arrested and convicted for a burglary in which he was sentenced to a four to six year jail term. He was paroled from Green Haven in August of 1959. The defendant was then thirty-one years old. From the above, one can see clearly that the client's youth, i.e. the ten years from twenty-one to thirty-one were spent almost totally in jail. The impact and environment of prison life was so depressing for Mr. W_____, that it was difficult for him to adjust in society, and he found himself in jail again. This time it was a sixty day sentence for Petit Larceny. He was again arrested in 1968, but the case was dismissed.

### III.  PRESENT COURT INVOLVEMENT

In April, 1972, Mr. W_____ was arrested for instant offense, Attempted Possession of a Dangerous Weapon, to which he pled guilty on August 14, 1975.

He told us that he regrets having possession of the weapon, but had no intention of using it. The total record of this forty-seven year old man is, in essence, limited to a list of various offenses committed in his twenties, and he served time on all of them. In the last fifteen years since then he has shown a marked improvement in his ability to cope and live in society.

### IV.  DIAGNOSTIC ASSESSMENT

J_____ W_____ is a responsible, soft-spoken, motivated and concerned man. He was very cooperative while working with the Pre-Sentence Service Group. He is also a lonely, quiet and reserved person. He drinks at times to forget his problems, but he has realized that drinking cannot solve his problems. Mr. W_____ has never depended on anyone or anything. He has always supported himself and has always worked with the people around him to help make their lives and their surroundings a little better.

Mr. W_____ has expressed a desire to learn a trade because he feels it is almost impossible to be employed without a skill. Therefore, we feel he can benefit from the services the Office of Vocational Rehabilitation has to offer.

Although limited because of his lack of education and his criminal record, Mr. W_____ continues to strive for better training and a healthier life.

## V. RECOMMENDATIONS

Mr. W_____ has been in no trouble since the late 1950's, and we do not believe that he will be before this Court in the future. We feel that he has made a tremendous effort in adjusting to our society and has shown a great improvement.

When talking to Mr. W_____ concerning this case, he has stated on several occasions that he regrets ever posessing the weapon that has led him to this Court. Due to the fact that he has suffered a great deal because he fears incarceration, we feel that it has been a punishment in itself. We therefore strongly recommend Probation for Mr. Williams.

We hope the Court will take our recommendation into consideration.

Respectfully submitted:

N_____ A_____
Social Worker
Legal Aid Pre-Sentence Service
Group

# H

Outline for Action
Representative Personal History
Fifth Judicial District Department of Court
Services*

> NAME:        Michael Doe
> AGE:         19
> SENTENCE:    180 days
> DATE:        October 31, 1972

I. Behavioral Functioning

**FAMILY**

The dominant figure in this family is May Doe, age 49. She is currently working on her Ph.D. in Special Education. She views Michael as having an organic or perceptual problem. She has interpreted his actions and problems in this way, both to him and to others throughout his life. She has a history of interference and

*Sample of a case assessment report which serves as a basis for the treatment plan in the Des Moines Pre-Trial Services Program. Source: Law Enforcement Assistance Administration A Handbook on Community Corrections in Des Moines. (Washington, D.C.: United States Government Printing Office, 1973), pp. 141-44.

noncooperation with schools, Eldora, and probation. She has sheltered Michael to a ridiculous extreme, i.e., supplying him with his own condiments at Eldora. She explains her marriage as merely a Catholic "till death do us part" commitment. She explains her husband as an alcoholic having an "irregular EEG" and has in the past year committed him to Lutheran psychiatric. In conversation with her she has confined herself to Michael's past rather than expressing interest in his present treatment.

Robert Doe, 56, is a retired mailman who earned $171.00 per week. He has a high school education. He has in the past made attempts to be more directive with his son, i.e., after Eldora, but apparently these were short lived. From information gathered from Ann Marie (daughter) and DVR files it appears, Mr. Doe is an alcoholic and unstable. He is slight in build and has felt threatened by Michael.

Gregory, 21: Works as a parking lot attendant and lives upstairs at his parents home. He has engaged in some delinquent behavior while growing up, but was not caught. He is married and the father of two children. It appears he enjoys a limited family life. His attitude toward Michael is violent.

Ann-Marie, 18: She is a senior at South High. She appears very mature and is active socially and in extracurricular activities. She states she has raised herself and spent the overwhelming majority of her time outside the home. She does not express condemnation of her family but acknowledges that it is abnormal. It appears that the home has the atmosphere of a circus. Mr. and Mrs. Doe, Gregory and Michael are the primary participants, with Ann being an observer.

## PEERS

Michael is quite obvious in his attempts to "be cool" and to "get in" with his peers. He is regarded by some facility clients as quite immature and is avoided a majority of the time. One client has observed that he thinks it's cool to "mouth-off", i.e., calling someone a punk, and appears oblivious of the extent to which he is aggravating them.

Ann states he had no friends while in school, was teased and almost tortured by school mates. He then began affiliating with youths who had been in trouble. He often misplaced his trust, losing clothing and in one case, a guitar and amplifier.

## EDUCATION

Michael attended parochial schools until entering Urbandale in 9th grade, he was expelled in February of 1969 for "truancy, violation of rules, disrespect, and poor attitude". After this he attended Dowling briefly. He also attended Drop-In but was expelled due to truancy and poor attitude.

Michael has always had the tools to do well in school, and maintains that potential now.

He received his GED as part of his probationary period. DVR records show his IQ as high bright-normal.

### EMPLOYMENT

Michael has never shown motivation toward obtaining or maintaining employment. He remained on a car wash job for five weeks, 3½ years ago, when influenced by his probation officer. He has now worked for 1½ weeks, suspecting that quitting this job means a return to jail.

His immediate employment goals are both unrealistic and contradictory.

Again, he has the potential to eventually secure an interesting and well-paying job but does not possess the attitude or sense of reality necessary.

### MEDICAL AND PSYCHIATRIC

This is included, as Michael seeks to avoid responsibility, get attention, and shelter himself by presenting himself as psychotic or brain-damaged.

On July 1, 1970, Michael was released from Eldora and sent to the State Psychopathic Hospital at Iowa City. He has just turned 17 at this time and has been using drugs heavily since age 14. At this time Michael *termed himself* "egocentric, schizophrenic, having split-second mood changes, intelligent, paranoid and always trying to manipulate everyone." Dr. Jones states, "on testing this patient's mental status today, there is no evidence of organicity or psychosis . . ." He continued, "our diagnosis at this time was sociopathic—drug addiction (psychologic) with possible periods of psychosis probably secondary to chronic drug usage."

On August 19, 1971, Michael was admitted to Lutheran Hospital for evaluation.

At this time, "general physical and neurological examinations were within normal limits." He was of estimated below normal intelligence without any gross sensorum changes." "Michael Doe was classified as a personality disorder, dysocial behavior." There was some evidence of a convulsive disorder. It was at this time that Michael was placed on Mysoline.

Ann has stated doubt regarding Michael's drug use. She

states he has seen drug use as something to brag about and may have exaggerated his own history.

II. Behavior Assessment:

A. DVR counselor has described Michael as having, "an apathetic attitude toward involvement with authority, completing assignment of jobs and relating with peer group." He is extraordinarily ambivalent in terms of long- and short-range goals and in his attitude toward himself and others.
B. He employs a wide variety of unsophisticated attention-getting devices and attempts to manipulate the staff. He denies any knowledge of doing this when called on specific actions.
C. He chooses to present himself as handicapped, mentally and physically, rather than accepting the responsibilities of adulthood.
D. He changes his goals and priorities, both immediate and long-range, quite frequently, i.e., several times a day.

Through his behavior, he almost creates a caricature of himself, effectively hiding the fact that he is a healthy adult male with the ability to assume responsibility for himself and his actions.

III. Treatment Goals and Plans

The primary goal is to force Michael into acting maturely in all the above areas. The broad method of achieving this is to condemn all his immature and childishly manipulative actions and to provide penalties rather than rewards for them.

A. His contacts with staff should be reported. When he is merely seeking attention, i.e., "taking a poll" for advice he does not need, he should incur a penalty. When he is manipulating to achieve a specific thing, he should receive the reverse. An example: When complaining of muscle aches, he should be made to exercise.
B. He should be treated at all times as healthy and normal. He must hold employment, this being the main gauge of his progress. Rewards should be based primarily on employment. He should not be given any assistance in tasks he himself can complete, i.e., deciding time and location of a weekend pass.
C. He must be made to follow-up on any commitments he makes, even unrealistic. For example: he states his first day at F.W. Means, that he would "work for a month."

The separation between himself and his parents should be continued, hopefully after he leaves the facility.

A transfer to a male counselor or inclusion on a triad may be advisable in the future.

John Jones

I

## Counseling Rape Victims*

### ROLE OF THE COUNSELOR

In counseling and/or interviewing rape victims the following skills and abilities can be extremely useful in getting necessary information, putting the victim at ease and recognizing the limits of the counseling effort.

Compassion—be aware that the victim is experiencing mental and physical trauma. Be acquainted with myths and the resultant responses they may engender in the victim and her friends and family.

Knowledge—of the procedural matters involved regarding the medical, law enforcement and judicial systems.

General Counseling Skills—be on guard to recognize what is important to victim. Encourage her to express her feelings. Do not attempt to redefine the situation as being more or less critical than she sees it. Only the victim can determine how critical the situation is, since determination must be based on her values.

*Source: Gerald Bryant and Paul Cirel, Polk County Rape/Sexual Assault Care Center, Des Moines, Iowa (Washington, D.C.: United States Government Printing Office, 1977).

*Maintain Reasonable Expectations*—for both the counselor and the victim. Communicate immediately what can and cannot be done. Pre-existing life problems will persist and may, in fact, be brought into sharper focus by the crisis.

*Assist in Decision-making*—the victim must, of course, make all the decisions herself. However, she should be made aware that decisions need to be made regarding medical treatment, reporting to the police, child care, and informing relatives. The counselor must be aware of the available alternatives to be effective.

*Institutional Advocacy*—know all the procedures followed by all agency personnel that the victim might contact. Although they have their own SOP's that are sensitive to the rape victim, those SOP's might be overlooked. Be prepared to explain all procedures.

*Family Contacts*—the counselor can help the victim find support from other people in her life. The victim will often have a good intuitive idea who to tell or not and how they will react. Offer to help her tell family/friends if she wants you to. Sometimes a third party can be a buffer during the initial period of revelation.

The following excerpts from the guidelines present counselors with specific information concerning the emotional state of the victim, needs for counseling during the trial and overall "do's and don'ts" of counseling.

### FEELINGS FREQUENTLY FELT BY RAPE VICTIM

*Fear of the Rapist*—The rapist overcame the victim's resistance and forced her to submit to his sexual demands. Either because of direct threats of the rapist or because media rape stories give the impression, it is likely that she felt that she would either be brutally injured or had only a few moments to live. Normal fear response may be quite generalized or specific to the rapist. The victim's fear may be particularly strong if the rapist threatened to harm her again, as often happens if he suspects she will report to the police. Fear of attack under these circumstances is a normal human fear. She is not crazy or paranoid to fear the attacker. She needs positive assurance from those around her that life is worth living and she needs to explore alternate ways of coping with her fear of attack. Help her express and specify her fear. Encourage her to list all the things she can do to protect herself including some things that are unacceptable to her such as staying home all the time behind heavily locked doors. Whatever she decides, her plan should be clear in her mind and simple to put into operation even when she is emotionally upset.

*Guilt*—the rape victim's feelings of guilt are difficult for her to deal with and will likely have an effect on her decision to contact the police. Many women have internalized the prevalent mythology which emphasizes the idea that women are to blame for having been raped. No matter how strongly you feel that it was not the woman's fault, it is important to let her talk and try to help her define in precise terms what she might have done "wrong"—and what she might have done differently.

*Loss of Control Over Her Own Life*—the rapist has forced her to submit to something she did not want to do. Possibly, she harbored some ideas before the rape that rape couldn't happen to her, that she would be able to resist or that she could take care of herself. Since the rapist overcame her resistance by force or fear, she no longer feels sure of anything about herself and her self-determination. Sometimes even little decisions like whether to have a cigarette or whether to eat become momentous things. The victim practically has to repossess herself after the rapist took possession by force. She has to reassert the value of doing things for herself, she has to insist to herself that she is worthwhile and that she still has willpower and control over herself.

If the victim has followed a life style of trusting people, leaving doors open, talking to strangers, making friends in odd places, hitchhiking across country, and so on, she may feel that in addition to body, the rapist has stolen her whole way of life.

*Embarrassment*—she may be embarrassed to discuss the physical details of the assault. Our bodies and sexual activity have always been regarded as private and her privacy has been stripped from her by another. Telling anyone at all may be painful.

It is likely that the rapist verbally abused her with offensive sexual language, and she is embarrassed to say these words. She may also not know acceptable terminology to describe what happened sexually.

The medical exam is especially embarrassing. Her body is again exposed and is an object of attention and inspection by strangers. She is likely to feel that her body, her appearance, and her *whole being* is offensive and disgusting. She may even feel sorry for the doctor who "has to look at it." She may even be too embarrassed to admit her embarrassment. Help her recognize that you and any person would be embarrassed under such circumstances. What she is feeling is normal.

*Anxiety, Shaking, Nightmares*—Victims often react after physical attack with shaking and anxiety. The relief of having made it, the shuddering at the thought of how close to death she was are expressed in this way. The victim remembers the incident. The trauma goes so deep that she may have nightmares. She thinks what she could have done and she thinks what he could have done. Continued support from all around her and reassurance that she is physically safe and can do things to protect herself will help these symptoms of trauma dissipate. The nightmares will continue, perhaps, but will not be as vivid.

*Concern for the Rapist*—many victims express a concern about what will happen to the rapist if he is reported to the police. Some victims want psychiatric help for the rapist rather than jail. She may have very negative attitudes towards the criminal justice system and jail and may feel guilt in reporting the crime. Perhaps these attitudes are the result of the victim's effort to understand what happened and what her contributions were to the assault. If no physical beating or other violence occurred, some victims even say that it is not worth sending a man to jail. It is human to show concern for another human, especially one in trouble. But she must not let this feeling obscure the fact that he did attack her. In feeling sorry for him, she should not repress her anger for the indignities she has suffered just as most robbery victims wouldn't think of forgiving and forgetting someone who robbed them.

*Wondering—Why Me?*—some women wonder why the rapist chose them. What is it about them that separates them from other women? These feelings arise from the common mistaken belief that rape happens to women who "ask for it," or who in some other way made themselves noticeable. It may help her to know that this is a common normal feeling of rape victims and that anyone can be raped. To help the victim see this, try to get her to tell you how she came in contact with the rapist and what contact she had with the rapist before the rape occurred. He probably manuevered the situation to lead to the rape. In short, she should be reminded that the rapist made the decision to assault her.

*Shame*—the destruction of self-respect, the deliberate efforts by the attacker to make her do things she knows she and society detest, to make her feel dirty and disgusting, may make her ashamed. That she submitted at all, even if at knife point, may make her feel ashamed. Society's attitudes toward sex and different sexual acts are all reflected in her shame. The victim who feels she has been violated needs to see the rape as an attack, not her choice. She need not feel shame where no choice was involved.

*Stupidity*—the extent of her mistake that led to the point of rape determines how really stupid she feels. If she was hitchhiking, for instance, she may blame herself for the rape because she knew it would be risky. It is good to admit an error and to try to be more cautious in the future. But admission of error must not hide the fact that she was attacked. She was not the attacker. No person asks or deserves to be raped no matter how thoughtless or careless they were. Remind her that we all go about our daily lives in a spirit of trust and that we all, after any accident or tragedy, can think of countless things we should or should not have done.

*Anger*—this is the most appropriate attitude, and it is a healthy response. When someone burglarizes our homes or runs into our cars, we are angry. The victim has been attacked and humiliated, so she should be angry. She can vent this anger in several ways, such as pressing charges, or telling other women about the attacker or the situation he created leading up to the attack. She may tend to generalize and extend the anger to all men.

*In Summary*—the victim needs calm, reassuring, unwavering support. She needs to know that she is not crazy. She needs help to restore her dignity and self-respect. She need not feel ashamed or guilty. She needs to see the total rape experience for what it was, an attack on her whole being. The rape cannot be allowed to become a dominant factor in her life. Such an assault is a terrifying experience that she must incorporate into her life, and then continue living as a stronger woman. It would be damaging to repress the experience or to negate her own part in it, however small.

### COUNSELING AT THE TIME OF THE TRIAL

As the trial approaches, many of the victim's initial feelings will resurface and may even intensify. She faces seeing and accusing her attacker and telling about what happened before a jury and open court. The defense will be either that she has incorrectly identified the rapist, that sexual intercourse did not take place, or that she consented to the intercourse. Any line of defense will make her feel that she is not believed. The questioning will be embarrassing in its detail and frustrating and irritating as the attorney will attempt to confuse her and cast doubt on her credibility and character.

   She will be helped by recognizing that it will all be over soon. She will no longer have to keep details fresh in her memory and can allow herself to forget. The prosecuting attorney should become acquainted with the victim prior to trial and should explain courtroom procedures to her and discuss with her the likely defense. The sexual assault counselor is invaluable at time of trial. The victim needs to recognize and express her feelings and not suppress them in her attempt to view the trial objectively.

   She should be prepared for the possibility of acquittal and encouraged to recognize that successful prosecution of rape is very difficult, and acquittal does not necessarily mean that she was not believed. "Proof beyond a reasonable doubt" is a necessity for conviction. Technical and legal problems are also often factors in acquittal.

She should not be present in the courtroom except when testifying. Hearing the other testimony will intensify her negative feelings, and the jurors may be distracted by her presence or influenced by her reaction/nonreaction.

### TIPS FOR COUNSELORS

1. Just listening and indicating that you understand is very important to the victim. By trying to share her feelings of the moment she is, in essence, helping herself.
2. During the impact period, the victim is hypersensitive to any action or statement which you might make and often fears "pressure" from you even when she is asking for advice.
3. Even if the woman states that she is a relative or friend of the victim, keep in mind that it might be the victim herself. Some women cannot bring themselves to admit to the fact immediately.
4. For the victim who has difficulty in communicating, the counselor can usually begin by asking her how she feels.
5. Assure the victim that she has not been singled out for an attack, but that what has happened to her has happened to thousands of other women.
6. Do not phrase questions in a manner which will inhibit the victim, such as "Are you using a form of birth control?" Say instead, "Do you have any physical concerns right now?"
7. It helps the victim to be told that this experience will cause a disruption to her life for a while.
8. If she feels guilt because she failed to fight, tell her that fear inhibits most people or that survival is the most important thing—depending upon the individual situation.
9. If she is alone, offer to call someone for her. If she does not want anyone called, assure her that you will be avilable if she needs to call again.

# J

## A Review of Pretrial Diversion Programs and a Glossary of Terms*

Pretrial alternatives can be offered at points increasingly "deeper" into the criminal justice system. Generally, the point at which the decision to opt for an alternative is made—the locus of authority—determines how long an arrested person will remain in custody (Figure J-1). Options made available early in the justice process (e.g., at the point of police contact) thus are cheaper and have a greater impact on jail populations than those offered at later stages. There are trade-offs, of course. While early decisions to release or divert may save more in terms of time and money, they may be less protective of either the rights of the suspects or the safety of the community.

Terms used in the figures are defined in the glossary which follows. Several of these alternative practices and arrangements are illustrated in the section which follows, as are various pretrial diversion programs. It should be emphasized that the examples cited below rep-

*Source: John J. Galvin, Walter H. Busher, William Green-Quijano, Gary Kemp, Nora Harlow, and Kathleen Hoffman, Instead of Jail: Pre- and Post-trial Alternatives to Jail Incarceration, Volume 1. (Washington, D.C.: United States Government Printing Office 1977), pp. 9–19, and 55–59.

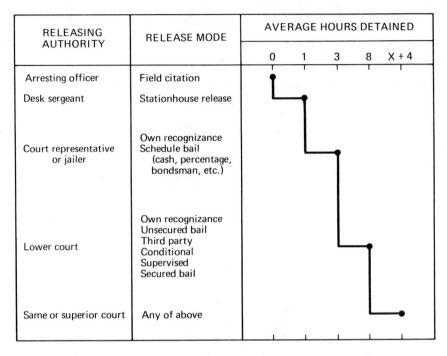

| RELEASING AUTHORITY | RELEASE MODE | AVERAGE HOURS DETAINED 0  1  3  8  X + 4 |
|---|---|---|
| Arresting officer | Field citation | |
| Desk sergeant | Stationhouse release | |
| Court representative or jailer | Own recognizance Schedule bail (cash, percentage, bondsman, etc.) | |
| Lower court | Own recognizance Unsecured bail Third party Conditional Supervised Secured bail | |
| Same or superior court | Any of above | |

**Figure J-1.** Locus of Authority to Release and Detention Time

resent only a handful of the alternative programs operating today in American communities. These few were selected simply to demonstrate the range of practices and to indicate some of the variations in administrative arrangements.

### ALTERNATIVE: POLICE CITATION

In New York City, under the desk appearance ticket system, the suspect is brought to a precinct stationhouse where he goes through a booking procedure which varies with the charge—that is, he may or may not be fingerprinted or photographed. Where the charge is a misdemeanor he may be released by the desk sergeant on his promise to appear in court. The expensive alternative requires the arresting officer to deliver him to a court detention cell. He then confers with a deputy prosecutor and, if a charge is to be pressed, with a court calendar clerk. The officer and the defendant wait their turn to appear for arraignment (courts are in session daily until after midnight) where the arrest report is presented orally to the judge. The entire procedure consumes an average of eight hours of police officer time.

Desk appearance tickets are issued in a majority of misdemeanant cases. Although rates of failure to appear have approached unacceptable levels in one or two of the city's boroughs, very substantial savings in law enforcement expenditures have accrued by reducing police manpower tied up in arrest procedures.

*California* law allows the release of misdemeanants by police in the field at any point prior to arraignment (pre- or post-booking). In each case, release takes effect upon written promise by the suspect to appear for an initial hearing at a time and place specified on the citation form. If release is not effected in the field, the officer may transport the suspect to the stationhouse or other facility for verification of information prior to issuing a pre-booking citation. Post-booking citation release, which occurs at the detention facility, is made by the officer in charge of booking or his superior. In some counties, selection of persons for release is assisted by release-on-recognizance staff.

The decision to release or detain is guided by statutory provisions and departmental policies. A recent amendment to the California code requires the arresting officer to state his reasons for not using citation release in the field or before or after booking. In some counties, arrest reports also are reviewed by superior officers and conferences are scheduled with officers who appear to avoid reasonable use of citation release. Both of these arrangements tend to encourage more liberal use of the citation alternative.

*In Washington, D.C.,* a unique arrangement for release decision-making exists: In cases eligible for citation release, the police desk sergeant calls the D.C. Bail Agency, supplies the available facts, and then puts the arrestee on the telephone for an interview. Following the verification process, the interviewer calls back with his recommendation regarding release which generally is accepted and acted upon by the desk sergeant.

### ALTERNATIVE: PRETRIAL RELEASE

*The Brooklyn Pretrial Services Agency* is one of four such programs in New York City boroughs operated by the Vera Institute of Justice. All arrestees are brought to a central booking center in a building which houses the criminal court. Those not "cited out" (most misdemeanants are) are interviewed by an agency staff member. Round-the-clock coverage is provided and release decisions are recommended in a series of "waves". Release on recognizance is recommended whenever the individual meets selection criteria, as determined by interview and verification process. Those not released at first appearance may be recommended for ROR the following day as verifications are completed or new information becomes available. When release is still denied by the court after full investigation, the agency seeks to arrange for release to the custody of a person known to the defendant or a selected volunteer. If third-party release is denied, the agency may recommend release to its own direct supervision.

ROR releasees are monitored. Reminders of court appearance dates are sent, appearances are verified, and efforts are made to locate any absentees and encourage them to report immediately to court. These procedures, as well as the agency's screening function and its third-party and supervised release programs, have been found cost-effective in terms of detention costs saved and low failure rates.

In Indianapolis, Ind., the Pretrial Services Agency of the Marion County Municipal Court employs law students on a part-time basis to provide round-the-clock coverage of the jail at lower cost than would be possible with full-time salaried employees. Experienced inter-viewers in their senior year of law school are appointed bail commis-sioners. They have the authority to release misdemeanants on recog-nizance without referral to court—greatly reducing the time required for release decision-making. Bail commissioners may recommend ROR, supervised release, or reduced bail (that is, less than that provided for in the bail schedule). In addition, they investigate eligibility for indi-gent defense services, handle diversion of public inebriates, and per-form initial screening for drug-dependency services. From its inception the agency has been dynamic and innovative, adding new features and options and expanding its capacity to meet the needs of the commu-nity.

In Washington, D.C., the D.C. Bail Agency monitors and super-vises not only recognizance and conditional release cases, but persons released on percentage bail. Private social service agencies and self-help groups are used extensively in third-party release cases. Recently, the agency has experimented with a mobile field unit, which can be contacted by radio. The functions of this unit are diverse—from help-ing to verify facts in the case of a person just arrested, to contacting absentees from court, or making supervisory or service contacts with persons on conditional release.

In Albuquerque, N.M., three detention facilities once operated by the city-county corrections director. The former county jail is the pri-mary pretrial detention center. The jail has a staff of five counselors who perform a variety of social service tasks, including emergency services, referral to diversion agencies, release planning, and adminis-tration of a work-release program. One of their functions is to interview unsentenced prisoners on admission and recommend ROR, where appropriate, to the judges. They give this function top priority, interviewing all unsentenced prisoners booked into the jail and supplying reports to the magistrate on all who do not "bail out" before first court appearance.

*The tri-county Regional Probation Department in El Paso, Texas,* offers an integrated court services program covering not only pretrial release, but diversion screening, presentence investigation, and probation supervision. In the pretrial area, the agency screens arrestees and recommends release on "personal bond"—a form of non-monetary supervised release. Supervision requirements vary from infrequent contacts by telephone to frequent reporting in person, depending on the assessed risk level and need for services. Supportive counseling and referral services are provided where indicated. All releasees are reminded of court appearance dates and appearances are verified. In the event of failure to appear, the agency makes investigations, obtains warrants if necessary, and may make arrests. The program is partially supported by service fees assessed against releasees who can afford to pay them.

*The Berkeley pretrial services program* offers a model for small or medium-sized cities in which universities or colleges are situated. Most of the jail interviewing and community contact with pretrial releasees is handled by unpaid college student volunteers who are recruited, trained, and supervised by a four-person paid staff. Agency interviewers are present in the jail early each weekday morning. Reports of their interviews and verification efforts are supplied to judges. Releasees are reminded by telephone the night before each scheduled court appearance. Court dockets are checked daily. If a defendant fails to appear, persistent efforts are made to locate him and persuade him to appear voluntarily before a warrant is issued. The agency also arranges acceptance of drug-dependent arrestees by residential drug treatment centers as a condition of pretrial release.

### ALTERNATIVE: PRETRIAL DIVERSION

Pretrial release allows the individual his freedom pending appearance in court. It is an alternative to jail pending trial. Pretrial diversion is an alternative to prosecution. It takes many forms and may occur at any point following receipt of a criminal complaint. The range of possibilities is reflected in Figure J-2. Examples of different modes and methods follow.

**Figure J-2.** Levels and Kinds of Intervention in Relation to Criminal Justice Stage where Diversion May Occur

| Examples of Intervention Levels | STAGE AND AGENCY WHERE DIVERSION OCCURS | | | |
| --- | --- | --- | --- | --- |
| | Police | Prosecutor | Pros. or Court | Court |
| | Pre-Arrest | Pre-Arraingment | Pretrial | Pre-Judgement |
| 1. warning/reprimand | X | | | |
| 2. Referral to appropriate resource | X | X | | |
| 3. Problem solving service—counseling, mediation, arbitration, etc. | X | X | | |
| 4. (Referral for) civil commitment | X | X | X | X |
| 5. Conditional suspension of prosecution or final judgement of guilt, with or without supervision and helping services | | X | X | X |

*The Night Prosecutor Program in Columbus, Ohio,* handles interpersonal criminal charges (such as assault, threats, telephone harassment, criminal mischief, and larceny) arising from family or neighborhood disputes by attempting to resolve the complaint without resort to criminal processing. Referrals may come from complainants directly or from police, city prosecutor, or legal aid office. Project staff also select prospective cases by reviewing the court's summons docket each day. Cases diverted at an initial screening interview may be referred on to the detective bureau, scheduled for a mediation hearing, or referred to a community social service agency. Mediation hearings are designed to help the parties arrive at a resolution of their differences and achieve some basis for reconciliation. In cases where long-standing conflicts lie behind the complaint, family counseling services also are provided. Law students are employed part-time as interviewers and hearing officers and seminary students with special training conduct family counseling sessions. Very few cases must be referred on for prosecution.

In *Charlotte, N.C.,* public inebriates booked into the jail may be released without prosecution when they become sober enough or when a third party agrees to assume responsibility for them—usually in a matter of a few hours. An informal agreement with the prosecutor and the court provides the basis for release. In California, police have the statutory authority to release intoxicated persons if prosecution is deemed unnecessary or inappropriate. Once the arrestee is booked into the jail, county jailers make such release decisions through agreements with arresting agencies. Typically, arrestees who have not received such releases more than twice during the year are processed in this way.

In *Phoenix, Ariz.,* persons arrested for drunk driving may be diverted, at the prosecutor's discretion, to a program dealing with the problem underlying the offense (e.g., community college courses on driving and alcoholism or therapeutic treatment for problem drinking). The defendant signs an agreement to plead guilty in a specific courtroom on a named date to a lesser vehicle code charge. The prosecutor also signs and agrees to recommend a specified fine. If the defendant is not re-arrested within a set time period, usually sixty days, and participates in the prescribed program, the bargain is carried out in open court, with the judge ordinarily accepting the prosecutor's recommendation as to the penalty. Failure of the defendant to meet his obligations can result either in reinstatement of the original charge or a recommendation of a heavier penalty by the prosecutor if the defedant is allowed to plead to the lesser offense.

A *diversion program called TASC* (Treatment Alternatives to Street Crime) offers an unusually effective approach to case selection, service referral, and monitoring in a score of jurisdictions across the country. TASC works to identify arrestees who are addicted to drugs and to engage them immediately following arrest in services which might help them overcome their dependency on drugs. Although its original goal was to select and monitor cases for pretrial diversion, the program also attempts to gain conditional pretrial release for persons not selected for diversion and probation conditioned on participation in drug treatment for convicted offenders.

With a few exceptions, TASC does not provide drug treatment services, but arranges for treatment by existing community agencies. TASC then monitors client performance and keeps the court, prosecutor's office, or probation department advised of the individual's progress in the program. Considerable attention is devoted to generating, mobilizing, and evaluating community resources for the rehabilitation of drug-dependent offenders. An information or tracking system assists in both individual case monitoring and in program evaluation.

*The Citizens Probation Authority in Flint, Mich.,* one of the oldest formal diversion programs in the country, selects "situational lawbreakers" for participation in an alternative program. The program requires that the defendant "accept moral responsibility" for the crime, pay a service fee of $100 (unless waived for indigence), pay restitution (if appropriate), accept probation supervision for up to one year, and become involved in a contractual agreement with the agency to participate in recommended rehabilitative programs or undertake other steps to improve daily functioning. In return, along with any benefits derived from services, the defendant has a 90 percent chance of avoiding prosecution and the assurance that efforts will be made to expunge his arrest record.

*Vocationally disadvantaged defendants are diverted to Project Intercept,* a program operated by a private nonprofit corporation in San Jose, Calif. The criteria for selection favor young property offenders who appear to have difficulty in finding or maintaining employment. A project staff member attends court daily and screens persons scheduled for arraignment on misdemeanor charges. In cases where a defendant who meets the criteria expresses an interest in the program, the court is requested to grant a ten-day continuance. During this period, project staff assess the needs and motivation of the defendant and acquaint him with the program in detail. Where participation in the program seems warranted, diversion to the agency is recommended to the judge, the prosecutor, and the defense attorney. With concurrence of these officials, the defendant enters a plea of nolo contendere and the case is set down for three to six months. Assistance to accepted clients includes placement in a job or job training, individual tutoring for high-school equivalency exams, family or personal counseling, child care and transportation. Successful program participants tend to incur less serious charges than do those who fail in or are ineligible for the program.

In *California*, Section 1000 of the penal code provides for diversion of persons charged with any of several drug possession offenses and a few other specified offenses indicative of drug use. Eligibility screening to determine whether the individual meets statutory requirements is the responsibility of the District Attorney. Qualified defendants are offered the opportunity to waive their right to speedy trial and apply for diversion. Those who apply are referred to the county probation department for a determination of suitability for the program. Results are reported to the court, which, in the process of making final selection, assures itself of the voluntary and informed agreement of the defendant. For those approved, further criminal proceedings are suspended for six months to two years, with progress reports to the court required at six-month intervals. Participation in a drug education or treatment program is a standard condition of diversion. Satisfactory completion of the program—in the absence of conviction for a new felony or serious misdemeanor during the diversion period—results in dismissal of charges.

This massive state-wide diversion program, which is administered at the county level, has been well tracked statistically and subjected to numerous evaluative studies. The program has been successful, as judged by dismissal of charges—86 percent of program terminations during 1973–74.

# Glossary[*]

Summons—The summons is a request or instruction to appear in court to face an accusation. As an alternative to the arrest warrant, it is used in cases where complaints are registered with the magistrate or prosecutor's office.

Field Citation—Citation and release in the field is used by police as an alternative to booking and pretrial detention. This practice reduces law enforcement as well as jail costs.

Stationhouse Citation—Under the alternative of stationhouse citation, the arrestee is escorted to the precinct police station or headquarters rather than the pretrial detention facility. Release, which may occur before or after booking, is contingent upon the written promise of the defendant to appear in court as specified on the release form.

Release on Recognizance (ROR)—ROR refers to release without monetary bail or other special conditions and without supervision or services. The arrestee is placed on his honor to appear in court when scheduled.

Conditional Release—The defendant who is conditionally released

*Source: John J. Galvin, Walter H. Busher, William Greene-Quijana, Gary Kemp, Nora Harlow, and Kathleen Hoffman, Instead of Jail: Pre- and Post-trial Alternatives to Jail Incarceration, Volume I (Washington, D.C.: United States Government Printing Office.)

agrees to specified conditions in addition to appearing in court. Such conditions may include remaining in a defined geographical area, maintaining steady employment, avoiding contact with the victim or with associates in the alleged crime, avoiding certain activities or places, participating in treatment, or accepting services. Conditional release is often used in conjunction with third-party or supervised release.

*Third-party Release*—Third-party release extends to another person the responsibility for insuring the defendant's appearance in court. This may be a person known to the defendant or a designated volunteer. Third-party release may be a condition of unsecured bail, with the third party as a co-signer.

*Monitored Release*—Monitored release is recognizance release with the addition of minimal supervision or service, i.e., the defendant may be required to keep a pretrial services agency informed of his whereabouts while the agency reminds the defendant of court dates and verifies his appearance.

*Supervised Release*—Supervised release involves more frequent contact than monitored release. Typically, various conditions are imposed and supervision is aimed at enforcement of these conditions and provision of services as needed. Some form of monetary bail also may be attached at a condition of supervised release, especially in higher-risk cases.

*Unsecured Bail*—This form of release differs from ROR only in that the defendant is subject to paying the amount of bail if he defaults. Unsecured bail permits release without a deposit or purchasing a bondsman's services.

*Cash Bail*—Cash bail generally is used where the charge is not serious and the scheduled bail is low. The defendant obtains release by paying in cash the full amount, which is recoverable after required court appearances are made.

*Bondsman-secured Bail*—Under this traditional bail arrangement the defendant purchases security service from a bail bondsman. The fee for this service ranges upward from 10 percent and is not refundable. The bail bondsman system, which permits a private entrepreneur to share with the court the decision on pretrial release, has been criticized for many years and is becoming obsolete in more progressive jurisdictions.

*Privately-secured Bail*—This arrangement is similar to the bail bondsman system except that bail is provided without cost to the defendant. A private organization provides bail for indigent arrestees who meet its eligibility requirements.

*Personally-secured Bail*—If bail is personally secured, the defendant or his family puts up the security. This arrangement is generally out of reach of the less affluent defendant.

*Percentage Bail*—A publicly managed bail service arrangement, percentage bail requires the defendant to deposit a percentage (typically 10 percent) of the amount of bail with the court clerk. The deposit is returned to the defendant after scheduled court appearances are made, although a charge (usually 1 percent) may be deducted to help defray program costs.

*Unconditional Diversion*—Unconditional diversion involves the cessation of criminal processing at any point short of adjudication with no continuing threat of prosecution. This type of diversion may involve the voluntary referral to a social service agency or program dealing with a problem underlying the offense.

*Conditional Diversion*—Conditional diversion at the pretrial stage refers to suspension of prosecution while specific conditions are met. If conditions are not satisfied during the specified time period, the case is referred for continued prosecution.

*Citizen Dispute Settlement*—Charges arising from interpersonal disputes are mediated by a third party in an attempt to avoid prosecution. If an agreement between the parties cannot be reached and the complainant wishes to proceed with criminal processing, the case may be referred to court for settlement.

*Partial Confinement*—An alternative to the traditional jail sentence, partial confinement may consist of "weekend" sentences which permit the offender to spend the work week in the community, with his family, and at his job; furloughs, which enable the offender to leave the jail for a period of a few hours to a few days for specified purposes—e.g., to seek employment, take care of personal matters or family obligations, or engage in community service; or work/study release, under which the offender holds a job or attends school during the day and returns to the detention facility at night and on weekends.

*Alternative Facilities*—A sentence to confinement in alternative facilities may be an option for certain kinds of offenders. Such facilities may include treatment settings for drug-dependent offenders, minimum-security facilities in the community which provide treatment and services as needed, work/study release centers, and halfway houses or shelter-type facilities. All of these are less secure than the traditional jail, but offer a more stimulating environment for the individual.

*Early Release*—Early release to supervision means less jail time and, with more rapid turnover, lower jail populations and capacity requirements. Early release may come about through parole, time off for good behavior or work performed, or modification of the sentence by the court. The last procedure is usually associated with sentences to jail with a period of probation to follow. Although there are some objections to its use, "probation with jail" is a very common disposition in some jurisdictions. More often than not these sentences are in lieu of a state prison term.

*Unconditional Discharge*—Discharge without conditions as a post-trial disposition is essentially the same as unconditional diversion. No savings are obtained in criminal justice processing costs, but jail populations may be reduced; conditions of release are imposed for an offense in which the defendant's involvement has been established.

*Suspended Sentence*—This is essentially a threat to take more drastic action if the offender again commits a crime during some specified time period. Where no special conditions are attached, it is assumed that the ends of justice have been satisfied by conviction and no further action is required as long as the offender refrains from involvement in new offenses. Suspended sentences may be conditioned on various limitations as to mobility, associates, or activities or on requirements to make reparations or participate in some rehabilitation program.

*Fine*—The fine is a cash payment of a dollar amount assessed by the judge in an individual case or determined by reference to a published schedule of penalties. Fines may be paid in installments in many jurisdictions.

*Restitution*—Restitution generally is a cash payment by the offender to the victim of an amount considered to offset the loss incurred by the victim or the community. The amount of the payment may be scaled down to the earning capacity of the offender and/or payments may be made in installments. Sometimes services directly or indirectly benefitting the victim may be substituted for cash payment.

*Community Service*—Community service often is used as a substitute for, or in partial satisfaction of, a fine. Generally this disposition is a condition of a suspended or partially suspended sentence or of probation. The offender volunteers his services to a community agency for a certain number of hours per week over a specified period of time. The total number of hours, often assessed at the legal minimum wage, is determined by the amount of the fine which would have been imposed or that portion of the fine which is suspended.

*Probation*—A requirement to report to a designated person or agency over some specified period of time. May involve special conditions as discussed in the definition of suspended sentence. Probation often involves a suspended sentence—but may be used in association with suspension of final judgement or deferral of sentencing.

# Bibliography

ABADINSKY, HOWARD. *Probation and Parole.* Englewood Cliffs, N.J.: Prentice-Hall, 1977.

ABRAHAMSEN, DAVID. *Crime and the Human Mind.* Montclair, N.J.: Patterson Smith, 1969.

ALEXANDER, FRANZ and HUGO STAUB. *The Criminal, the Judge, and the Public.* Glencoe, Ill.: Free Press, 1956.

AMERICAN FRIENDS SERVICE COMMITTEE. *Struggle for Justice.* New York: Hill Wang, 1971.

AMERICAN PSYCHIATRIC ASSOCIATION TASK FORCE on Behavior Therapy. *Behavior Therapy in Psychiatry.* New York: Jason Aronson, 1974.

ARMORE, JOHN R. and JOSEPH D. WOLFE. *Dictionary of Desperation.* Washington, D.C.: Communications Department of the National Alliance of Businessman, 1976.

BAILEY, ROY and MIKE BRAKE, eds. *Radical Social Work.* New York: Pantheon, 1975.

BASSIN, ALEXANDER, THOMAS E. BRATTER, and RICHARD L. RACHIN, eds. *The Reality Therapy Reader.* New York: Harper & Row, 1976.

BECKER, HOWARD. *Outsiders: Studies in the Sociology of Deviance.* New York: Free Press, 1963.

BLOCK, PETER B. and DAVID SPECHT. *Neighborhood Team Policing.* Washington, D.C.: United States Government Printing Office, 1973.

BLUMBERG, ABRAHAM. *Criminal Justice.* Chicago: Quadrangle, 1970.

BOORKMAN, DAVID, et al. *Community Based Corrections in Des Moines.* Washington, D.C.: United States Government Printing Office, 1976.

BOTTOMORE, TOM, ed. *Karl Marx.* Englewood Cliffs, N.J.: Prentice-Hall, 1973.

BRENNER, CHARLES. *An Elementary Textbook of Psychoanalysis.* Garden City, N.Y.: Anchor Books, 1974.

BRODYAGE, LISA, MARGARET GATES, SUSAN SINGER, and RICHARDSON WHITE. *Rape and Its Victims: A Report for Citizens, Health Facilities and Criminal Justice Agencies.* Washington, D.C.: United States Government Printing Office, 1975.

BROMBERG, WALTER. *Crime and the Mind.* New York: Macmillan, 1965.

BROWN, B. CURTIS, ed. *Frances Smart: Neurosis and Crime.* New York: Barnes & Noble, 1970.

BRYANT, GERALD and PAUL CIREL. *Polk County Rape/Sexual Assault Care Center, Des Moines, Iowa.* Washington, D.C.: United States Government Printing Office, 1977.

CANNAVALE, FRANK J., JR. and WILLIAM D. FALCON. *Improving Witness Cooperation.* Washington, D.C.: United States Government Printing Office, 1976.

CARKHUFF, R. R. *The Development of Human Resources.* New York: Holt, Rinehart & Winston, 1971.

CASPER, JONATHAN D. *American Criminal Justice:* The Defendant's Perspective. Englewood Cliffs, N.J.: Prentice-Hall, 1972.

CAVAN, RUTH SHONLE. *Juvenile Delinquency.* Philadelphia: Lippincott, 1969.

CENTER FOR RESEARCH IN CRIMINAL JUSTICE. *The Iron Fist and the Velvet Glove: An Analysis of the United States Police.* Berkeley, Calif.: Center for Research in Criminal Justice, 1975.

CLARK, RAMSEY. *Crime in America.* New York: Simon & Schuster, 1970.

CLARK, ROBERT E. *Reference Group Theory and Delinquency.* New York: Behavioral Publications, 1972.

CLEMMER, DONALD. *The Prison Community.* New York: Holt, Rinehart & Winston, 1958.

CLINARD, MARSHAL B., ed. *Anomie and Deviant Behavior.* New York: Free Press, 1964.

CLOWARD, RICHARD, et al. *Theoretical Studies in Social Organization of the Prison.* New York: Social Research Council; reprinted by Kraus Reprint Co., Millwood, N.Y., 1975.

CLOWARD, RICHARD A. and LLOYD E. OHLIN. *Delinquency and Opportunity.* New York: Free Press, 1960.

COFFEY, ALAN, EDWARD EDELFONSO, and WALTER HARTINGER. An Introduction to the Criminal Justice System. Englewood Cliffs, N.J.: Prentice-Hall. 1974.

COFFEY, ALAN R. Juvenile Corrections. Englewood Cliffs, N.J.: Prentice-Hall, 1975.

COHEN, ALBERT K. Delinquent Boys, New York: Free Press, 1955.

COHEN, HAROLD L. and JAMES FILIPCZAK. A New Learning Environment. San Francisco: Jossey-Bass, 1971.

DAWSON, ROBERT O. Sentencing. Boston: Little, Brown 1969.

DENZIN, NORMAN K. The Research Act. Chicago: Aldine, 1970.

DINITZ, SIMON, RUSSELL R. DYNES, and ALFRED C. CLARKE, ed. Deviance. New York: Oxford University Press, 1975.

DRESSLER, DAVID. Sociology: The Study of Human Interaction. New York: Knopf, 1976.

DURKHEIM, EMILE. Suicide. New York: Free Press. 1951.

EISSLER, K. R., ed. Searchlights on Delinquency. New York: International Universities Press, 1956.

ERIKSON, KAI T. Wayward Puritans. New York: John Wiley, 1966.

EYSENCK, HANS J. Crime and Personality. London: Routeledge and Kegan Paul, 1964.

FEDERICO, RONALD C. The Social Welfare Institution. Lexington, Mass.: Heath, 1973.

FENICHEL, OTTO. The Psychoanalytic Theory of Neuroses. New York: W. W. Norton, 1945.

FENSTERHEIM, HERBERT. Help Without Psychoanalysis. New York: Stein and Day Publishers, 1971.

FILSTEAD, WILLIAM, ed. An Introduction to Deviance. Chicago: Markham Publishing, 1972.

FINK, ARTHUR E., C. WILSON ANDERSON, and MERRILL B. CONOVER. The Field of Social Work. New York: Holt, Rinehart & Winston, 1968.

FOGEL, DAVID. We Are the Living Proof: The Justice Model for Corrections. Cincinatti: W. H. Anderson, 1975.

FOX, VERNON. Introduction to Criminology. Englewood Cliffs, N.J.: Prentice-Hall, 1976.

FRANK, BENJAMIN, ed. Contemporary Corrections: A Concept in Search of Content. Reston, Va.: Reston Publishing, 1973.

FREUD, SIGMUND. A General Introduction to Psychoanalysis. New York: Washington Square Press, 1961.

FRIEDLANDER, WALTER H., ed. Concepts and Methods of Social Work. Englewood Cliffs, N.J.: Prentice-Hall, 1976.

FROMM, ERICH. *The Crisis in Psychoanalysis.* New York: Holt, Rinehart & Winston, 1970.

GAGE, NICHOLAS. *The Mafia Is Not An Equal Opportunity Employer.* New York: McGraw-Hill, 1971.

GALDSON, IAGO, ed. *Psychoanalysis in Present-Day Psychiatry.* New York: Brunner/Mazel, 1969.

GARFINKEL, HAROLD. *Studies in Ethnomethodology.* Englewood Cliffs, N.J.: Prentice-Hall, 1967.

GIBBONS, DON C. *Society, Crime and Criminal Careers.* Englewood Cliffs, N.J.: Prentice-Hall, 1973.

GIBBONS, DON C. and JOSEPH F. JONES. *The Study of Deviance.* Englewood Cliffs, N.J.: Prentice-Hall, 1975.

GLASSER, WILLIAM. *Reality Therapy.* New York: Harper & Row, 1975.

———. *The Identity Society.* New York: Harper and Row, 1975.

GOFFMAN, ERVING. *Asylums.* Garden City, N.Y.: Doubleday, 1961.

GOLD, MARTIN. *Status Forces in Delinquent Boys.* Ann Arbor: Institute for Social Research, 1963.

GOTTFREDSON, DON M., et al. *Decision-Making in the Criminal Justice System: Reviews and Essays.* Rockville, Md.: National Institute of Mental Health, 1975.

GOVERNOR'S SPECIAL COMMITTEE on CRIMINAL OFFENDERS. *Preliminary Report.* Albany: State of New York, 1967.

HALLECK, SEYMOUR L. and WALTER BROMBERG. *Psychiatric Aspects of Criminology.* Springfield, Ill.: Charles C Thomas, 1968.

HALLECK, S. L. *Politics of Therapy.* New York: Science House, 1971.

———. *Psychiatry and the Dilemmas of Crime.* New York: Harper & Row, 1967.

HAZELRIGG, LAWRENCE, ed. *Prison Within Society.* Garden City, N.Y.: Doubleday, 1969.

HERAUD, BRIAN J. *Sociology and Social Work.* Oxford: Perganon Press, 1970.

HERBERT, W. L. and F. V. JARVIS. *Dealing With Delinquents.* New York: Emerson Books, 1962.

HILTS, P. J. *Behavior Mod.* New York: Harpers Magazine Press, 1974.

HIPPCHEN, LEONARD J., ed. *Correctional Classification and Treatment.* Cincinatti: W. H. Anderson, 1975.

HIRSCHI, TRAVIS. *Causes of Delinquency.* Berkeley, Calif.: University of California Press, 1972.

HOSFORD, RAY E. and C. SCOTT MOSS. *The Crumbling Walls.* Urbana, Ill.: University of Illinois Press, 1975.

HUNT, JAMES W., JAMES E. BOWERS and NEAL MILLER. *Laws, Licences and the Offender's Right to Work*. Washington, D.C.: American Bar Association, 1974.

IANNI, FRANCIS A. J. *The Black Mafia*. New York: Simon & Schuster, 1974.

IRWIN, JOHN. *The Felon*. Englewood Cliffs, N.J.: Prentice-Hall, 1970.

JACKSON, GEORGE. *Soledad Brother: The Prison Letters of George Jackson*. New York: Bantam Books, 1972.

JACOBY, JOAN. *Pre-trial Screening in Perspective*. Washington, D.C.: United States Government Printing Office, 1976.

_____. *The Prosecutor's Charging Decision: A Policy Perspective*. Washington, D.C.: United States Government Printing Office, 1977.

KATZ, LEWIS. *Justice is the Problem*. Cleveland, Ohio: Press of Case Western Reserve, 1972.

KENISTON, KENNETH. *Youth and Dissent*. New York: Harcourt Brace Janovich, 1971.

KITTRIE, NICHOLAS N. *The Right to Be Different*. Baltimore: John's Hopkins University Press, 1971.

KNUDTEN, RICHARD D., ANTHONY C. MEADE, MARY S. KNUDTEN, and WILLIAM DOERNER. *Victims and Witnesses: Their Experiences With Crime and Criminal Justice System*. Washington, D.C.: United States Government Printing Office, 1977.

KONOPKA, GISELA. *Social Group Work: A Helping Process*. Englewood Cliffs, N.J.: Prentice-Hall, 1972.

KU, RICHARD and CAROL HOLLIDAY BLEW. *A University's Approach to Delinquency: The Adolescent Diversion Project*. Washington, D.C.: United States Government Printing Office, 1977.

LEMERT, EDWIN M. *Social Pathology*. New York: McGraw-Hill, 1951.

_____. *Human Deviance: Social Problems and Social Control*. Englewood Cliffs, N.J.: Prentice-Hall, 1971.

LEONARD, ROBERT F. and JOEL B. SAXE. *Screening Criminal Cases*. Chicago: National District Attorneys Association, 1973.

MATZA, DAVID. *Delinquency and Drift*. New York: John Wiley, 1964.

McCALL, GEORGE J. *Observing the Law: Application of Field Methods to the Study of the Criminal Justice System*. Rockville, Md.: National Institute of Mental Health, 1975.

MEYER, VICTOR and EDWARD S. CHESSER. *Behavior Therapy in Clinical Psychiatry*. New York: Science House, 1970.

MILAN, MICHAEL A., LARRY F. WOOD, ROBERT L. WILLIAMS, JERRY ROGERS, LEE HAMPTON and JOHN M. McKEE. *Applied Behavior Analysis and the Imprisoned Adult Felon, Project 1: The Cellblock Token*

*Economy.* Montgomery, Alabama: Rehabilitation Research Foundation, 1974.

MILLER, NEAL E. *Selected Papers on Conflict Displacement, Learned Drives and Therapy.* Chicago: Aldine-Atherton, 1971.

MORRIS, NORVAL. *The Future of Imprisonment.* Chicago: University of Chicago Press, 1974.

MULLEN, JOAN. *The Dilemma of Diversion.* Washington, D.C.: United States Government Printing Office, 1975.

NATIONAL ADVISORY COMMISSION on CRIMINAL JUSTICE STANDARDS and GOALS. *A National Strategy to Reduce Crime.* New York: Avon Books, 1975.

NEW YORK STATE SPECIAL COMMISSION on ATTICA. *Attica.* New York: Praeger, 1972.

NUTTIN, JOSEPH. *Psychoanalysis and Personality.* New York: New American Library, 1962.

OFFICE of the COMPTROLLER GENERAL. *State and County Probation: Systems in Crisis.* Washington, D.C.: General Accounting Office 1976.

OHLIN, LLOYD E., ALDEN D. MILLER and ROBERT B. COATES eds. *Juvenile Reform in Massachusetts.* Washington, D.C.: United States Government Printing Office, 1977.

O'LEARY, K. DANIEL and G. TERRENCE WILSON. *Behavior Therapy: Application and Outcome.* Englewood Cliffs, N.J.: Prentice-Hall, 1975.

OLSON, SHELDON R. *Issues in the Sociology of Criminal Justice.* Indianapolis, Ind.: Bobbs-Merril, 1975.

ORLAND, LEONARD and HAROLD R. TYLER, eds. *Justice in Sentencing.* Mineola, N.Y.: Foundation Press, 1974.

PARKER, WILLIAM. *Parole.* College Park, Md.: American Correctional Association.

PARSONS, TALCOTT. *The Social System.* New York: Free Press, 1951.

―――. *Social Structure and Personality.* New York: Free Press, 1970.

POLSKY, HOWARD A. *Cottage Six: The Social System of Delinquent Boys in Residential Treatment.* New York: John Wiley, 1962.

POPE, CARL E. *Sentencing of California Felony Offenders.* Washington, D.C.: United States Government Printing Office, 1975.

PRESIDENT'S COMMISSION on LAW ENFORCEMENT and ADMINISTRATION of JUSTICE. *The Challenge of Crime in a Free Society.* New York: Avon Books, 1968.

QUINNEY, RICHARD. *Critique of the Legal Order.* Boston: Little, Brown and Co., 1974.

RECKLESS, WALTER C. *The Crime Problem.* Englewood Cliffs, N.J.: Prentice-Hall, Inc., 1967.

RUBIN, TED. *The Future of the Juvenile Court.* College Park, Md.: American Correctional Association, 1971.

RUBINSTEIN, JONATHAN. *City Police.* New York: Ballantine Books, 1973.

RUTHERFORD, ANDREW and ROBERT McDERMOTT. *Juvenile Diversion.* Washington, D.C.: United States Government Printing Office, 1976.

SCHUESSLER, KARL, ed. EDWIN H. SUTHERLAND: *On Analyzing Crime.* Chicago: University of Chicago Press, 1973.

SCHUR, EDWIN M. *Radical Non-Intervention.* Englewood Cliffs, N.J.: Prentice-Hall, 1973.

SHELYAG, A.D., et al. *Military Psychology: A Soviet View.* Washington, D.C.: United States Government Printing Office, 1976.

SHORT, JAMES F. JR., ed. *Gang Delinquency and Delinquent Subcultures.* New York: Harper and Row, 1968.

SINGH, UDAI PRATAP. *Personality of Criminals.* Agra, India: Mehra and Co., 1973.

SLAVSON, S.R. *Reclaiming the Delinquent.* New York: Free Press, 1965.

SMITH, JOAN and WILLIAM FRIED. *The Uses of American Prisons.* Lexington, Mass.: Heath, 1974.

SULZER, BETH and G. ROY MAYER. *Behavior Modification Procedures for School Personnel.* Hindsdale, Ill.: Dryden Press, 1972.

SUTHERLAND, EDWIN M. *White Collar Crime.* New York: Dryden Press, 1949.

TASK FORCE on POLICING in ONTARIO. *The Police Are the Public and the Public Are the Police.* Ontario: Office of the Solicitor General, 1974.

TAYLOR, IAN, PAUL WALTON, and JOCK YOUNG. *The New Criminology.* New York: Harper & Row, 1973.

TURNER, JONATHAN H. *The Structure of Sociological Theory.* Homewood, Ill.: Dorsey Press, 1974.

VON HIRSCH, ANDREW. *Doing Justice.* New York: Hill & Wang, 1976.

WHEELER, HARVEY, ed. *Beyond the Punitive Society.* San Francisco: W. H. Freeman, 1973.

WILSON, JAMES Q. *Thinking About Crime.* New York: Basic Books, 1975.

WOLFGANG, MARVIN and FRANCO FERRACUTI. *The Subculture of Violence.* Tavistock Publications, 1967.

WOLPE, J., A. SALTER and L. J. REYNA, eds. *The Conditioning Therapies.* New York: Holt, Rinehart & Winston, 1964.

WRIGHT, ERIK OHLIN. *The Politics of Punishment.* New York: Harper & Row, 1973.

# Name Index

Schur, Edwin M., 28–29, 30–31
Schwartz, Michael, iv
Schwartz, Richard D., 31fn
Schwartz, William, 212
Schwitzgebel, Ralph K., 63–64
Sechenov, I. M., 51
Seeman, Melvin, 8–9
Sellin, Thorsten, 98
Shah, Saleem A., 62–63
Shectman, Frederick A., 49
Shelyag, V. V., 50fn
Shepard, George H., 130fn
Shireman, Charles, 190–91
Short, James F., Jr., 16, 17, 19fn
Sigler, Maurice, 115–16
Sigurdson, Herbert R., 194fn
Silber, David, 59
Silver, Isidore, 33
Simmel, Georg, 188
Simpson, George, 2
Singer, Susan, 184fn
Singh, Udai Pratap, 37
Siporin, Max, 31
Skinner, B. F., 14, 48fn, 59
Skolnick, Jerome, 31fn
Slavson, S. R., 43
Smart, Frances, 46, 47
Smith, Jack F., 104–5
Smith, Joan, 111fn
Specht, David, 90
Staub, Hugo, 37, 38–39
St. Pierre, C. André, 202–4
Stretch, John J., 183
Stuart, Richard E., 61, 64–65
Studt, Elliot, 210
Stumphauzer, Jerome S., 227–28
Sudnow, David, 68fn
Sulzer, Beth, 50fn, 58
Susman, Jackwell, 80fn

Sutherland, Edwin H., 10–12, 14
Sykes, Gresham W., 24–26
Szurek, S. A., 43

Taylor, Ian, 11, 15, 19fn, 32fn, 107fn
Taylor, Roy, 125fn
Tennyson, Roy A., 16
Tharp, Roland G., 221–27
Thomas, C. W., 166fn
Thorne, Gaylord L., 221–27
Turner, Jonathan H., 1fn
Tyler, Harold R., 34fn

Voit, Eckford, iii
Volkman, Rita, 187
von Hirsch, 107fn

Walton, Paul, 11
Weathers, Lawrence, 65
Weber, George H., 168–69
Weber, Max, 188
Weissman, James C., 241
Wellford, Charles, 32fn
Wetzel, Ralph J., 221–27
Wheeler, Harvey, 50fn
White, Richardson, 184fn
Whyte, William Foote, 16
Widen, Paul, 48fn
Williams, Hadley, 119–21
Williams, Robert L., 220fn
Wilson, James Q., 104
Wolfgang, Marvin E., iii
Wolpe, Joseph, 49fn, 61
Wood, Larry F., 220fn
Woolf, Donald A., 124fn
Wright, Erik Ohlin, 111fn

Young, Jock, 11

# Subject Index

Adjudicatory hearing, 80
Adolescent Diversion Project, 195
Advocacy in social service, 7, 35, 182, 190–99
Alienation, 6, 7–10
Anomie, 1–6, 7, 8, 190
Attica Correctional Facility, 111–12
Auburn Correctional Facility, 111
Authority in social service, 122–23, 128, 164, 165, 208–9

Bail, 150
Behavior modification, 61–65
  effectiveness, 62–64
  ethical considerations, 50
  (See also Learning theory)
Behavioral contracting, 64–65, 216–20
Bronx (N.Y.) District Attorney, 98–99

California, sentencing in, 107–8
Citizens Probation Authority, 141–43
Classification, 31, 112–14
Clinical sociology, 185
Community Arbitration Program, 132–35
Community Resources Management Team, 194
Confidentiality, 128, 131, 240–42
Containment theory, 23–24
Contract in social service, 211–13
Corrections, 110–14, 164–70
Court systems in United States, 246–49

Crime, ii, 5, 9, 37, 71, 193
  definition of, i, ii, 32, 70
  and mental illness, 44–45
  organized, 16
  "schools" of, ii
  white collar, 44, 86
Criminology, the new, 32
Crisis intervention, 123–29

Dade County (Fla.) Pre-Trial Intervention Project, 143–47
Dallas Police Department, 119–20
Defense, 99–102
Delinquents, female, 20
Desk appearance ticket, 274–75
Detectives, 72
Determinate sentencing, 107
Deterrence, 15, 111
Deviance, secondary, 31
Differential association, 10–15, 185fn
Differential identification, 12
Differential opportunity, iv, 15–17
Discretion defined, 82fn
Diversion, 82fn, 83–84, 89–90, 121–22, 141–42, 195, 273–81
Draper Correctional Center, 220
Drenk Memorial Guidance Center, 135–38
Drift, 24, 27–28
Drug addiction (See Narcotic)